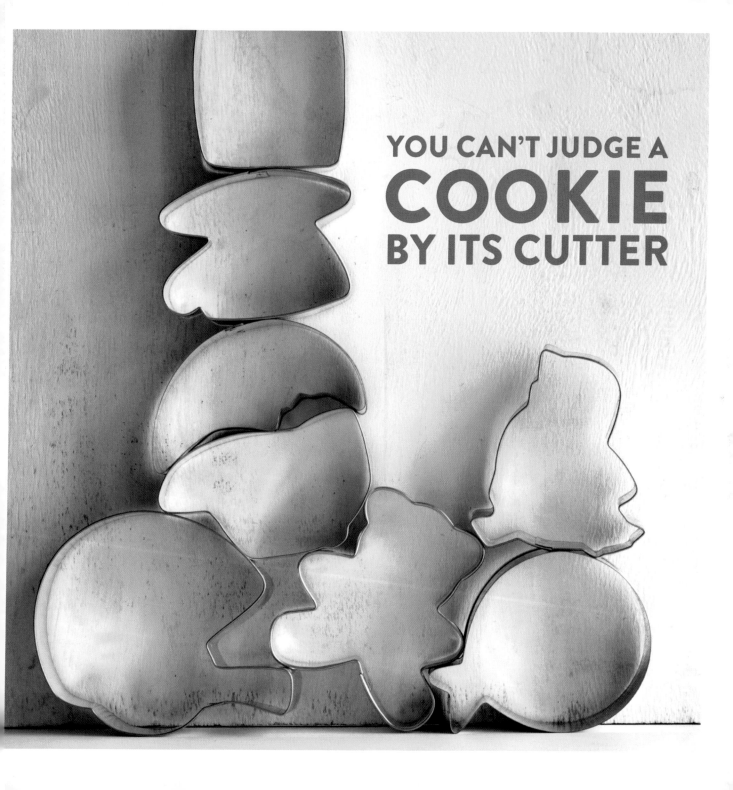

YOU CAN'T JUDGE A
COOKIE
BY ITS CUTTER

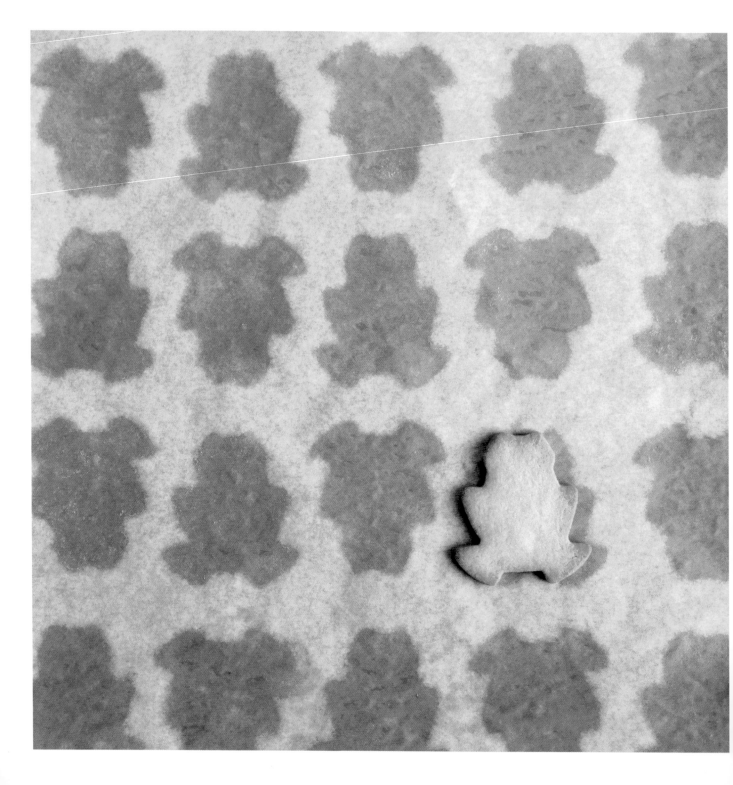

YOU CAN'T JUDGE A COOKIE BY ITS CUTTER

MAKE 100 COOKIE DESIGNS WITH ONLY A HANDFUL OF COOKIE CUTTERS

PATTI PAIGE

PHOTOGRAPHS BY JENNIFER CAUSEY

Developed and written with The Stonesong Press

GRAND CENTRAL
Life&Style
NEW YORK · BOSTON

Grand Central Life & Style
Hachette Book Group
1290 Avenue of the Americas, New York, NY 10104
www.GrandCentralLifeandStyle.com

Printed in the United States of America

Q/MA

First Edition: November 2014
10 9 8 7 6 5 4 3 2 1

Grand Central Life & Style is an imprint of Grand Central Publishing.
The Grand Central Life & Style name and logo are trademarks of Hachette Book Group, Inc.

The Hachette Speakers Bureau provides a wide range of authors for speaking events. To find out more, go to www.HachetteSpeakersBureau.com or call (866) 376-6591.

The publisher is not responsible for websites (or their content) that are not owned by the publisher.

Library of Congress Cataloging-in-Publication Data

Paige, Patti.

You can't judge a cookie by its cutter : make 100 cookie designs with only a handful of cookie cutters / Patti Paige photographs by Jennifer Causey.

pages cm

Includes index.

ISBN 978-1-4555-4849-1 (hardback)— ISBN 978-1-4555-4850-7 (ebook) 1. Cookie cutters. 2. Cookies. 3. Icings (Confectionery) I. Title.

TX657.C72P35 2014

641.86'54—dc23

To Nana

CONTENTS

INTRODUCTION

There's More Than One Way to Spin a Cookie Cutter

Here are the first four lines of a poem I wrote in second grade:

SOME COOKIES ARE ROUND,
SOME COOKIES ARE SQUARE,
SOME COOKIES HAVE ICING,
SOME COOKIES ARE BARE.

BEGINNINGS

It's a pretty good description of the adventure we are about to go on. But first, a little background.

Ever since I can remember, I have made things. Whether it was a house for worms or a game to play, I was always creating something new, crafty, or quirky. As a grade schooler, I was never satisfied eating commercially prepared food. I had to *make* something: a batch of rice, or a pot of tomato sauce, or potato chips from scratch.

Except when it came to cookies. I was invariably drawn to the colorful boxes and bags—Oreos, Mallomars, Fig Newtons, Lorna Doones, and Chips Ahoy!—that filled our cupboards. It was my grandmother's cookies, however, that made the deepest impression on me. Whenever she visited us on Long Island, she always showed up

with "Nana Cookies," the name my family affectionately called the treats she baked in her Brooklyn kitchen. Using cream cheese dough and a cookie gun, she made dozens of shapes that, to an eight-year-old, were nothing short of magic. The various circles she attached to the end of the gun formed the cookies, much like my cookie cutters define the shapes of my cookies today. When I popped one of Nana's cookies into my mouth, I was always thinking about that shape and noticing the simple embellishments—a maraschino cherry, a chocolate chip, an almond sliver. My grandmother eventually moved to Florida, gave up her cookie making, and left her pans and cookie gun to me.

Curiously, my mother never stepped foot in the kitchen; her favorite cookbook was *The I Hate to Cook Book* by Peg Bracken. But she did cultivate in me an intense love of games. After dinner, we always sat around the table to play card and board games. Bridge, Scrabble, gin rummy, Rack-O, and Sorry were among my favorites. I'm sure that's why games—not just playing them but appreciating their graphic designs—are such an important part of my life.

So my grandmother was all cookies and my mother was all games. I was lucky enough to inherit both passions.

Although it seemed from the start that I was going to be an artist or maker of some sort, I began college as an English major. Among my first electives was a class based on the work of Josef Albers, the father of modern color studies. The class assignments challenged me to play games with color relationships that would change the

viewers' perception of them. I was hooked. I loved working with shape, color, and design. This was the beginning of my obsession with transformation.

As a working artist, I made paintings in bold relief with major dimensionality. I layered paint thickly onto canvas, eliciting comments that my paint resembled frosting. As I pursued my dream of being a fine artist in New York City, I not only made paintings in my SoHo studio

but put Nana's pans and cookie gun to good use and made cookie gifts for friends. At parties, guests couldn't get enough of them.

Emboldened by these raves, I took my cookies to two nearby specialty food stores, both of which kept renewing their orders. Then I aimed even higher and made Dean & DeLuca my next client. I'll never forget walking into the original SoHo store, full of confidence and certain my cookies would sell. Soon, I was fielding requests for other varieties, and that's when I expanded to making classic chocolate chip and peanut butter cookies. Bloomingdale's called not long after, and in 1979 Patti Paige Baked Ideas was born.

Eventually, I needed to create something else entirely, beyond the cream cheese, chocolate chip, and peanut butter doughs, so I began to bake gingerbread and construct gingerbread houses. I've probably made every iconic building in New York City, along with dozens of private homes. Many of these made it into the *New York Times,* the *New York Daily News,* and numerous magazines.

When I was asked to bake a cake for an art opening, my two worlds suddenly collided. One commission led to several others, but it was the one for Acorn Press that moved me to think more inventively about cookie shapes. Unable to find the right acorn cookie cutter, I made one myself, which opened up endless possibilities. Making my own cutters distinguished me from every other baker; I made unique frames for unique cookies. Crazy custom cookie orders began to roll in—the iconic soldier that

stands outside the Cartier store, the face of Dennis Rodman, the box of Tide for a brand anniversary. My clients have included Hillary Clinton (who ordered NYC taxi cab cookies for one of her luncheons) *and* her husband, whose administration commissioned a batch of my Easter cookies for the annual White House Easter Egg Roll. Disney, Alicia Keys, David Hyde Pierce, Ina Garten (the Barefoot Contessa), and Martha Stewart have all ordered Baked Ideas confections.

People think it is magical to create an original cookie, especially when the shape is meant to become something else. You can never tell how many different shapes might come from a cutter shaped like the state of Texas or a baseball cap. I have discovered that great things can take shape within rigid confines, especially when you really use your imagination. You can take something nostalgic and make it modern, something disguised and make it familiar. By playing games with shapes, a little dough and colored icing can be transformed into dozens of different designs.

You Can't Judge a Cookie by Its Cutter is a cookie decorating game that anybody can play. In it, I have taken 25 cookie cutters and created four different, beautiful cookies from each one. I challenge you to see even more in the shapes that follow. It's a fun way of looking at a cookie cutter not just for what it is, but for what it could be. Indeed, I like to call them "cookies" cutters for their ability to produce multiple images.

WHY NOT JUDGE A COOKIE BY ITS CUTTER?

The inspiration for this book came—as most things that interest me do—rather serendipitously. My custom cookie cutters hang on a wall that spans the length of my studio. Whenever guests visit me there, they are immediately drawn to the wall and naturally begin guessing what each shape is supposed to be. "Is that a frog?" or "Does that make a car shape?" One day I suddenly realized that all of

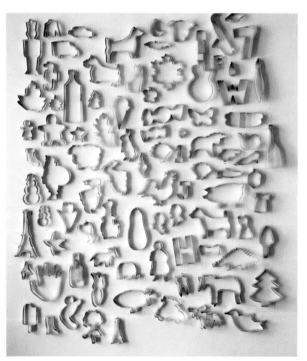

their guesses could be right. And as a lover of wordplay, I couldn't help but repeat to myself, "You can't judge a cookie by its cutter."

Being my mother's child, I began to play the game myself. And then it became an obsession. In a football helmet cutter, I saw a colorful bowl of fruit and an elephant head. In a wedding cake cutter, I found a stack of suitcases, a typewriter on a desk, and a pair of witch's shoes. I saw a cone of cotton candy, a paintbrush, and a ship in a bottle in a guitar cookie cutter.

> Thinking of the cutter simply as an outline opens up the entire frame to be filled. Turn it upside down, sideways, or at an angle. When you invert a teacup-and-saucer cutter, the outline looks just like a vintage rotary phone! You will be surprised by the possibilities when you let your eyes do the work.

As I was drawn deeper and deeper into coming up with transformations, I used a technique to help me "see." Trace the cutter on a piece of paper and draw inside the lines, ignoring what the cutter represents and sketching instead what you see. Try to keep it simple, with only the necessary lines involved so that the image comes to life. If it doesn't come to you in the moment, its next incarnation might just pop out at you when you least expect it. Make it a competition for the whole family to discover how many new cookie designs can come from just one cutter. Then bake the shape and fiddle around with the icing.

Involving friends and family was by far the best part of making this book. I enlisted the help of my assistants, my daughter, and plenty of friends. It was fascinating to see what people came up with, how everyone saw something so different in one cutter shape. Seeing through their eyes became great fun for me and provided a lot of inspiration for my own designs. Just when I thought there was nothing left to find within a shape, my eyes would shift and an image would appear. I never settle for a partial transformation; the cutter has to yield a well-formed and easy-to-translate cookie. It can be challenging, but that's the fun of it!

Admittedly, decorating cookies requires patience and perseverance. The key is to have fun and enjoy the process. Making both the dough and icing is easy; it's the decorating that takes practice. Be sure to read all of the chapters on techniques (starting on page 26) before you begin and then refer to them often as you create the cookies. The techniques are there to guide you, as are the cookie designs, but your cookies should look like *you* made them; they needn't look like mine, and whoever is lucky enough to receive them will always be impressed. (In truth, some of my best ideas and cookies have come from mistakes.) The keys to creating beautiful cookies are:

- Exercise restraint. Less is more. Don't feel overwhelmed.
- Step back. Give the designs you make a minute to rest before you edit.
- Let the cookies be what they are. Cookies are individuals. You can bake a dozen or two and

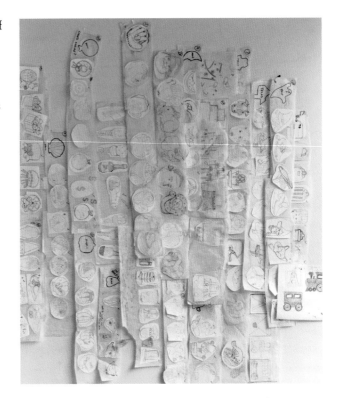

try out all of the options swimming around in your head. It's not a whole cake; cookie mistakes can easily be tossed into the garbage (or eaten!) and forgotten as a better idea surfaces.

Armed with a good attitude and the knowledge that, like a board game, there's always another chance to win, making amazing cookies will become second nature. Play to win, but remember that in the end it's just a game . . . and no matter how they look, your cookies will always taste great.

GETTING STARTED

BAKING SUPPLIES

You don't need much in the way of fancy tools and equipment for making rolled and cutout cookies. Chances are pretty good that you already own many of the essentials—a baking sheet or two, some mixing bowls and measuring cups and spoons. Anything you don't have is very easy to find in kitchenware stores and online. Check the Sources on page 275 to find out where you can find all the supplies used in this book.

I happen to have an odd assortment of baking tools and more kitchen equipment than any one baker could ever use, the result of years of going to yard sales and flea markets in Upstate New York. I have a tough time resisting a set of battered measuring cups, old tin measuring spoons, and timeworn graters. I've also amassed a huge assortment of very useful bowls, baking sheets, whisks, and enough rolling pins for a cookie decorating party of 20—one for each guest. Of course, you only need one rolling pin, but once you begin making and decorating cookies, the pull to own a few more may strike.

I've organized this section (and the Decorating Supplies section that begins on page 17) into essential and optional items. The nonessential tools are just that, but you will find them helpful in getting the most pleasure out of baking and decorating cookies.

ESSENTIAL

Baking Sheets or Cookie Sheets

If you didn't know there was a difference between *baking* and *cookie* sheets, that's okay because either will work. A baking sheet has a raised edge around the entire pan, whereas a cookie sheet has only one raised edge so that you can easily slide the cookies off the rimless edges of the pan. I use both interchangeably.

I still bake my cookies on my grandmother's 14 x 17-inch WearEver aluminum cookie sheets. Have on hand at least two inexpensive, light-colored (avoid dark, they cause cookies to burn) aluminum cookie or baking sheets. Insulated or nonstick baking sheets are not necessary if you line your sheets with parchment paper, which keeps the cookies from sticking and makes cleanup easy.

Cookie Cutters

You can make all 100 cookie designs in this book with 25 inexpensive, widely available cookie cutters (see Sources, page 275), many of which you may already own—heart, circle, square, crescent moon, ghost. If your cutters aren't exact replicas of those I use, but pretty close, you can still transform them the way I do by tweaking the decoration just a bit. I rarely spend more than $4 on an average size cutter (2 to 4 inches) but expect to pay more

for larger ones. Copper cutters can be a bit pricier; forgo them unless you are making very large cookies, in which case their firm, strong construction is useful.

When I can't find a cutter shape that I'm looking for, I make my own (see DIY Cookie Cutters, page 38). This may sound extreme, but I wouldn't suggest trying it if it wasn't so, so easy.

Cooling Racks

These are really useful if you have a limited number of baking sheets and a lot of cookies to make. What's more, transferring cookies to cooling racks allows air to circulate around them so that they cool evenly and quickly. Have several on hand, especially if you plan to bake large batches of cookies.

Standing or Hand-Held Mixer

A standing mixer with a paddle attachment is the ideal combination for making my cookie dough and royal icing. It is an excellent investment, particularly if you like to bake in general. Of course, a hand-held mixer will do the job too, but when making dough you'll have to switch to a wooden spoon when it comes time to add the flour mixture because the dough may be too stiff for the beaters.

Measuring Cups and Spoons

I personally can never have enough of these, but that has more to do with my habit of picking up different styles at yard sales than with necessity. You really only need a set of measuring cups for dry ingredients and a glass measuring cup for liquids. I like a simple set of nesting metal cups in 1-, ½-, ⅓-, and ¼-cup measures. A 1-cup spouted Pyrex measuring cup is all you need to measure liquids. I still use the classic metal measuring spoons that my grandmother gave me 40 years ago. I am pretty nostalgic about things that have a history! A basic set in measures ranging from ¼ teaspoon to 1 tablespoon is essential for accurately measuring both dry and liquid ingredients including vanilla, salt, and baking soda.

Mixing Bowls

You only need a basic set of mixing bowls and a stack of smaller bowls to make and decorate cookies. I especially love the nesting melamine bowls with spouts that I grew up with, but I also use metal and glass varieties.

Parchment Paper

I use parchment paper to line baking sheets to prevent cookies from sticking to the pan, to make piping bags (see How to Make a Parchment Piping Bag, page 54), and to roll out dough (see Parchment Paper Method, page 35). Parchment paper is available in 13-inch-wide rolls or in half-sheet (13 x 16-inch) pieces at supermarkets and kitchen supply stores.

Plastic Wrap

I triple-wrap my dough in plastic wrap to keep it airtight in the refrigerator so it doesn't dry out.

Rolling Pin

I have used a variety of rolling pins, but my current favorite is a wooden rolling dowel that's thick enough around to accommodate spacer bands (see Rolling Pin Spacer Bands, below).

Metal Spatula

A metal spatula is useful for transferring cutout dough to the baking sheet, especially when the cutout doesn't come up with the cutter. I also use it to move the baked cookies from the baking sheet to a cooling rack. I use an everyday offset metal spatula with a 3-inch-wide head.

Silicone Spatulas

I never seem to have enough of these—they are indispensable for scraping down the dry ingredients that cling to the bottom and sides of the bowl when mixing dough and icing. I like to have several on hand so that I'm not distracted with washing one during the baking and decorating process. Have at least two 12-inch silicone spatulas at your fingertips.

Whisk

I use a balloon whisk to combine the dry ingredients—flour, baking soda, salt, etc.—when making the various cookie doughs.

OPTIONAL

Digital Kitchen Scale

All of my recipes include measures for both volume and weight. A scale is not essential if you choose to measure strictly by volume, but my first choice is to measure by weight because it is more precise and the results are more consistent. If you decide to go the kitchen scale route, buy one that measures in both ounces and grams.

Pastry Cloth

Little more than a piece of thick cotton canvas upon which to roll out your dough, a pastry cloth greatly reduces the amount of flour you have to use to keep the dough from sticking to the work surface while rolling. Pastry cloths are sold usually as a 20 x 25-inch rectangle and are available at specialty baking supply stores and online. When you're finished rolling out your cookies, scrape the cloth down with the end of your metal spatula and store in a plastic bag or plastic wrap in the refrigerator. After using a few times, wash the cloth by hand with soap and water to prevent any oils that seep into it from turning rancid. Lay flat to dry. Parchment paper is a popular alternative, but a pastry cloth will last years if cared for properly.

Rolling Pin Spacer Bands

These rubber band–like attachments slide onto either end of most column-shaped rolling pins to assist in rolling dough to a uniform thickness without any guesswork. They generally come in a set with bands ranging from $\frac{1}{16}$ to $\frac{1}{2}$ inch thick and are available at specialty kitchen and baking shops or online. Alternatively, use a pair of 15- to 18-inch-long, $\frac{1}{4}$-inch-thick dowels. Full disclosure: I didn't use bands or dowels for the first few years I baked.

When I began to hire bakers for my business, I bought the rings for them to ensure consistency.

Sifter or Fine Mesh Strainer

The only time I sift flour is when I am making Gluten Free Lemon Lime Sugar Cookies (page 32), because the gluten free flour can be clumpy. For the most part, I weigh all of my dry ingredients because this ensures perfect results every time. Measured amounts vary depending on whether you sift or don't sift. Some bakers prefer sifting all of the dry ingredients together after combining them, but I find it easier to whisk them together using several small circular motions and then final big circular motions.

DECORATING SUPPLIES

ESSENTIAL

Ball Head Pins

These are ideal for unclogging piping tips: Insert the sharp end into the tip and twirl it around, squeezing the bag until icing flows freely again. If the tip continues to become clogged, make a new bag rather than constantly unclogging it, which can lead to frustration! Avoid using dressmaker pins, which are harder to hold and can easily slip into the icing. A pin also comes in handy if air bubbles rise to the surface after you paint in a cookie. Make them disappear with a gentle prick.

Bowls

I'm not too, too picky about the bowls I use for mixing up different colors of icing, but I prefer them to be dishwasher safe to make cleanup easy. A variety of small ones, six to eight about the size of cereal bowls, are enough. If I run out of bowls, I use teacups or coffee mugs.

Food Coloring

I prefer gel food coloring to liquid primarily because it results in much more intense, vibrant icing colors. A little gel goes a long way, which means it won't thin the icing (see Icing Consistencies, page 49). I use both AmeriColor Soft Gel Pastes and Chefmaster Liqua-Gel Colors (see Sources, page 275) because each brand offers different colors. You can buy basic colors to begin: bright red, sunset orange, lemon yellow, leaf green, bright blue, regal purple, chocolate brown, super black, and whitener. But I also choose specialty colors since they give me more options. Be sure to check the recipe before beginning.

All of the icing colors in this book are made with gels, but if you only have liquid food coloring on hand, keep in mind that the colors will be more pastel than saturated. And you'll need to start with a relatively stiff icing because liquid colorings dilute the mix substantially. If the icing becomes too thin, add more stiff icing or sifted confectioners' sugar.

Paintbrushes

The artist in me sees a cookie as a canvas, which is why I naturally reach for a paintbrush rather than the more conventional squeeze bottle and toothpick or pastry tube to apply icing, a method known as flooding. In fact, my workspace looks more like an art studio than a bakery; there are jars filled with various sizes of paintbrushes lining the counters. I like to use brushes because you can actually feel the icing going onto the cookie, can spread it

quickly with long strokes and can push it around efficiently. Round oil paintbrushes work best; the bristles are stiff enough to push the icing around with ease. It's worth spending some money on good-quality brushes—the better the bristles, the less likely they are to shed (it's no

fun fishing them out of a freshly iced cookie!) or lose their shape over time. Start with the three I use the most:

- Large: #4 or #5 round oil bristle brush for flooding the entire surface of the cookie
- Medium: #2 round oil bristle brush for flooding smaller areas such as the belly of a frog or the bow on a gift box
- Small: Size 0 or 00 watercolor brush for details such as painting the eyes on a cat, the antennae and dots on a ladybug, or metal latches on a suitcase

How do you know which one to use? It's best to look at the space on the cookie and then choose the appropriate-size brush.

To preserve brushes, gently massage them with warm water right after you use them. To keep the points of the bristles sharp, store them in a jar, bristles up. Good brushes will last more than five years with proper care and storage.

Piping Bags

I prefer parchment paper piping bags to disposable plastic versions because they can be cut to whatever size you need, and are nicer to touch than plastic. Parchment is very strong, convenient, and cheap, too. Admittedly, using parchment is a tad more complicated than using plastic in that you have to "make" the bags every time you decorate cookies, but once you learn how (see page 54), it becomes second nature. Parchment triangles are available at specialty baking supply stores and online (see Sources, page 275) or you can cut your own from a roll of parchment, which is available at most grocery stores.

There are ready-made and DIY plastic disposable piping bags. The ready-made plastic varieties, available at baking supply stores, are superconvenient. They're ready-to-use and transparent, so you can see the icing colors through them, making them a good choice when decorating cookies with kids.

DIY plastic piping bags, made by snipping a corner of a resealable plastic bag, are very floppy and, if used without a tip, will make less-than-smooth lines in your icing due to the seam in the bag and the imperfect opening for the icing.

Piping Tips

Like mixing bowls, you will always wish you had one more tip in a particular size than you have on hand. I tend to buy multiples of each of the tip sizes I use, because it allows me to make bags of every color I desire at one time and eliminates the need for using up one color before moving on to the next. Tips come in dozens of sizes and shapes, but you will need only round writing tips in just two hole sizes—#1 and #1.5—to create the cookies in this book. The smaller the number, the smaller the hole. I find that using tips with holes any larger than these results in lines that are too thick for outlining the cookies and for details.

Buy the best piping tips you can afford because you will use them forever. Keep in mind that the numbering system is not uniform and depends on what brand tip you buy. The sizes can vary slightly. They also can vary in other ways that can be frustrating. One tip might deliver the icing in such a way that it does not lie down in a straight line but rather curls upward, while another can give you results you really love.

Wilton and Ateco are the most common piping tip brands. They're inexpensive and will do the job just fine, but I prefer to pay just a little more for PME tips because they do not have a seam, which reduces the chances of icing curling as you work.

Plastic Wrap

I always have a roll of wrap on hand for covering the bowls of icing when they are not being used (if I'm not using terry cloth towels!—see below). It prevents the icing from drying out and forming a crust.

Scissors

If you keep one good pair of scissors in a drawer with your other baking supplies, you will be surprised by how often you reach for them. If you plan to give cookies as gifts, have a second pair on hand for cutting ribbon; you want this pair to stay extra sharp.

Spoons

You can't have enough of them. I use one small spoon in each bowl of icing, which means over the course of one day, I can go through dozens. These spoons don't have to be any style in particular—I've amassed most of mine from yard sales, flea markets, and thrift stores.

Terry Dish Towels

These are vital for preventing the master batch of royal icing—the one that is constantly dipped into and transferred to smaller bowls to make colored icings—from drying out when it is not in use. If exposed to air for too long, the icing begins to dry out and form tiny chunks I call "crunchies." These pellets are the culprits in most clogged piping tips, a huge annoyance that can easily be avoided. Cover the big bowl with a damp terry towel to prevent crunchies from ruining the batch. If using thinner cotton kitchen towels, use two.

Two-Sided Tip-Cleaning Brush

One of the most useful tools I own, this small stainless steel wire-handled brush (4 to 6 inches long) with nylon bristles is designed specifically for cleaning piping tips after they've soaked in water for a few minutes. It is available in baking supply stores and online. A small stiff-bristled paintbrush makes a good substitute.

Toothpicks

Toothpicks are indispensable for mixing food-coloring gels into icing. Rather than squeezing the gel directly into the icing, I dip the end of a toothpick into the gel and dab it into the icing, gradually adding more until I achieve the color I want. It is always better to

start with too little color and add to it rather than try to lighten up an icing that has gone too dark with more white icing.

X-ACTO Knife

There are many instances when a line or dot that I pipe does not fall perfectly into place. To remove it, I (patiently!) let the icing dry slightly (it will look more matte than shiny) and then very gently scrape it away with an X-ACTO knife.

OPTIONAL

Carafe

. . . or any narrow-necked jar or vase taller than a parchment piping bag comes in handy for holding the bag when filling it with icing. The opening at the top of a full roll of paper towels does the job, too.

Cocoa Powder

Cocoa powder allows me to use less black gel when making black royal icing. I start by adding sifted cocoa powder to the uncolored icing until it is a medium to dark brown, then I add only as much black gel as I need to turn it deep black.

Dropper

A liquid medicine dropper is the best tool for adding the tiny amount of extract or vodka needed to liquefy the luster dust.

Edible Markers

Fine-tip edible markers are great for sketching a template of your design directly on a bare cookie. They're also a fine substitute for royal icing when it comes to making small details—drawing faces, writing words, making tiny black dots on the ladybug's back (page 201). I began decorating before edible markers came on the market, but if you are new to decorating and want to develop your skills before using piping tips, they aren't a bad way to start. Edible markers are available at cake decorating supply stores and online (see Sources, page 275).

Extracts

Because luster dust is not water-soluble, any clear, alcohol-based extract (lemon and clear vanilla are the most readily available) or vodka must be used to thin it before painting with it on cookies. Add the liquid to the luster dust with a dropper for best results. Vodka is ideal for mixing with the dust if you plan to stack or package your cookies, since it doesn't smear the way luster dust mixed with lemon extract can if it comes into contact with other cookies.

Natural Food Coloring

Plant-derived food colorings are available in both liquid and powder forms. The liquid colorings are good to use if you do not need intense or specific colors. These must be mixed very carefully with icing as they can quickly thin it. Several cookies here, including the Swiss Cheese (page 240), Seashell (page 175), and Stork (page 263), can

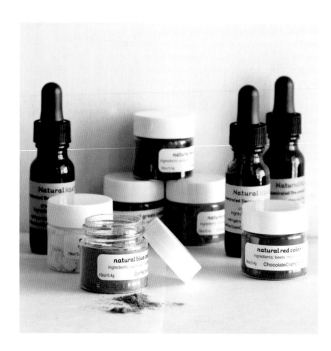

Luster Dust

I am from the less-is-more school when it comes to decorating cookies. I love using many different colors on a single cookie, so long as the results are clean and unfussy. For the cookies in this book I avoid any additional embellishments, including edible glitter, disco dust, sanding sugar, or even sprinkles. The one exception I do make is with edible gold, silver, and pink luster dust, which allows me to achieve a sheen on certain cookie designs that really benefit from it. For example, the metal details on the Stacked Luggage cookie (page 166) wouldn't look nearly as realistic without the luster dust. And Santa's cheeks (page 92) benefit from a dusting of pink luster dust.

be decorated using the natural liquid colorings, but the effect will be more subdued than if gels are used. Powdered natural colorings, on the other hand, will produce vibrant colors. They do not thin the icing any more than standard gels do.

Isomalt

A sugar substitute that comes in the form of crystals or nibs, isomalt is used to attach one cookie to another (see Playing with Your Cookies, page 70) or a lollipop stick to a cookie by first melting it and then using it like glue. I use the nibs exclusively because they are easier to work with; they just require a microwave and a glass measuring cup.

Painter's Palette

A ceramic palette is useful for mixing gel paste colors with water to make "watercolors" for painting onto iced cookies. A dinner plate can also be used.

MAKING, ROLLING, AND CUTTING OUT THE DOUGH

MY SIGNATURE GINGERBREAD COOKIES

MAKES ABOUT 32 (3-INCH) COOKIES

This is the cookie dough that started it all. When I first began baking cookies professionally, most of them were gingerbread, which led to many commissions for gingerbread replicas of New York landmarks and iconic architecture—the French/Gothic Sherry-Netherland Hotel, the original Dean & DeLuca store and dozens of other SoHo cast iron loft buildings, and many brownstones. I love this cookie for the delicious bite of ginger paired with sweet icing. For the first few years I made it, I ate at least five each day, dunked in coffee. It's the perfect cookie—sophisticated enough for adults and appealing to kids. This is the only cookie that benefits from chilling the dough regardless of the method used to roll it out. The dough can be a bit sticky, making it difficult to use directly from the bowl as is standard in the Parchment Paper Method (page 35). When decorating, keep in mind that any part of a gingerbread cookie that isn't covered with icing will appear dark.

3 cups plus 2 tablespoons (420 grams) unbleached all-purpose white flour

1 teaspoon baking soda

½ teaspoon baking powder

⅔ cup (1 stick plus 3 tablespoons, or 151 grams) unsalted butter, softened

½ cup packed (100 grams) brown sugar

1 tablespoon ground ginger

1½ teaspoons ground cinnamon

¼ teaspoon ground cloves

1½ teaspoons salt

1 large egg

¾ cup molasses

Whisk together the flour, baking soda, and baking powder in a medium bowl and set aside. In the bowl of a standing mixer fitted with the paddle attachment, combine the butter, brown sugar, ginger, cinnamon, cloves, and salt and mix on medium speed until the ingredients are thoroughly incorporated, about 1 minute. Reduce the speed to low, add the egg, and mix until thoroughly incorporated, about 1 minute. Raise the speed to medium and mix

for 5 seconds more. Do not overbeat. Pour in the molasses and mix until thoroughly combined, about 30 seconds. Reduce speed to low.

Gradually add the flour mixture, scraping down the sides of the bowl as needed, and beat until the dry ingredients are just incorporated.

Divide the dough into two equal parts, flatten into discs, and double-wrap in plastic wrap. Refrigerate for at least 2 hours. Roll out the dough using the Pastry Cloth Method (page 34).

Preheat the oven to 350°F. Cut out shapes from the dough (see page 36). Bake the cookies until they are slightly firm to the touch, 8 to 14 minutes, depending on the size. Do not let the edges darken. Let the cookies rest on the baking sheet for 5 minutes, then transfer to a rack to cool completely before decorating.

2½ cups plus 2 tablespoons (340 grams) unbleached all-purpose white flour

½ teaspoon baking powder

½ teaspoon salt

¾ cup (1½ sticks or 170 grams) unsalted butter, softened

1 cup plus 2 tablespoons (225 grams) granulated sugar

1 large egg

1½ teaspoons vanilla extract

SUGAR COOKIES

MAKES ABOUT 24 (3-INCH) COOKIES

This dough is not overly sweet so it pairs well with the royal icing. That said, unfrosted, these cookies taste amazing. If you are new to cookie decorating, this is the perfect dough to get you started. Not only is it easy to work with, but it is sturdy enough to stay intact when using intricately shaped cookie cutters.

Whisk together the flour, baking powder, and salt in a medium bowl and set aside. In the bowl of a standing mixer fitted with the paddle attachment, combine the butter and sugar and mix on medium speed for 1 to 2 minutes, until thoroughly combined. Reduce the speed to medium low and add the egg and vanilla, mixing until thoroughly combined, about 40 seconds. Reduce speed and gradually add the flour mixture, scraping down the sides of the bowl as needed and beating just until the dry ingredients are incorporated.

If using the Pastry Cloth Method (page 34) to roll out the dough, divide the dough into two equal parts, flatten into discs, and double-wrap in plastic wrap. Refrigerate for at least 3 hours. If using the Parchment Paper Method (page 35), roll out the dough straight from the mixing bowl, working in three batches.

Preheat the oven to 350°F. Cut out shapes from the dough (see page 36). Bake the cookies until the edges begin to brown slightly, 9 to 15 minutes, depending on the size. Let the cookies rest on the baking sheet for 5 minutes, then transfer to a rack to cool completely before decorating.

ANDREA'S WHOLE WHEAT COOKIES

MAKES ABOUT 24 (3-INCH) COOKIES

This dough, named for my assistant Andrea, who helped create it, is made with stone-ground whole wheat flour (not to be confused with whole wheat pastry flour, which results in a fragile cookie) and hazelnut extract. It's perfect if you love earthy flavors and a bit more texture to your cookie. If you do not like the flavor of hazelnut, replace it with vanilla extract.

2½ cups plus 2 table-spoons (340 grams) unbleached all-purpose white flour

1⅓ cups plus 1 tablespoon (252 grams) stone-ground whole wheat flour

1½ teaspoons salt

1 teaspoon baking powder

1½ cups (3 sticks or 340 grams) unsalted butter, softened

1¾ cups (354 grams) granulated sugar

1 large egg

2 teaspoons vanilla extract

2 teaspoons hazelnut extract

Whisk together the all-purpose and whole wheat flours, salt, and baking powder in a medium bowl and set aside. In the bowl of a standing mixer fitted with the paddle attachment, combine the butter and sugar and mix on medium speed until thoroughly combined, 1 to 2 minutes. Reduce the speed to low, add the egg and extracts, and beat for 1 minute.

Gradually add the flour mixture, scraping down the sides of the bowl as needed and beating just until the dry ingredients are just incorporated.

If using the Pastry Cloth Method (page 34) to roll out the dough, divide the dough into two equal parts, flatten into discs, and double-wrap in plastic wrap. Refrigerate for at least 2 hours. If using the Parchment Paper Method (page 35), roll out the dough straight from the mixing bowl, working in three batches.

Preheat the oven to 350°F. Cut out shapes from the dough (page 36). Bake the cookies until they just begin to darken around the edges, 8 to 14 minutes, depending on the size. Let the cookies rest on the baking sheet for 5 minutes, then transfer to a rack to cool completely before decorating.

CHOCOLATE COOKIES

MAKES ABOUT 24 (3-INCH) COOKIES

Yum. These are delicious straight from the cooling rack because of their distinctive rich chocolate flavor. Not only do they taste incredible, but they are a gorgeous dark brown color, making them a great background for certain cookies, including the Ghost (page 158) and the Indian Corn (page 159).

CHOCOLATE COOKIES CONTINUES

3 cups (390 grams) unbleached all-purpose white flour

1 teaspoon baking powder

½ teaspoon salt

1 cup (2 sticks or 227 grams) unsalted butter, softened

1½ cups plus 3 tablespoons (338 grams) granulated sugar

½ cup plus 2 tablespoons (57 grams) sifted unsweetened cocoa powder

2 large eggs

Whisk together the flour, baking powder, and salt in a medium bowl and set aside. In the bowl of a standing mixer fitted with the paddle attachment, combine the butter and sugar and mix on medium speed for 60 seconds. Reduce the speed to low, add the cocoa, and mix until thoroughly incorporated, about 30 seconds. Add the eggs, one at a time, scraping the bowl after each addition until thoroughly incorporated.

Gradually add the flour mixture, scraping down the sides of the bowl as needed and beating just until the dry ingredients are incorporated.

If using the Pastry Cloth Method (page 34) to roll out the dough, divide the dough into two equal parts, flatten into discs, and double-wrap in plastic wrap. Refrigerate for at least 3 hours. If using the Parchment Paper Method (page 35), roll out the dough straight from the mixing bowl, working in three batches.

Preheat the oven to 350°F. Cut out shapes from the dough (page 36). Bake the cookies until the centers are slightly firm, 8 to 14 minutes, depending on the size. Let the cookies rest on the baking sheet for 5 minutes. Transfer to a rack to cool before decorating.

VEGAN GINGERBREAD COOKIES

MAKES ABOUT 24 (3-INCH) COOKIES

This cookie is a favorite of my longtime yoga teacher, for whom I developed the recipe. It's a wet dough; it will never harden to the same stiffness as doughs made with butter, no matter how long you chill it. The trick here is to use the Pastry Cloth Method (page 34) to roll it out, so that you can help yourself to lots of flour as you go. I like unsweetened soy milk for these, but if you can't find it, the more readily available sweetened version is perfectly fine.

2 cups (260 grams) unbleached all-purpose white flour

1½ teaspoons ground ginger

½ teaspoon ground nutmeg

½ teaspoon ground cloves

½ teaspoon ground cinnamon

½ teaspoon baking soda

½ teaspoon baking powder

½ teaspoon salt

⅓ cup plus 1 tablespoon canola oil

¾ cup (169 grams) vegan sugar

¼ cup molasses

⅓ cup unsweetened soy milk

Whisk together the flour, ginger, nutmeg, cloves, cinnamon, baking soda, baking powder, and salt in a medium bowl and set aside. In the bowl of a standing mixer fitted with the paddle attachment, combine the oil and sugar and beat on medium speed for about 3 minutes. Reduce speed to low, add the molasses and soy milk, and mix until incorporated.

Gradually add the flour mixture, scraping down the sides of the bowl as needed and beating just until the dry ingredients are incorporated. The dough will be very wet.

Divide the dough into two equal parts, flatten into discs, and double-wrap in plastic wrap. Refrigerate for at least 3 hours. Roll out the dough using the Pastry Cloth Method (page 34).

Preheat the oven to 350°F. Cut out shapes from the dough (page 36). Bake the cookies until the centers are slightly firm, 8 to 14 minutes, depending on the size. Let the cookies rest on the baking sheet for 5 minutes, then transfer to a rack to cool completely before decorating.

OATMEAL COOKIES

MAKES ABOUT 24 (3-INCH) COOKIES

Yes, you can make a rolled and cut oatmeal cookie, which, when decorated, will come as a pleasant surprise to anyone who takes a bite. Kids love their flavor, making them a good choice because the oats and whole wheat flour add nutritional value. Use only old-fashioned rolled oats (not instant). Grind the oats until you can still see small pieces of them but not so finely that they become a powder.

1¾ cups (227 grams) unbleached all-purpose white flour

1 cup (100 grams) old-fashioned rolled oats (not instant), ground fairly fine

½ cup (60 grams) stone-ground whole wheat flour

½ teaspoon baking powder

1¼ teaspoons ground cinnamon

¼ teaspoon ground ginger

¾ teaspoon salt

1 cup (2 sticks or 227 grams) unsalted butter, softened

¾ cup packed (150 grams) light brown sugar

1 large egg

2 teaspoons vanilla extract

Whisk together the all-purpose flour, oats, whole wheat flour, baking powder, cinnamon, ginger, and salt in a medium bowl and set aside. In the bowl of a standing mixer fitted with the paddle attachment, combine the butter and brown sugar and beat on medium speed until thoroughly combined, about 1 minute. Add the egg and vanilla and beat on low until smooth, about 1 minute.

Gradually add the flour mixture, scraping down the sides of the bowl as needed and beating just until the dry ingredients are incorporated, 45 to 50 seconds. The dough will be slightly soft.

If using the Pastry Cloth Method (page 34) to roll out the dough, divide the dough into two equal parts, flatten into discs, and double-wrap in plastic wrap. Refrigerate for at least 3 hours. If using the Parchment Paper Method (page 35), roll out the

OATMEAL COOKIES CONTINUES

dough straight from the mixing bowl, working in three batches.

Preheat the oven to 350°F. Cut out shapes from the dough (page 36). Bake the cookies until the centers are slightly firm to the touch, 8 to 14 minutes, depending on the size. Let the cookies rest on the baking sheet for 5 minutes, then transfer to a rack to cool completely before decorating.

· ·

GLUTEN FREE LEMON LIME SUGAR COOKIES

MAKES ABOUT 24 (3-INCH) COOKIES

Gluten free flour tends to make a very tender dough, which means that it was a challenge to create a gluten free recipe for rolled and cut cookies. After testing dozens of variations, I found this one to be excellent, though a tad more fragile than other doughs. It keeps its shape well and is a great combination of texture and flavor. I experimented using 1 cup rice flour in place of 1 cup of the gluten free flour, and it worked beautifully, too. I use Bob's Red Mill xanthan gum, the stabilizer and thickener that gives the cookies their sturdiness, as well as the company's gluten free flour. This turned out to be a huge favorite among my friends and samplers, who had no idea it was gluten free. It also happens to be my happiest discovery among the recipes I developed for this book.

3 cups (408 grams) Bob's Red Mill All-Purpose Gluten Free Baking Flour, sifted before measuring

1½ teaspoons baking powder

¾ teaspoon xanthan gum

½ teaspoon salt

1 large egg

2 tablespoons heavy cream

2 teaspoons lemon extract

1 teaspoon lime zest

1½ teaspoons lime juice

1 cup (2 sticks or 227 grams) unsalted butter, softened, at room temperature

1 cup plus 2 tablespoons (225 grams) granulated sugar

Whisk together the flour, baking powder, xanthan gum, and salt in a medium bowl and set aside. In a small bowl, gently whisk together the egg, heavy cream, lemon extract, lime zest, and lime juice and set aside.

In the bowl of a standing mixer fitted with a paddle attachment, combine the butter and sugar and beat on medium speed until just smooth, less than a minute. Reduce the speed to low, gradually add the egg mixture, and mix until thoroughly incorporated. (The mixture may look curdled. This is okay.)

Gradually add the flour mixture, scraping down the sides of the bowl as needed and beating just until the dry ingredients are incorporated and the dough comes together on the paddle, 45 to 50 seconds.

If using the Pastry Cloth Method (page 34) to roll out the dough, divide the dough into two equal parts, flatten into discs, and double-wrap in plastic wrap. Refrigerate for at least 3 hours. If using the Parchment Paper Method (page 35), roll out the dough straight from the mixing bowl, working in three batches. Cut out shapes from the dough (page 36). Refrigerate cutout cookies for at least 30 minutes.

Preheat the oven to 350°F. Bake the cookies until they are firm to the touch, 12 to 17 minutes, depending on the size. Let the cookies rest on the baking sheet for 5 minutes, then transfer to a rack to cool completely before decorating.

BAKING PERFECT COOKIES: TIPS AND A TIMESAVER

Measuring Flour: Every baker has a preferred method for measuring flour. I generally weigh my flour, but on the occasion that I measure it by volume, I use the scoop and scrape method, but not before I pour the flour into a large bowl and fluff it with a fork to aerate it. Next I dip my cup into the flour and scoop it to overflowing, then hold the cup over the bowl and scrape the excess off with a knife or any straightedge.

Staying in Shape: If the temperature in the kitchen is especially warm or if you want to help ensure that the cutout shapes won't spread as they bake, chill them on the baking sheet in the refrigerator for 15 to 20 minutes before putting them in the oven.

Baking Times: These will vary depending on the size—and shape—of the cookie. The more intricate the shape, the quicker the cookies will bake. For example, circle or square cookies take longer than guitars or ghosts.

Underbaked Cookies: There have been times when I've pulled the cookies from the oven a touch too soon, but didn't discover it until they cooled completely. This is fine if the shape is not too intricate. You want your cookies to be firm for decorating, so put the more fragile ones back in the preheated oven and bake for 3 to 5 minutes more.

Yields: Since cookie cutters vary in size, you will often have dough left over after rolling out my suggested number of cookies. Do not be concerned! You can always bake more cookies and freeze them for future decorating or freeze the unbaked dough.

Timesaver: You can prepare the dough more than a day in advance; just double-wrap it very well and refrigerate for up to 4 days or freeze for up to 2 months.

ROLLING OUT THE DOUGH

I like two methods for rolling out dough—the Pastry Cloth Method and the Parchment Paper Method. Choosing a method is strictly a matter of taste and comfort. Try them both and decide for yourself which one feels right.

THE PASTRY CLOTH METHOD

This is my go-to method for rolling out dough, probably because it's the one I used when I started my cookie business so many years ago. It still works for me because I roll out large swaths of dough (I am usually making at least 4 dozen cookies at a time and often many more), and I like the simplicity of going from pastry cloth to baking sheet to oven. I rarely refrigerate the unbaked, cutout cookies (unlike in the Parchment Paper Method), but rather work quickly so that the dough does not get too warm before it goes into the oven. Admittedly, it seems a bit quaint— old-fashioned even—but I go for the tactile approach. You touch the dough, sprinkle flour around, and rub it into the pastry cloth. And I never get tired of looking at the faint linear images the cutters leave behind. Yes, it incorporates some flour into the dough, and yes, I do have to throw out a small piece of dough at the very end, but still, it feels right to me, however messy. I highly recommend this method when rolling out My Signature Gingerbread Cookies (page 26) and Vegan Gingerbread Cookies (page 30), both of which love more than a dusting of flour.

what you need

Baking sheets

Parchment paper, for lining baking sheets

Pastry cloth (see page 16)

Unbleached all-purpose white flour

Rolling pin fitted with ¼-inch silicone rings or accompanied by 2 (15-inch-long) ¼-inch-thick dowels

Dough of choice (pages 26–33), chilled in the refrigerator and set out at room temperature until it gives under the rolling pin (Note: If the dough was refrigerated more than 4 hours, or overnight, it must be set out at room temperature for at least 30 minutes.)

1. Line four baking sheets with parchment paper and set aside.

2. Place the pastry cloth on a clean work surface and sprinkle flour over it. Gently rub the flour into the pastry cloth. Unwrap one batch of dough and set it in the center of the pastry cloth. Set the rolling pin fitted with the silicone rings in the center of the dough. Alternatively, arrange the dowels on the cloth perpendicular to you and far enough apart so that both ends of the rolling pin just sit on them. Roll up and away from your body. Pick up the pin, place it back in the center, and roll down toward you. Repeat rolling in this manner, checking after a few rolls to be sure the dough is not sticking. If it is sticking on either the bottom or the top, sprinkle a little flour onto the pastry cloth or the top of the dough and spread it around. Rotate the dough 45 degrees, and roll as above. To rotate the dough as it grows larger, slide both hands underneath it toward the center and gently lift. Roll until the rings on the pin hit the counter, at which point you will have a rectangle or circle of dough that is ¼ inch thick.

Cut out the cookies (see Cutting Out Cookies, page 36) and bake. If not quite ready to bake, freeze them in an airtight container (see page 37).

THE PARCHMENT PAPER METHOD

This method, in which the dough is rolled out between two pieces of parchment, allows you to begin rolling straight from the mixing bowl. It's ideal if you are the neat, clean, orderly type, or if you are impatient for the dough to chill before cutting out your cookies and want to get going right away. That said, you still have to chill the dough after it is rolled out and again after the cookies are cut out (right on the baking sheet), so it isn't necessarily a timesaving option. This technique doesn't add flour to the dough during rolling, which means there's no waste; you'll use every last speck of it, unlike in the Pastry Cloth Method (opposite), which yields some unusable scraps since the dough ends up drying out.

what you need

Dough of choice (pages 26–33)

13 x 18-inch sheets of parchment paper

Rolling pin fitted with ¼-inch silicone rings or accompanied by 2 (15-inch-long) ¼-inch-thick dowels

Baking sheets

1. Place a piece of dough between two sheets of the parchment. Use the rolling pin fitted with the silicone rings, or place the dowels on top of the top parchment sheet perpendicular to you and far enough apart so that both edges of the rolling pin just sit on top of them.

PARCHMENT PAPER METHOD CONTINUES

the same manner, then set it directly on top of the previous package. If you are not planning to bake the cookies the same day you roll out the dough, wrap the whole stack—the layers of parchment and doughs and baking sheet—in plastic wrap and refrigerate.

3. Remove one piece of dough from the refrigerator at a time. Flip it over and loosen the top piece of parchment until it comes completely away from the dough, then set it back on top of the dough. This will prevent your cutout cookies from sticking to the parchment. Flip the whole thing back over and remove the top piece of parchment altogether.

CUTTING OUT THE DOUGH

1. To cut out the cookies, place the cutter as close to the edge of the dough as possible and press firmly to cut through the dough. Lift it out of the dough, set it on the baking sheet, and push the dough out by pushing your index finger around the edge, being careful with the intricate parts. If the design is super-intricate, you may want to dip the cutter into flour first. If you're using the Pastry Cloth Method and the dough does not easily come up off the cloth, slide a wide, flat metal spatula under the cutout and transfer it onto the baking sheet. If using the Parchment Paper Method, re-chill the dough in the refrigerator.

Set the rolling pin in the center of the dough and roll up and away from your body. Pick up the rolling pin, place it back in the center, and roll down toward your body. Repeat rolling in this manner, rotating the whole parchment paper–dough sandwich. Roll until the rings on the pin hit the counter, at which point you will have a rectangle or circle of dough that is ¼ inch thick.

2. Slide the whole package (parchment /dough/ parchment) onto a baking sheet and refrigerate until firm, about 30 minutes. Roll the remaining dough in

2. Whichever method you are using, gather up the scraps and press them together into a disc. Reroll using preferred method and cut out as above if there is enough. If not, add them to the next batch.

Tip: When I'm cutting the dough, there are inevitably small patches of dough left over. And if I don't feel like rolling it up into a ball, chilling and rerolling and cutting, I use a mini cutter to use up the dough. A graduated set of cutters is great for this, or any mini cutter that will fit the space. And then I have something to munch on while I decorate other cookies.

Timesaver: Rolling and cutting out dough can be done in advance of baking the cookies. Arrange the cutout shapes between sheets of parchment in a rigid container, seal tightly, and freeze up to 2 months. To bake them, put them on parchment-lined baking sheets while they're still firm. Bake as directed in the recipe, or an extra minute if the dough is still frozen.

DIY COOKIE CUTTERS: HOW TO MAKE YOUR OWN

I make all of my own cutters, which may sound a bit extreme, but it's actually very easy—and it allows me to cut out any cookie shape I can dream up. Cookie-friendly images are all over the place—in art and children's books, on greeting cards, wrapping paper, and fabrics, and, of course, on the Internet. Once you begin to look at everything with an eye toward turning it into a cookie, you will find inspiration in places you would least expect. Aluminum cookie cutter strips are available online (see Sources, page 275).

what you need

Paper and pencil

¾- to 1-inch-wide aluminum cookie cutter strips

Needle-nose pliers

Clear adhesive tape

1. Hand-draw or trace your design on a piece of paper. Cut a length of the aluminum strip at least 2 inches longer than you will need to make the shape. This may be difficult to judge, so estimate more than you may need. Using the outer edge of the drawing as your guide, use your fingers and needle-nose pliers to bend the aluminum strip to conform to the shape of your drawing, setting the strip against the drawing throughout. The pliers work best to create sharp turns, while your fingers will shape curves. When you come to a sharp turn, mark the spot on the strip with a pencil and, using the pliers, bend the metal to make a crisp angle.

2. When the metal ends meet, allow them to overlap by ½ inch and cut with an old pair of scissors (so you don't ruin a new pair). Wrap tightly with the tape at the overlap, making sure that the two sides of the cutter strip line up.

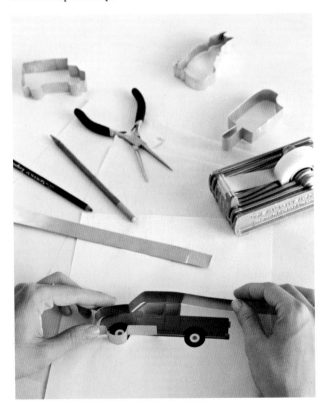

MAKING ICINGS

I like to think of my cookies as inspiration; they're suggestions that exemplify my personal decorating style. My hope is that once you understand the basic techniques of cookie decorating, you will develop your own style, changing up the colors and patterns—and finding even more designs in the cookie shapes here. Paint the spider whatever color you like, choose team colors for the football helmet, and decorate the wedding cake with polka dots and stripes. Vary the colors and designs within each batch. The pear can be a Bartlett, Anjou, Comice, Bosc, or Red Williams, depending on how you color the icing. The possibilities are unlimited.

THE ICING RECIPES

I always make sure I have plenty of uncolored royal icing on hand—more than I need, in fact. I strongly suggest that you make extra royal icing for each recipe. It will come in handy if you want to practice decorating techniques on paper or spare cookies, need to lighten up a color that you accidentally made too dark, or even remake a color that can't be rescued. You might also want to make three different colors of Baseball Caps (page 242), or Cars (page 176), or Rotary Phones (page 260). It is a lot easier to have extra icing on hand than it is to make more in the middle of a cookie decorating session. What's more, royal icing is inexpensive and can be stored in the refrigerator, wrapped properly, for up to a week. Throughout, I note that you can reserve lining icing in its bag, properly wrapped, for use the following day. Depending on the storage conditions, the icing may or may not keep properly, but it's worth a try. If the reserved icing is difficult to use, simply make more and don't worry about the colors matching perfectly.

Tip: Every recipe can be directly doubled or tripled (as long as your mixer can accommodate it) if you are making several batches of cookies.

Tip: Be sure to use sifted confectioners' sugar in the icing recipes. If you don't, your pastry tips may clog.

ROYAL ICING WITH EGG WHITES

MAKES 2 CUPS

I invariably use this version of royal icing, simply because it's the recipe I've long been accustomed to. Pasteurized egg whites come in pints or larger cartons in the refrigerated section of grocery stores. You can store the whole carton in the fridge, or you can freeze the egg whites in small containers if not using all at once.

5½ cups (562 grams) sifted confectioners' sugar

7 tablespoons pasteurized egg whites

½ teaspoon lemon juice, optional

Combine the confectioners' sugar and egg whites in the bowl of a standing mixer fitted with the paddle attachment. Beat on low until smooth, about 30 seconds. Add lemon juice, if using. With the mixer on medium speed, beat until thick, soft peaks form, scraping down the sides of the bowl, 1 to 2 minutes.

- **Don't let the icing dry out.** Keeping icing from drying out and crusting over is essential throughout the entire decorating process. Leave the beater right in the bowl, then drape a damp terry cloth dish towel over it. Be sure the *bowl is covered at all times* apart from when you are transferring icing to smaller bowls to make colored icing.

- **Do give the icing enough time to dry on the cookie.** This is crucial, especially dark colors on light; it's not as risky with two pale colors. The majority of the cookies in the following pages take more than a day to complete (typically two) because the flooding icing (the icing in the larger areas of color) must set for 6 to 8 hours. It is best to let the icing set until it is hard. To determine whether it is completely dry, do my **Ball Pin Test:** If a ball pin can't puncture the surface, your icing is dry and you can proceed. Drying times can vary considerably depending on how thick or thin you paint on the icing. Use your best judgment.

- **Do achieve the right consistency.** Royal icing should form a soft peak that will fall over when you pull the beater away from it—it might fall back into itself, but it will never dissolve back into the bowl. If the icing is too stiff (the peak does not fall over), add more egg whites or reconstituted egg white powder. If it is too loose, add more confectioners' sugar or thick royal icing to thicken it.

- **Don't skimp on the royal icing.** Note that I call for more icing than is likely needed in the decorating instructions because it's always better to have leftover icing than to have to stop in the middle of decorating to mix up more.

- **Do *refresh* the icing.** In every cookie recipe, I tell you to do this; *refresh* is simply the word I use for beating the icing in the mixing bowl after it has been sitting in the bowl for any longer than 3 or 4 hours.

ROYAL ICING WITH DRIED EGG WHITES

MAKES 2¼ CUPS

Dried egg whites can be kept at room temperature, which makes them a convenient option for making royal icing.

3 tablespoons dried egg white powder

6 tablespoons warm water

4½ cups minus 1 tablespoon (454 grams) sifted confectioners' sugar

Combine the egg white powder and warm water in the bowl of a standing mixer fitted with the paddle attachment. Before placing the bowl under the paddle, use a hand whisk to break up as many large clumps of dried egg white as you can. (Don't worry if all of them don't dissolve.) Let sit for 2 minutes. Beat the mixture on medium-high speed until frothy, about 2 minutes. Reduce speed to low and gradually add the confectioners' sugar, scraping the sides of the bowl as needed. Raise the speed to high and beat until smooth, about 2 minutes longer.

VEGAN ROYAL ICING

MAKES 3 CUPS

Because this icing replaces egg whites with water, it has a somewhat different texture than non-vegan versions. It may take slightly longer to dry than the instructions for the cookies suggest. If you use vegan confectioners' sugar, the icing may appear slightly gray. Add whitener to lighten it to the desired color.

2 tablespoons Ener-G egg replacer

½ cup plus 4 teaspoons warm water

1 tablespoon orange or lemon juice

1 teaspoon almond extract (optional)

10½ cups (908 grams) sifted vegan confectioners' sugar

Combine the egg replacer powder and water in the bowl of a stand mixer with the whisk attachment. Beat on medium speed for 4 minutes, until thickened. Switch to the paddle attachment. Add the orange or lemon juice and almond extract if using, and beat for 1 minute on medium. Reduce speed to low. Gradually add the confectioners' sugar, scraping the bowl as needed. Beat on medium-high speed until well mixed and smooth.

Tip: Saving Icing. Storing icing requires special care. I've come up with a way of keeping the mixing bowl of royal icing overnight that works every time. First, push any icing on the sides of the bowl that is still soft back down into the bowl. Place a piece of plastic wrap directly onto the icing so that it is touching it. Lay a piece of slightly dampened paper towel, gathered into a very loose ball, on the plastic, then cover the bowl itself tightly with a second piece of plastic wrap. The icing will keep in the refrigerator overnight. Refresh before using; if too thick, add a little egg white or water.

You can try storing colored icings, but I find I often have such small amounts of them left that I prefer to start fresh each day. If you do keep them, use the same technique as used with uncolored, but be sure to beat or mix them *very* well before using, as the colored icing may dry splotchy if you do not.

COLORING THE ICING

I have a narrow-necked carafe in my studio that pretty much tells the story of my love for color. Its ostensible use is as a holder for the piping bag as I fill it with colored icing, but I also invariably squeeze a bit of icing from the bag onto it to check out the color and, more importantly, the consistency. As time passes, the colorful strands of icing build up to make it a beautiful object reminiscent of the candle drip–covered Chianti bottles so ubiquitous in red sauce Italian restaurants. Everyone who comes into my studio notices it right away.

You don't need to be an artist to make wonderful colored royal icings. That said, I tend to border on obsession when it comes to mixing my own. If I want to make a blue the precise color of the Caribbean, I might mix together regal purple, neon green, and royal blue. But it's really not necessary; simply mixing a drop of turquoise into the white royal icing will yield equally pretty results. Once you become familiar with how the gels behave in the icing, mixing colors will become second nature. Patience, practice, and experimentation are key, as is a willingness to start over if you've taken a color too far in the wrong direction, so make sure you have extra ingredients! Sometimes, mistakes turn out to be the happiest accidents of all. The best colors are surprises—and even now, after years of stirring them up, I love to come up with icing colors I have never seen before.

MIXING COLOR DOS AND DON'TS

Do work quickly. Air is icing's nemesis, so if you are mixing several small bowls of icing simultaneously, cover those that you have not yet colored with plastic wrap so that it touches the surface of the icing. This will prevent a crust from forming. Alternatively, lay a damp kitchen towel over all of the bowls, allowing it to drape over the rims without touching the icing.

Do squeeze food color gel bottles carefully. Different colors have different consistencies and come out of the bottle at different rates, so be vigilant at this step.

Do check the color label on the bottle. Dark colors, including green, navy, red, brown, and blue, all look like black in the bottle. It is very easy to grab the wrong one—and discover when it's too late that it's not the color you intended.

Do intensify color very gradually. It is far more difficult to lighten a dark color than the other way around. When working with dark gels (blue, green, red, black), add gel to the icing *by toothpick, one dot at a time*. Add more color in this fashion until you get the desired shade. In fact, any gel color can have a dramatic effect on a small amount of icing.

Don't stir in the color too vigorously... or you'll end up with air bubbles in the icing. Rather, stir gently but thoroughly with a spoon, constantly scraping the icing from the sides of the bowl to keep it together; if icing remains on the sides of the bowl, it will dry out in no time and you'll risk introducing the dried-out pieces into your smooth, wet icing.

Do look at your colored icing in daylight, near a window, to get the truest version of the shade you are shooting for.

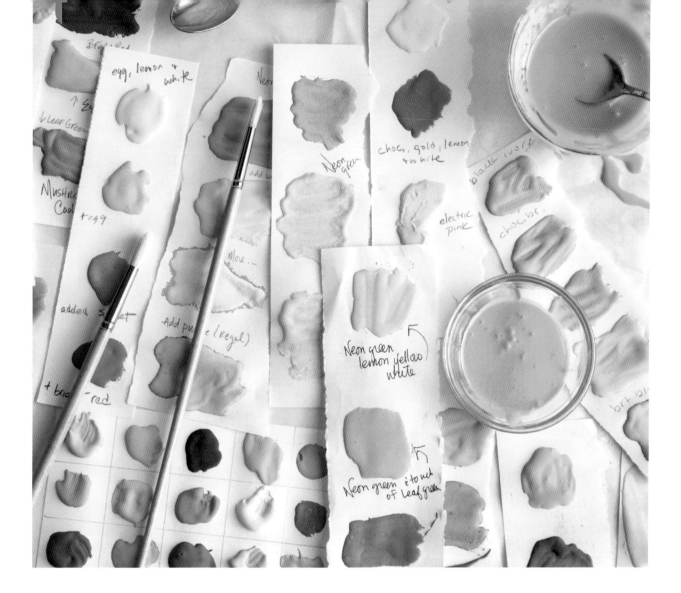

Food Coloring

Without a doubt, gel food colorings (see Sources, page 275) are superior to the liquid versions available in most grocery stores. They're more concentrated, which delivers two benefits: Your icing colors will be more intense, and the gels don't thin the icing the way liquids, which must be added in greater quantity to achieve deep color, do. So, what if liquid colorings are all that is available to you? You'll make perfectly fine pastel icings, but they will never be as vibrant as those made with gels.

Swatches: A Cookie Decorator's Color Chart

Mixing the exact same color twice can be elusive, which is why swatches of color are tacked up all over my studio. Whenever I make a color that I really like, I brush a postage stamp–sized swatch of it onto a piece of paper and scribble down the gel colors used to make it. To make color swatches, dip a toothpick into each gel paste color and mix dots of each color into a tablespoon of royal icing. Keep the ratio of gel paste to icing consistent with each color. For example, if you use 2 toothpick dots of gel paste with 1 tablespoon of icing, use those same amounts for every color. Dab each mixed color onto a sheet of paper, and write down what colors you used.

MIXING COLORS: THE BASICS

Throughout the cookie section, I instruct you to mix gels with royal icing to make certain colors. The detailed steps you need to take are here, and apply to mixing all manner of colors. In instances in which I list several gels to make a color, use more of the first gel listed, and gradually less of those listed second, third, and so on.

MIXING LIGHT COLORS

The lighter the color you want to make, the less gel you need to add. In fact, always use less than you think you need to get the color you want. Squeeze a tiny bit of the coloring onto the parchment, dip a toothpick into the gel, and swab it into the icing. Stir thoroughly with a spoon after each addition, digging down to the bottom of the bowl and around the sides to be sure the color is fully incorporated. Continue adding the gel to the icing, one toothpick dot at a time, and stirring, until the desired color is reached. Add a small drop of white food gel, which I call whitener (see page 48), and stir thoroughly. Of course, if you are coloring a large batch of royal icing, squeeze the gel from the bottle a drop at a time.

MIXING DARK COLORS

Making dark colors doesn't require as subtle a touch as do light colors—until you get close to the color you want.

1. When making deep, saturated colors, add the gel directly into the royal icing one drop at a time, stirring thoroughly after each addition. Be sure to dig down to the bottom of the bowl and around the sides to fully incorporate the color.

2. When you are close to the desired color and it seems one full drop will darken it too much, add a half drop of gel by touching the tip of the bottle to the icing and squeezing ever so gently. Alternatively, dip a toothpick into the gel and add pinpricks of color, stirring thoroughly after each addition, until you are satisfied with the color. Add a few drops of whitener (see page 48) to give the icing a lovely opacity but not so much as to lighten it considerably unless you want it lighter.

Tip: Mixing Skin Tones. Throughout, I call for a food gel called copper (flesh) for making light skin tones (see Santa, page 92; Gnome, page 231). If you can't find it, make your own skin tones using brown, pink, and yellow gels in the smallest amounts possible—pinpricks, really. For light skin tones, combine brown, pink, and yellow in the teeniest tiniest amounts possible (add whitener if you've gone too dark). For dark skin tones, use brown only.

Tip: Dark Colors Dry Darker. When in doubt, leave the icing color slightly lighter than the one you have in mind because it will dry somewhat darker. This is especially true of icings made with gel paste blues (bright blue, royal blue), browns (chocolate brown, buckeye brown), reds (bright red, red red), greens (leaf green, teal green, neon green), and purple (regal purple). They will darken quite a bit while drying on the cookie, so be aware of that as you make your flooding icing.

Tip: A Word About Black Food Gel. I find that black food gel has a somewhat different consistency from other gels, which is not readily obvious when you add it to the royal icing. But if you thin it to normal flooding consistency, it won't spread easily. To ensure that icing colored with black gel lies down nicely, I always make it slightly thinner than standard flooding icing when using it to paint on a cookie (it's so dark, it covers the cookie beautifully). If it is used for undercoating, as in the open mouth of the Hippo (page 196) and the background for the keys of the Typewriter (page 169), I make it even thinner and rub it into the cookie with the brush, which has the added benefit of a faster drying time.

Tip: Cocoa Is the New Black. If I have to use a lot of black gel to make black flooding icing, I sometimes use cocoa to color the icing to the point where only a little of the black gel is needed at the end. You can use this same technique for making large amounts of brown, too. To do this, spoon sifted cocoa into the royal icing and stir, adding more until it is a bit darker than milk chocolate. As you add cocoa, the icing may dry out, so add a little egg white or water to maintain its consistency. Then add the black food gel, one drop at a time, stirring thoroughly, and continue adding until you reach the desired color.

MIXING VINTAGE COLORS FOR DISTINCTIVE COOKIES

My personal taste leans toward colors that are slightly "off." The best examples include the wonderful green desk blotter under the Typewriter (page 169), the various greens on the Turtle (page 149), and the Stacked Luggage (page 166) in ochre, avocado, and dusty blue. One way to achieve these colors is to add a toothpick of ivory gel color to your colored royal icing. It tones down a color to give it sort of a vintage feel. If you don't have ivory, you can try brown or a complementary color to do the trick. Just remember to use toothpick dots of color.

Tip: Gel Stains Rx. Food gels are water-soluble, which means any stains you get on your hands will eventually disappear over the course of several washings with soap and water. If you want to remove stains immediately, use an abrasive cleaner such as Ajax and warm water. Stains on clothing will come out in the wash.

LIGHTEN UP: WHEN YOU MAKE A COLOR TOO DARK

If you are a beginning cookie decorator (and even if you're not!), you will almost certainly put too much gel paste into a bowl of royal icing at one time or another and wind up with a color that's too dark. This is not a big deal, especially because mixing up a new batch of icing in the right color is easy.

There are two ways to lighten up a color:

Spoon ¼ cup fresh icing into a small bowl. Next, gradually spoon a little of the too-dark color into the white icing and stir. Continue adding the darker icing in small portions until you reach the desired color. Adjust consistency as needed.

OR

Add white gel and stir until incorporated and you reach the desired color. Adjust consistency as needed.

WHAT IS WHITENER?

For years, I piped plain royal icing in its natural state onto cookies, satisfied with the not-exactly-white color, but once I discovered that whitener makes royal icing *bright white*, I never turned back. Whitening is not all the addition of whitener can do, though. I love the way a few toothpicks of it subtly mute an otherwise garish color and lend an opacity to it. My experience has also been that whitener gives colored icing body and seems to help keep colors from bleeding into each other. You will notice that many of the instructions for mixing color read like this: "Thin to flooding consistency, add whitener, and cover with plastic wrap." This always means a toothpick dot or a drop or two of whitener, which should be stirred in thoroughly.

ICING CONSISTENCIES: GETTING IT RIGHT

More than any other step, getting the consistency of royal icing right is key to successfully decorating cookies. Much of achieving this is a judgment call, and your judgment will grow keener the more you make the icings. After all these years, sometimes it still takes me several tries to get the icing the way I want it. When outlining or re-outlining, if your icing consistency is only slightly off, you can compensate by moving the piping tip a little more slowly (if it's too tight) or more quickly (if it's too loose).

There are essentially two icing consistencies—lining and flooding—that you will use repeatedly in cookie decorating. There are variations in thickness and thinness within each, but if you master these two, making the other subtly different versions will come easily.

Tip: One Bowl, Same Color, Two Icings. In many instances, you will make the same color icing for lining and flooding, in which case you can use the same bowl for both. Begin with stiff royal icing in a small bowl, mix it to the desired color, and thin to lining consistency. Spoon the amount you need to outline the cookies into a piping bag, then thin the remaining colored icing in the bowl to flooding consistency. Cover the bowl of flooding icing with plastic wrap to prevent it from drying out while using the lining icing to outline your cookies.

HOW TO MAKE LINING ICING

Icing that is thinned to **lining consistency** is the perfect thickness for easily outlining, re-outlining, and making details on a cookie. Lining icing is almost always applied to a cookie through a piping bag fitted with a tip. It should emerge from the piping tip in a smooth line without breaking and should hold up without spreading when it drops onto a cookie. I use the term **tight lining consistency** when an icing should be just slightly stiffer to achieve a finer line that gives more definition. Tighter lining icing comes in handy for writing a name or re-outlining a cookie. In some cases, you will want a **loose lining consistency,** in which the icing flows more quickly and with less pressure applied to the piping bag. Icing mixed to this consistency should fall more easily off the spoon into the mixing bowl, yet still retain its shape. I use loose lining consistency when lines sit on a bare cookie, as in the legs of the Spider (page 86). I also use it to make fatter lines, as in the ladybugs on the Leaf (page 200) and the cheese strands on the Pepperoni Pizza (page 155), by spooning it into a piping bag fitted with a #1.5 tip.

Here's how to thin icing to lining consistency:

1. Spoon the royal icing into a small bowl and stir. If it is too stiff to stir, add a touch of egg white or water. I generally use egg white, but either is fine.
2. Gradually add drops of the food gels in the order listed, using more of the first color, less of the second, and even less of the third (where applicable). (See Coloring the Icing, page 43.) Stir thoroughly after each addition until the desired color is reached. The icing should be only *slightly* thinner than it was when you started due to the addition of the gels.
3. Thin it to lining consistency by very gradually adding egg white or water to the bowl, gently stirring after each addition until the icing is a similar consistency to toothpaste. To test, lift the spoon out of the bowl. A soft peak should form and then fall back into itself.

Another way to test: If a spoonful of icing, dropped back into the bowl, begins to disappear into the icing in 10 seconds and disappears entirely after 60 seconds, you have lining icing in the correct consistency.

4. If you are unsure, spoon 1 tablespoon into a piping bag and practice making lines on a piece of parchment paper or on a spare cookie. The line of icing should be stiff enough to hold its shape and it should not be a struggle to squeeze the bag.

Tip: Too Much Egg White? If you accidentally pour too much egg white into the bowl of icing (and you will realize this just seconds after the fact), tip the bowl into the sink and let it drizzle out.

Troubleshooting: When Lining Icing Is Too Thick or Too Thin

Your lining icing is *too thick* if:

- The piping bag is way too difficult to squeeze.
- The line of icing breaks as it comes out of the tip.
- The icing does not adhere to the bare cookie.

To fix it, open the piping bag and squeeze the icing into a clean bowl. Thin with egg white to desired consistency and spoon into a new piping bag.

Your lining icing is *too thin* if:

- It drips out of the tip without your applying any pressure to the bag.

THINNING DOS AND DON'TS

- **Do be patient with yourself!** Knowing when you've reached lining consistency can involve lots of trial and error. Eventually, you will know when you're there by simply stirring the icing and dropping it from a spoon.

- **Don't stir in the egg white or water too vigorously.** This will create air bubbles in the icing.

- **Do cover the small mixing bowls with plastic wrap.** When making multiple bowls of lining icing at one time, use plastic wrap to cover those not immediately being thinned to prevent them from drying out.

- **Do leave the spoon in the small bowl of flooding icing as you are painting in cookies with the flooding icing** so that you can give it a stir and scrape down the sides often to prevent the icing from crusting over.

- The icing forms blobs when it comes out of the tip and the line you make does not hold its shape. You should be able to make sharp corners with the icing.

To fix it, open the piping bag and squeeze the icing into a clean bowl. Gradually add more royal icing or sifted confectioners' sugar to the bowl until you achieve lining consistency. Add gel and stir until the desired color is achieved.

Timesaver: Leftover Lining Icing. If you run out of flooding icing and have some unused lining icing in the same color, tear open the piping bag, spoon the icing into a bowl, and thin it to flooding consistency (below).

HOW TO MAKE FLOODING ICING

Flooding consistency is much thinner than lining consistency and is used to paint in the designs on the cookie. Conventional cookie decorating has you apply the flooding icing through a piping bag or squeeze bottle, but I have always used a paintbrush to put it on the cookie. I like the control and ease this offers, and using a brush allows you to apply a thinner coat. Royal icing that is thinned to flooding consistency should settle evenly and smoothly on the cookie's surface.

You can make flooding icing either with a fresh batch of stiff royal icing or from the colored icing that has been thinned to lining consistency. For the most part, you will make it the latter way.

Here's how to thin icing to flooding consistency:
- Spoon fresh royal icing into a small mixing bowl or use a bowl of icing already thinned to lining consistency.
- Gradually add egg white or water to the bowl, stirring gently but thoroughly after each addition until the icing reaches a consistency somewhere between honey and maple syrup. To test, drop a spoonful back into the bowl. It should fall off the spoon in a ribbon and disappear into the bowl after 6 to 8 seconds.

Troubleshooting: When Flooding Icing Is Too Thick or Too Thin

Your flooding icing is *too thick* if:
- It does not settle smoothly onto the surface of the cookie.
- The surface is bumpy after drying on the cookie (hold it at eye level to get the best view).
- It does not flow easily to the outline of the cookie when you gently nudge it with the brush.

To fix it, add more egg white to the bowl, stirring in the icing that has adhered to the sides of the bowl.

Your flooding icing is *too thin* if:
- It is the consistency of heavy cream or thinner.
- It runs over the outline when you paint it in.
- The cookie shows through.

To fix it, stir more fresh royal icing or sifted confectioners' sugar into the mixing bowl.

DECORATING COOKIES

I once had an assistant who put flooding icing on cookies using the back of a spoon instead of a brush. Another held the piping bag with one hand. And while I always suggested using two hands, I could not get her to change her ways, which turned out fine because her cookies were beautiful! There are basic techniques that will make decorating with a piping bag a pleasurable experience, but you will eventually find methods that are ultimately comfortable for you and result in beautiful creations. The point is not whether your technique is perfect but rather that you get the results you want. When there are five different people working in my studio, no two are using exactly the same techniques. The most important thing is to get started, keep at it, and don't let the process intimidate you. Sometimes accidents turn out to be the most memorable cookies. In fact, I once was working with children, making gingerbread houses, and the icing was so tight that the roofs popped off. The kids decided to decorate the insides of the houses by making tiny furniture out of candy and painting the walls!

PIPING BAGS

I use parchment paper bags exclusively because I find them easier to work with, I like the way they feel in my hand, and they're biodegradable. Admittedly, they are less convenient than plastic bags, but on the other hand, they are less expensive—a consideration if you are going to make lots of cookies in dozens of colors the way I do. Whatever bag you choose, get comfortable using it by practicing—*a lot*. I sometimes even use a bag and tip instead of a pencil when sketching out ideas. I like the three-dimensionality of the icing line compared to the flatness of a pencil. The more you use a piping bag, the better at it you will become.

HOW TO MAKE A
PARCHMENT PIPING BAG

These are remarkably simple—and satisfying—to make, once you get the hang of it. The first few may not be perfect, but persevere—after several successes, putting them together becomes second nature and goes quickly. Before I mix any royal icing, I fold a bunch of cones and stack them in a tall glass carafe so that they are ready when I need them. You can buy pre-cut parchment triangles or make your own from a 13-inch-wide roll of parchment.

1. Cut a 13-inch square piece of parchment from a roll. Fold it in half on the diagonal and run your finger or the flat side of a knife along the fold to make a sharp crease. Cut along the crease to make two triangles. Hold one triangle in both hands so that the longest side is at the top.

2. With your left hand, bring the left point down to meet the right angle to form a cone shape.

3. Turn the cone right side up and hold it in your left hand.

4. Using your right hand, grab the remaining point and wrap it around to meet the other points, fiddling with them so that they overlap. You will have three points at the top.

5. Fold the three points into the cone and make a sharp crease to create a smooth rim. Flatten the crease of the fold with your fingernail. The cone should stay together when you let go.

6. Using a pair of scissors, snip ½ to ¾ inch from the tip of the cone.

7. Drop the piping tip into the cone.

HOW TO FILL A PIPING BAG

1. Set the parchment bag, tip side down, into a carafe, vase, or paper towel tube (anything with a narrow neck will do). If using a disposable plastic piping bag, snip off about ½ inch of the tip of the cone with scissors, drop in the piping tip, and roll the top half of the bag down to form a cuff to make it easier to spoon the icing into it.

2. Spoon the icing into the center of the bag. Do not fill it more than halfway to prevent it from oozing out the top when you use it.

3. To seal the parchment bag, bring the top edges together, fold the corners down toward each other, and roll down until you reach the icing. Squeeze the bag gently from the top to remove any air pockets inside the bag. To seal a disposable plastic bag, cinch it shut with a rubber band, sealing it as close to the icing as possible to remove any air pockets.

4. Test the consistency of the icing by trying out a few lines on a piece of paper, the table, or a spare cookie.

Tip: A Tip About Tips. If you run out of tips, you can try to use the parchment bag without a tip. Just be sure that when you make the bag, the pointed end is entirely closed. Using small scissors, snip the smallest hole possible at the tip. This won't give you the same precision as a metal tip, but it works in a pinch.

Timesaver: What's in the Bag? It can be difficult to see color through a parchment piping bag, especially when colors are similar. To make it easier to distinguish one from another, use a Sharpie to write the name of the color on the outside of the bag.

HOW TO HOLD A PIPING BAG

Grasp the bag from the top only. You will find the bag far simpler to use holding it this way than if you apply pressure in the middle or anywhere else. Holding the bag this way serves two purposes: It puts pressure on the icing, pushing it down into the bag and out through the tip. It also serves to hold the top of the bag shut so that the icing doesn't ooze out the top.

1. Grasp the piping bag at the top with your dominant hand and wrap your fingers over the top, holding it tightly shut with your grasp. Use your thumb to apply added pressure to the side of the bag. Hold the bag so that the tip is at a 45-degree angle to the cookie.

2. Use one or several fingers of your other hand to support and steady the pastry bag while you work. Resist the temptation to work one-handed!

USING LINING ICING

Otherwise known to many as piping icing, I have always called the icing used to outline shapes and re-outline cookies lining icing. Using lining icing is a real pleasure when it is flowing smoothly out of the tip.

SEEING THE SILHOUETTE

My cookie decorating instructions invariably begin with outlining the silhouette of the design on the cookie without any interior lines. For example, the silhouette of the bow of the Gift Box (page 85) does not include the interior loops. Likewise, the silhouette of the box does not include the lines made to create the middle corner or the lid. The simplest example is the Kitty (page 162); the silhouette does not include the lines that delineate the arms and all of the interior details.

LINING: OUTLINING, RE-OUT-LINING, AND MAKING DETAILS

Getting lining right relies on balancing three components—speed, icing consistency, and applied pressure—every time you pick up the piping bag. Outlining, typically the first decorating step, is always done in the same color

as the flooding icing (except if you are Speed Outlining, page 60), so that when viewed from the side, you see the same color that's on the top of the cookie. For some people, it takes weeks of practice to become proficient at lining, but others pick it up instantly. As with every other aspect of cookie decorating, practice makes perfect. Make sure the tip is clean by wiping it off between your fingers before you begin and as you decorate the cookies.

1. **Starting a line.** As a right-hander, I find it easiest to begin lines on the left and move right (the opposite is true for lefties) or start at the top and go to the bottom. This allows you to see the icing coming out of the bag and gives you a better chance to drop it in the right place. Touch the piping tip to the surface of the cookie and squeeze gently. The icing should attach to the cookie and should not form a tiny ball when you begin.

2. **Dropping a line.** Continue to squeeze gently while lifting the tip about ½ inch above the cookie and holding the bag at a 45-degree angle. The icing should fall in a smooth line from above the cookie as you move the piping bag in the direction you want to go. The longer the line you are making, the higher above the cookie the tip can be.

3. **Ending a line.** I always say that learning how to do this is much like learning how to stop on a bicycle. Eventually, muscle memory takes over. Ending a line involves anticipating at what point you should ease pressure on the piping bag and

ultimately stop squeezing it altogether. To do this, you must reconcile the length of the line of icing falling from the tip with how much more cookie it needs to cover. Once you begin to ease pressure on the bag, guide the line of icing into place while lowering the tip down to touch the surface of the cookie. When you touch the piping tip to the surface of the cookie to end a line, do not squeeze the bag at all, and pull the tip away. If you continue to squeeze, a tiny ball of icing will form at the end of the line. Mastering this technique means that no one will ever know where your lines begin and end.

4. **Making sharp corners.** I use a technique called "touching down" to make sharp corners and avoid curved ones. To make sharp corners, always end your line by touching the pastry tip to the cookie and then continuing on until the next sharp angle. If you try to turn the corner without stopping, you will get a curve where you want an angle.

5. **Outlining curves.** Use the same techniques you would for outlining straight lines, but keep your eyes on the icing where it meets the cookie to help you better place the line. To outline short curves, bring your tip closer to the surface of the cookie; this gives you more control over where the line drops than if you are working higher above it. Slowly guide the icing to fall around the curve.

6. **Drying.** Let outlines dry for 5 minutes before painting them in with flooding icing. At times, I have waited just 2 minutes or so and painted

inside them very gently. If you are making two dozen cookies, by the time you are finished outlining the last cookie, the first cookie will be dry.

Tip: In a Word, Practice. I love to practice on spare cookies because I often end up with a design that really pleases me when I wasn't trying to design anything at all. If you don't have any cookies, practice on paper. Trace a cutter onto a piece of paper and outline the shape with the lining icing. Practice dropping horizontal, vertical, diagonal, and curved lines of all lengths.

TROUBLESHOOTING: IMPERFECT OUTLINES AND DETAILS

Wiggly line: You are holding the piping tip either on or too close to the cookie. It should hover about ½ inch above the cookie and the bag should be held at a 45-degree angle. There are times, however, when you *want to* make a jagged line (see Leaf, page 200; and

Flower, page 194)—in which case, holding the piping tip close to the cookie does the trick.

Broken line: If you move your hands too quickly and are not squeezing the piping bag hard enough, you can pull the line of icing to the point where it breaks. Slow down and squeeze harder.

Thick, wavy line: This is generally caused by moving too slowly and/or squeezing the piping bag too hard. Speed up and ease up on the piping bag.

Timesaver: Speed Outlining. As mentioned, outlining the silhouette and interior details is usually done in the same color used to flood that space. But to save time, especially if a cookie features many different colors, use white lining icing to outline everything. Paint in with the specified colored flooding icing, taking care to cover up the white lines.

DRAWING WITH A PIPING TIP

I use the term **drawing** to describe a technique I use to make thin or short lines and small details on a cookie that's been painted in and thoroughly dried (see the Ball Pin Test, page 41). Drawing with a tip is a lot like using a pencil. Set the tip directly on the cookie and squeeze the bag more gently than you would if you were outlining. Drawing comes in handy when writing a word in very small letters: Use the technique when you have less space to work in and you really want to make thin lines. Drawing also allows you to get a thinner line from a fat tip.

Tip: Steady On. To keep the cookie from sliding around

while you are pushing the tip against it, place it on top of a small terry cloth towel.

ERASING A LINE

Imperfect lines shouldn't be a cause for worry since by the time the cookie is completely decorated, this kind of mistake is barely noticeable. But if you put a line in the wrong place or just want to start over, remove it with an X-ACTO knife. To do this, scrape the errant line away by sliding the side of the blade underneath the line and working along the line; it will come off in pieces. Once the line is removed, scrape away any sign of the line with the side of the X-ACTO.

RE-OUTLINING

Almost every single cookie in this book is re-outlined, which means that I go over the silhouette and make any interior details with a colored lining icing (usually a shade darker, but not always). Generally the final step in the decorating process, it is similar in concept to framing a photo—re-outlining tends to pull together the look of the cookie. It is not absolutely necessary; there are times when I am certain I will re-outline, but when I get to that point and the cookie doesn't look like it needs it, I don't do it. It's really a matter of taste—there are no hard-and-fast rules. Re-outlining is especially useful when you want to define specific parts of the cookie (for instance, the tie on the Balloon, page 118; the veins on the Leaf, page 200; and the individual fries in the French Fries, page 78). The technique for re-outlining is exactly the same as that for outlining.

Timesaver: Speed Re-Outlining. To save yourself some time in the final step, re-outline the cookies in all black. This gives the design a graphic, illustrated look. That said, you have to be confident piping lines this dark because every single one shows. Make sure your lining icing is tight enough to make a nice thin line.

USING FLOODING ICING

Flooding icing is used for **painting in** the cookies, a technique most cookie decorators call flooding. Painting in the cookies is a very soothing, relaxing process, particularly when your icing consistency is just right, the brush feels good in your hand, and there's a good program on the radio. The trick here is to get the icing to cover the cookie so that you see no cookie through it but in as thin a layer as possible. Throughout, I give generous drying times for flooding icing. These are general guidelines; drying times depend on many factors, including how thick or thin you've painted on the icing, humidity, and the room temperature. Use your best judgment.

PAINTING IN WITHIN AN OUTLINE

Painting in a lined cookie is the technique I use to fill in an outlined area with flooding icing. The trick here is to apply a solid layer of icing onto the cookie but not more than is necessary. This is very important to the success of the cookie—it's crucial to its good looks—and satisfying when done well. Invariably, I am asked how I get my icing to look so smooth, and this is how. I call it painting, but it's really pushing.

1. Depending on the size of the area you are painting in, choose the appropriate-size brush (see Decorating Supplies, page 17). Dip the brush into the bowl of prepared flooding icing and load it up so that the bristles are completely covered. Do not let the excess icing drip off; twirl it around to prevent this.

2. Hold the cookie with the fingers of your non-painting hand so that it is level. Very quickly lay the brush on its side onto the cookie and twirl the bristles, applying gentle pressure, to release all of the icing onto the surface. If it looks like it is not enough to cover the area, dip the brush back into the flooding icing and repeat.

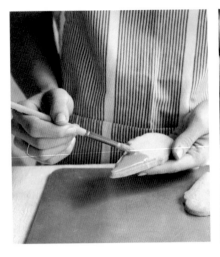

3. Working in one section at a time, gently push the icing around, gliding over the surface of the icing without touching the brush to the cookie itself. Paint the icing in so that it is as high as the outline—no lower or higher (hold the cookie up at eye level to accurately check this). If you paint it on too thinly, the cookie will show through; too thickly, and the icing may flow over the lined edge. Push the icing into tight spaces using the tip of the brush. As you approach the edge near the outline, nudge the icing so that it just covers the line to create a seamless painted surface.

4. Let the flooding icing dry 6 to 8 hours or overnight. Cookies are hard when a ball pin, pressed into the icing surface, will not puncture it. (See Ball Pin Test, page 41.)

PAINTING IN WITHOUT AN OUTLINE

There are instances when there is no outline into which you paint in the flooding icing. For example, the grass on the Building (page 217) and the grass on the Tombstone (page 212) are not outlined before the flooding icing is applied.

1. Depending on the size of the area you are painting in, choose the appropriate-size brush (see Decorating Supplies, page 17). Dip the brush into the bowl of prepared flooding icing and twirl to coat the bristles. Do not overload the brush with icing. Twirl the brush over the bowl a few times to let the excess drip off.

2. Hold the cookie with the fingers of your nonpainting hand. Lay the brush on its side on the cookie and twirl the bristles, applying gentle pressure, to release all of the icing onto the surface.

When painting in features that will be painted over, press the brush firmly against the surface of the cookie and brush the icing onto it in a thin layer, thinning it out beyond the area that will show on the cookie. Let dry to the touch, about 30 minutes. When painting in entire cookies without an outline, carefully paint to the edge of the cookie, pulling away from the edge with your brush so that the icing ends up slightly thinner around the edge. Let dry overnight.

Timesaver: Quick Dry. Decorated cookies dry best in a dry environment. Air-conditioning or a fan will help (any time of year!), as humidity can cause the icing to dry slowly and can result in splotchy colors.

Troubleshooting: Popping Air Bubbles. Sometimes, small air bubbles form in the icing as you paint it onto the cookie. To get rid of them, gently glide your brush across the surface of the icing a few times. If large bubbles form, pop them with a toothpick or pin.

PAINTING IN DOS AND DON'TS

- **Do dip your brush into the icing as many times as you need to transfer icing to a cookie.** It won't take long before you will be able to cover the entire surface of the cookie in just a few dips of the brush. But in the meantime, dip it as many times as you need to.

- **Do look closely at your cookie.** Hold it up to the light. If it looks bumpy, it may mean your flooding icing is too thick. Add egg whites and stir to thin to flooding consistency. The beauty of working from a bowl is that you can easily change the consistency of the icing as necessary.

APPLYING TWO DIFFERENT COLORS NEXT TO EACH OTHER

There are two main techniques for applying two different colors next to each other on a cookie: thinning out and butting up.

Thinning Out

This is the deceptively simple term for one of the key techniques in making these cookies look the way they do. It's the basis of a building process with lines and different colors of icing that I developed to add dimension, which makes the decoration look more realistic, lively,

and animated. It also makes it very difficult to detect how the cookie was made. For example, the beard and hat on Santa (page 92) look like they are actually sitting on his face because I thin out the pink icing for his face, then paint the beard and hat on top of the pink. This makes sense visually because in reality, his hat and beard would sit in front of his face. The cone on the Ice Cream Cone (page 227) is painted on this way, too.

To thin out flooding icing, use a paintbrush to push some icing beyond the area you are painting into the areas that will be covered with other colors. Make sure to extend the thinned-out icing far enough on the cookie: It shouldn't show on the finished cookie. Paint

it in a thin layer and let dry thoroughly.

Timesaver: Color, Side by Side. Though thinning out is my preferred method for applying two different colors of icing next to each other, if I am strapped for time, I will butt up the colors next to each other (see Butting Up, below). The cookies do not have the same dimensional look as when the icings are thinned out, but you don't have to wait for layers to dry before putting more icing on top.

Butting Up

Butting up is a technique used to paint one color next to another so that they exist on the same plane. It makes sense in such cases as the red and white stripes on the Cookie Jar (page 131), the beak on the Chick (page 77), and the black and orange on the face of the Swan (page 126). Once you've outlined the areas for each color, the corresponding flooding icings can be painted in at the same time.

1. Outline the different areas of color on the cookie with lining icing. It can be tricky to put two different outlines next to each other, but do the best you can.
2. Using the appropriate brush for the size of the area you are painting, paint each section with the corresponding flooding icing, using the Painting In Within an Outline technique (page 61). Paint in the area so that the icing sits at the level of the outline without covering it. You don't want the icing to overflow the outlines.

SPECIAL DECORATING TECHNIQUES

WET-ON-WET DOTS

This is an easy technique for making dots that are flush with the surface of the surrounding flooding icing. Because the dots are dropped into wet icing, they settle into it instead of sitting *on top* of it the way they would if piped onto dried icing. (Keep in mind that dark colors may bleed into light colors, so avoid putting dark dots on a light background if you want to ensure that color bleeding doesn't happen.)

1. To make wet-on-wet dots, prepare the flooding icing for the background color and the dots at the same time, thinning the icing for dots to slightly tighter than flooding consistency. Spoon it into a piping bag fitted with a #1 or #1.5 tip, depending on the size of the dots you want to make.
2. Paint in two or three cookies at a time with the flooding icing, and while the background color is still wet, squeeze the dots onto it (holding the piping bag at a 90-degree angle to the cookie), with the tip as close to the surface as possible without touching it. Gently squeeze the piping bag to release the icing; the dot will spread slightly and settle smoothly into the background icing. Keep this in mind when spacing the dots.

3-D DOTS

If you love dots but don't want to use the wet-on-wet technique, make them on a dried, painted-in surface instead. They will stick up off the cookie and will be smaller, but you have more control over the end result. What's more, they are brilliant for camouflaging splotches and a multitude of other icing sins such as bumpy icing. I use this kind of dot to add texture to a design: the center of the Flower (page 194), the berries on the Wreath (page 119), and anywhere there is an eye (Bird in Nest, page 137; Turtle, page 149; Spider, page 86).

To successfully make a dot, fill a piping bag fitted with a #1 or #1.5 tip with lining icing. Touch the piping tip to the surface of the dried flooding icing, holding the bag at a 45-degree angle. Squeeze gently until you get the size dot that you like. Stop squeezing the bag before removing the tip from the cookie. If packing in bags or shipping, the dots must be thoroughly dried, 6 to 8 hours or overnight. If serving the same day, let dry until they are crusted over, about 15 minutes.

Troubleshooting: If your 3-D dots have pointy tips, you can eliminate them by wetting a small brush with a little water and carefully patting the points on the dots with the brush to make them disappear.

CREATING DIMENSION WITH BLACK FLOODING ICING

There are instances when a cookie can really benefit from a thin layer of black flooding icing, in particular when you want to create the illusion of depth. For example, the earhole in the Football Helmet (page 134), the inside of the Hippo's mouth (page 196), the interior of the Bird in Nest (page 137), and the space behind the keys of the Typewriter (page 169). In each of these cases, black flooding icing is used to create the illusion of a hole.

WATERCOLORS

This technique is a nice alternative when you want to give your cookies a painterly look. It's a super-easy way to make them look just as special without having to mix

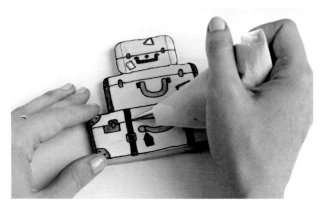

different colors of icing, so it is especially useful if you do not have enough time for several steps of lining and flooding. All you need is a white iced cookie, your gel food color, a plate or ceramic mixing palette, a cup of water, a watercolor brush, and a paper towel.

Watercoloring an Entire Cookie

1. Mix a small bowl of white royal icing and add whitener to make white icing. Thin to lining consistency and spoon ¼ cup into a piping bag fitted

with a #1 tip. Thin the remaining icing to flooding consistency and cover with plastic wrap. Using the lining icing, outline the cookie and let dry for 5 minutes. Using a paintbrush and the flooding icing, paint in cookie and let set until hard, 6 to 8 hours or overnight. It is essential that the icing be rock solid (do the Ball Pin Test, page 41).

Tip: When using watercolors, always make an extra cookie to use as your tester cookie. This way you will know if you like the color and consistency of the "paint" before you apply it to the main cookie. These tester cookies are always among my favorite by-products of cookie decorating.

2. Squeeze dots of desired food gel colors onto a plate or a ceramic palette. Dip a paintbrush into a little water, then gently touch the brush to the gel and swipe the brush onto the plate next to it to create a swatch of watercolor. The watercolor should be primarily water because if you paint with too much gel paste, it does not dry on the cookie. Test the color on your tester cookie. If you want it to be more intense, repeat the process.

3. Dip the brush into the watercolor, then lightly dab it onto a paper towel before applying to the cookie. Too much water in the watercolor can dissolve the icing on the cookie. The brush should be wet enough to paint with, but the watercolors should not puddle on the cookie. Lightly brush the watercolor onto the cookie. Let dry at least 30 minutes.

4. Leave the cookie as is to look more like a watercolor or, to make it look more graphic, re-outline in black lining icing. Spoon black royal icing thinned to lining consistency into a piping bag fitted with a #1 tip and use the drawing technique to make lines as thin as possible.

Timesaver: To speed up the process of making cookies decorated with watercolors, paint in the flooding icing early in the morning. It will harden sufficiently to paint on by evening.

WATERCOLOR DOS AND DON'TS

- **Don't ever use straight gel in place of watercolors.** The impulse is especially strong when you want to make dark watercolors. Don't succumb because the colors will not dry.

- **Don't worry if the watercolor beads up on the cookie.** Let it dry and go over it again. Or, just consider it a textural element of the design!

- **Do add royal icing to watercolors.** If you want to give the watercolor a little body and don't want the results to be super-transparent, try adding just a dab of icing to the mix.

- **Don't overwork the watercolors.** Going over the same spot repeatedly will cause the icing to wear thin, resulting in a pitted surface.

COMBINING STYLES: A MIX OF FLOODING ICING AND WATERCOLORS

Sometimes I like to include the watercolor technique in flooded cookies because it simply makes the design better and more interesting. For instance, on the Seashell (page 175), I flooded the entire cookie first. Then, to make it look opalescent, it made sense to apply color with watercolors. On the Cat and Fish cookie (page 250), I painted the water and fish in the bowl with watercolors to distinguish

them from the solid elements of the other parts of the cookie. I also used watercolor to paint the cat's stripes.

ADDING SHIMMER: EDIBLE GOLD AND SILVER LUSTER DUST

There is no combination of gel colors for making gold or silver icing that can compete with the metallic effects of gold and silver luster dust. I never cease to be amazed by the magical transformation that happens when I squeeze a drop of lemon extract or vodka onto the dust and a gorgeous metallic liquid ball forms.

Using gold and silver luster dusts for details on cookies is fun and can bring certain cookies to life, especially if used very sparingly (see the decorations on the Wedding Cake, page 165; the metal parts on the Stacked Luggage, page 166; and the halo on the Angel, page 254; and you could use it on the buckles on the shoes of the Witch, pages 97, 172; and the button of the Graduation Cap, page 261). Because luster dust is not water-soluble, you must dilute it with colorless alcohol-based extracts or vodka, which evaporate very quickly, making cookies featuring them still child-friendly.

Tip: Vodka or Extracts? You can use either to dilute luster dust. With vodka, the dust adheres to the cookie and will not rub off when touched. If you use extract, the dust does tend to come off on your hand if you touch the cookie. It's not really an issue unless you're packaging the cookies in cellophane bags or stacking them.

How to Paint In with Luster Dust

1. Using the flat end of a spoon or the tip of a knife, put a little luster dust in a small bowl. Using a liquid medicine dropper or the cap of the bottle, add a few drops of either vodka (cheap is fine!) or an alcohol-based clear extract such as lemon or clear vanilla to the edge of the pile. Using your brush, gradually draw the dust into the liquid until the mixture is the consistency of nail polish.

If it is too thick, add more vodka or extract. If it is too thin, add more luster dust.

2. Using the watercolor brush, paint in the desired areas with the liquefied luster dust. If the coat looks too transparent or thin for your liking, let it dry and paint over it. Let the luster dust dry completely, about 5 minutes.

3. When finished, wash the paintbrush with dishwashing soap, massaging the bristles gently until all of the dust is washed away.

Tip: The alcohol in the mixture evaporates quickly, so the paint may dry out while you are decorating your cookies. Just add more vodka or extract.

Tip: Leave the diluted luster dust out and uncovered when you are finished using it to allow the remaining alcohol or extract to evaporate. A dry powder will remain in the bowl, which you can use the next time you use luster dust.

EDIBLE MARKERS

There are instances when edible markers can save time, especially for making details on cookies. I generally opt not to use them, but in a pinch, you might find them convenient when making a black dot for an eye as on the Stork (page 263); drawing in stripes as on the Chair (page 245); or writing words, as on the Gift Tag (page 205). Use the finest-tipped version you can find to get the most control.

PLAYING WITH YOUR COOKIES

It's amazing how simple it is to transform a cookie into something else entirely—a table decoration, centerpiece, place card, or game piece. When you think about them standing upright, the cookies become animated and tell a story in a different way.

COOKIES ON A STAND

These are so fun and versatile; I've used the Turkey (page 95) to make place cards for Thanksgiving, the Tombstone (page 212) for a Halloween party, and put the Stork (page 263) on a stand for a baby shower favor. In fact, every holiday cookie could be "glued" onto a stand and used for decoration on a mantel, windowsill, hallway table, or dinner table. I prefer using isomalt over royal icing to adhere the cookies to the stands. It sticks immediately and dries clear.

what you need

Cookie dough of choice (pages 26–33), prepared, chilled, if necessary, and rolled out

3-inch square cookie cutter

Isomalt nibs or Royal Icing of slightly thicker than lining consistency

Decorated cookies

1. Cut out the squares from the dough, then cut each square in half to make two rectangles. Bake as directed. These will be the bases for your cookies.

2. If using isomalt nibs, melt ¼ cup—following the directions on the package—in a small skillet over medium-high heat until completely liquefied, stirring gently. If using a microwave, place nibs in a microwavable cup and melt in 20-second increments until liquid and bubbles form. Dip the bottom of the decorated cookie into the melted isomalt and place on the base. Hold in place for 5 seconds. Be careful—isomalt is a liquid sugar that can burn your skin.

3. If using the royal icing, apply it thickly to the bottom of the decorated cookie with your finger and set it on the base. Hold the cookie in place until it can stand on its own. Alternatively, prop it up with two cans so that you can move on to the next cookie.

Tip: You can substitute regular melted sugar for isomalt if you don't mind that it has a brownish hue. It may take just slightly longer to harden.

COOKIES ON A STICK

I prefer to use mini cookies when putting them on sticks, primarily because the scale is more reminiscent of a classic lollipop. These make special birthday party favors or cake decorations. I love the idea of passing them around at a party—they're witty and delicious. In the first option, the stick is baked right into the cookie, so you will need more baking sheets than called for in the recipe to accommodate all of the cookies on sticks.

what you need

Cookie dough of choice (pages 26–33), prepared, chilled, rolled, and cut out

Or decorated cookies

Isomalt nibs

8-inch or 6-inch lollipop sticks

To insert a stick before baking:

1. Working with one cutout shape at a time, place on a clean work surface or parchment. Insert the stick by slowly "rolling it" into the chilled dough, at least halfway into the cookie.
2. Slide a spatula under the cookie, hold the stick in your other hand, and place on the baking sheet.
3. Bake as directed, cool, and decorate as desired.

To attach a stick after baking and decorating:

1. Lay your cookies decorated side down. Melt ¼ cup isomalt nibs in a small skillet over medium-high heat until completely liquefied, stirring gently. Do not overheat. If using a microwave, place the nibs in a microwavable cup. Melt in 20-second increments until liquid and bubbles form.
2. Using the tip of a heatproof rubber spatula, scoop out a little isomalt and drizzle onto the cookie where the stick will go. Immediately place the stick on the isomalt and hold it there for 10 to 20 seconds. If necessary, add isomalt on top of the stick. Isomalt can burn if it gets on you, so have some ice water nearby just in case!

THE
COOKIE
DESIGNS

CHICK CUTTER

This is one of my favorite groupings because it's especially challenging to see the outline of a chick in the other images. Sometimes I even forget which came first, the Chick or the egg-laying Hen!

If the French Fries cookie makes you think of ketchup, you can always add a drizzle of red icing onto the fries themselves, and maybe a few grains of sugar for salt!

CHICK

● beginner   ○ intermediate   ○ advanced

what you need

TO MAKE THE COOKIES
3-inch chick cookie cutter

Cookie dough of choice (pages 26–33), prepared, chilled, and rolled out

Cooling racks

TO DECORATE
1¾ cups Royal Icing (pages, 40–42)

Pasteurized egg white or water

Gel food colors: lemon yellow, sunset orange, whitener, super black

4 plastic or parchment paper piping bags (see page 53)

4 #1 tips

Assorted paintbrushes

Black edible pen (optional)

1. **Make the cookies.** Cut out 24 cookies from the dough. Bake and cool as directed.

2. **Make yellow lining and flooding icing for the chick; outline and paint in.** Mix 1 cup royal icing in a bowl with a toothpick of lemon yellow gel to make pale yellow for the chick. Thin to lining consistency and spoon ¼ cup into a piping bag fitted with a #1 tip. Thin the remaining icing to flooding consistency, add whitener, and cover with plastic wrap. Using the lining icing, outline the silhouette of the chick. Let set for 5 minutes. Using a paintbrush and the flooding icing, paint in the chick. Let set until hard, 6 to 8 hours or overnight.

3. **Make yellow lining icing to re-outline the chick; re-outline and make interior details.**

Refresh the royal icing on medium speed for 30 seconds. Mix ¼ cup in a bowl with lemon yellow gel to make bright yellow to re-outline the chick. Thin to lining consistency and spoon into a piping bag fitted with a #1 tip. Re-outline the chick and make the wing and tail feathers.

4. **Make lining and flooding icing for the beak and feet.** Mix ¼ cup royal icing in a bowl with sunset orange gel to make bright orange for the beak. Thin to lining consistency and spoon 3 tablespoons into a piping bag fitted with a #1 tip. Thin the remaining icing to flooding consistency, add whitener, and cover with plastic wrap. Using the lining icing, outline the beak and make the feet. Let set for 5 minutes. Using a small

CHICK CONTINUES

paintbrush and the flooding icing, fill in the beak.

5. **Make lining icing for the eye.** Mix 2 tablespoons royal icing with super black gel. Thin to lining consistency and spoon into a piping bag fitted with a #1 tip. Make a black dot for the eye by touching the tip to the cookie, holding the bag at a 45-degree angle, and squeezing without moving the bag. Let set for 5 minutes. Alternatively, make the eye with the black edible pen.

• **MAKES 24** •

FRENCH FRIES

○ beginner ● intermediate ○ advanced

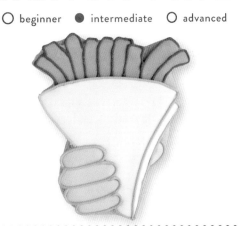

what you need

TO MAKE THE COOKIES
3-inch chick cookie cutter

Cookie dough of choice (pages 26–33), prepared, chilled, and rolled out

Cooling racks

TO DECORATE
3 cups Royal Icing (pages 40–42)

Pasteurized egg white or water

Gel food colors: gold, whitener, copper (flesh), chocolate brown, super black

6 plastic or parchment paper piping bags (page 53)

6 #1 tips

Assorted paintbrushes

1. **Make the cookies.** Cut out 24 cookies from the dough. Bake and cool as directed.

2. **Make lining and flooding icing for the French fries; outline and paint in.** Mix ¾ cup royal icing in a bowl with gold gel to make golden brown for the French fries. Thin to lining consistency and spoon ¼ cup into a piping bag fitted with a #1 tip. Thin the remaining icing to flooding consistency and cover with plastic wrap. Position the cookie so that the chick's feet and tail are the top. Using the lining icing, outline the top and sides of the silhouette of the French fries. Let set for 5 minutes. Using a paintbrush and the flooding icing, paint in the fries, thinning the icing where the paper cone overlaps the fries. Let set until hard, 6 to 8 hours or overnight.

3. **Make white lining and flooding icing for the paper cone; outline and paint in.** Refresh the royal icing on medium low for 30 seconds. Mix ¾ cup icing in a bowl with whitener to make paper white for the cone. Thin to lining consistency and spoon ¼ cup into a piping bag fitted with a #1 tip. Thin the remaining icing to flooding consistency and cover with plastic wrap. Using the lining icing, outline the paper cone, leaving a space on the left where the fingers overlap. Using a paintbrush and the flooding icing, paint in the cone, thinning the icing where the hand overlaps the cone. Let set until hard, 6 to 8 hours or overnight.

4. **Make skin tone lining and flooding icing for the hand; outline and paint in.** Refresh the royal icing on medium low for 30 seconds. Mix ¾ cup icing in a bowl with the copper (flesh) or brown gel to make desired skin color. Thin to lining consistency and spoon ¼ cup into a piping bag fitted with a #1 tip. Thin the remaining icing to flooding consistency and cover with plastic wrap. Using the lining icing, outline the silhouette of the hand and thumb. Let set for 5 minutes. Using a paintbrush and the flooding icing, paint in the hand and thumb and let set until hard, about 3 hours.

5. **Make lining icings: brown to re-outline the fries, light gray to outline the cone, and copper (flesh) or brown to re-outline the hand.** Refresh the royal icing on medium low for 30 seconds. Spoon ¼ cup icing into each of three bowls. Cover two with plastic wrap. To the remaining bowl, add gold and chocolate brown gels to make brown for re-outlining the tops of the fries and outlining each one. Thin to lining consistency and spoon it all into a piping bag fitted with a #1 tip. Re-outline the tops of the fries. Outline each fry so that they look like they are overlapping. Let set for 5 minutes.

   a. To the second bowl, add super black and whitener gels to make light gray for the paper cone. Thin to lining consistency and spoon all of it into a piping bag fitted with a #1 tip. Using the light gray lining icing, re-outline the paper cone including the fold detail on the right side.

   b. To the third bowl, add copper (flesh) or brown to re-outline the hand and thumb. Thin to lining consistency and spoon it all into a piping bag fitted with a #1 tip. Re-outline the hand and thumb and let set for 5 minutes.

HEN

○ beginner   ● intermediate   ○ advanced

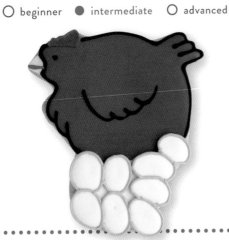

what you need

TO MAKE THE COOKIES
3-inch chick cookie cutter

Cookie dough of choice (pages 26–33), prepared, chilled, and rolled out

Cooling racks

TO DECORATE
2½ cups Royal Icing (pages 40–42)

Pasteurized egg white or water

Gel food colors: chocolate brown, bright red, whitener, lemon yellow, super black

6 plastic or parchment paper piping bags (page 53)

6 #1 tips

Assorted paintbrushes

1. **Make the cookies.** Cut out 24 cookies from the dough. Bake and cool as directed.

2. **Make terra cotta lining and flooding icing for the hen's body.** Mix 1 cup royal icing in a bowl with chocolate brown and bright red gel pastes to make terra cotta for the hen's body. Thin to lining consistency and spoon ¼ cup into a piping bag fitted with a #1 tip. Thin the remaining icing to flooding consistency, add a little whitener, and cover with plastic wrap.

3. **Outline and paint in the hen's body.** Position the cookie so that the chick's tail and feet are the top. Using the terra cotta lining icing, outline the hen, leaving unlined the point where the beak is and at the bottom where the eggs

overlap. Using a paintbrush and the flooding icing, paint in the hen, thinning out the icing where the eggs overlap the hen. Let set until hard, 6 to 8 hours or overnight.

4. **Make lining and flooding icings: white for the eggs and yellow for the beak.** Refresh the royal icing on medium low for 30 seconds. Mix ½ cup icing in a bowl with whitener gel to make bright white for the eggs. Thin to lining consistency and spoon ¼ cup into a piping bag fitted with a #1 tip. Thin the remaining icing to flooding consistency and cover with plastic wrap. Mix ¼ cup icing in a bowl with lemon yellow gel to make yellow for the beak. Thin to lining consistency and spoon 2 tablespoons

into a piping bag fitted with a #1 tip. Thin the remaining 2 tablespoons of icing to flooding consistency and cover with plastic wrap.

5. **Outline the eggs and beak and paint in.**
Using the white lining icing, outline the silhouette of the cluster of eggs—do not outline each individual egg. Using the yellow lining icing, outline the sides of the beak that are not attached to the face.

Let set for 5 minutes. Using a paintbrush and the white flooding icing, paint in the egg area. Using a paintbrush and the yellow flooding icing, paint in the beak, butting up the icing (see page 64) to the outline of the hen's face. Let set overnight.

6. **Make lining icings: red for the comb and black to re-outline the hen and eggs.**

HEN CONTINUES

Refresh the royal icing on medium low for 30 seconds. Mix ¼ cup icing in a small bowl with bright red gel to make bright red for the comb. Thin to lining consistency and spoon all of it into a piping bag fitted with a #1 tip. Mix ¼ cup icing in a small bowl with super black gel to make black for outlining the hen. Thin to lining consistency and spoon all of it into a piping bag fitted with a #1 tip. Mix ¼ cup icing in a small bowl with super black and whitener gels to make light gray for the eggs. Thin to lining consistency and spoon all of it into a piping bag fitted with a #1 tip.

7. Re-outline the hen and draw details. Outline the individual eggs. Outline and paint in the comb. Using the black lining icing, re-outline the hen and draw the feathers and wing. Make a dot for the eye and a line across the beak for the mouth. Using the light gray lining icing, outline the individual eggs, with some overlapping slightly. Using the red lining icing, outline the comb on top of the hen's head and draw in the comb. Let set for 5 minutes.

MAKES 24

DOG'S HEAD

● beginner ○ intermediate ○ advanced

what you need

TO MAKE THE COOKIES
3-inch chick cookie cutter

Cookie dough of choice (pages 26–33), prepared, chilled, and rolled out

Cooling racks

TO DECORATE
2¼ cups Royal Icing (pages 40–42)

Pasteurized egg white or water

Gel food colors: gold, regal purple, whitener, chocolate brown, super black

5 plastic or parchment paper piping bags (page 53)

5 #1 tips

Assorted paintbrushes

1. **Make the cookies.** Cut out 24 cookies from the dough. Bake and cool as directed.

2. **Make golden brown lining and flooding icing for the dog's head; outline and paint in.** Mix 1 cup royal icing in a bowl with gold gel to make golden brown for the dog's head. Thin to lining consistency and spoon ¼ cup into a piping bag fitted with a #1 tip. Thin the remaining icing to flooding consistency and cover with plastic wrap. Position the cookie so that the chick's feet are the top left and the feathers are the bottom left. Using the lining icing, outline the dog's head, skipping the bump where the nose will be and leaving the neck unlined where it meets the bow. Using a large paintbrush and the flooding icing, paint in the dog's head, thinning it out where the bow overlaps. Let set until hard, 6 to 8 hours or overnight.

3. **Make purple lining and flooding icing for the bow tie; outline and paint in.** Refresh the royal icing on medium low for 30 seconds. Mix ½ cup icing in a bowl with regal purple gel to make purple for the bow tie. Thin to piping consistency and spoon ¼ cup into a piping bag fitted with a #1 tip. Thin the remaining icing to flooding consistency, add a little whitener, and cover with plastic wrap. Using the lining icing, outline the silhouette of the bow, following the left and bottom edges of the cookie. Using a paintbrush and the purple flooding icing, paint in the bow and let set until hard, about 4 hours.

4. **Make lining icings: dark brown to re-outline the dog's head and purple for the bow tie; make black lining and flooding icing for the nose and eye.** Refresh the royal icing on medium low for 30 seconds. Spoon ¼ cup icing into each of two bowls. Cover one with plastic wrap. To the other, add gold and chocolate brown gels to make darker brown to re-outline the dog's head. Thin to lining consistency and spoon all of it into a piping bag fitted with a #1 tip. To the remaining bowl, add regal purple gel to make purple for the bow tie. Thin to lining consistency and spoon all of it into a piping bag fitted with a #1 tip. Mix 2 tablespoons icing in a bowl with super black gel to make black for the nose and eye. Thin to lining consistency and spoon all of it into a piping bag fitted with a #1 tip.

5. **Re-outline the dog's head and bow tie. Outline and paint in the nose and eye.** Using the darker brown lining icing, re-outline the dog's head, including detail on the ear, and make dots for the whiskers. Using the purple lining icing, re-outline the bow. Using the black lining icing, make the nose and fill in the eye. Let set for 15 minutes.

GIFT BOX CUTTER

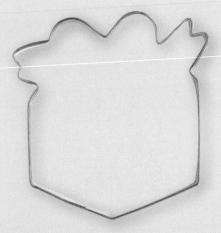

Decorate the Easter Bunny's egg any way you like; I love the way painting watercolor on the hardened flooding icing gives the effect of a traditional colored Easter egg.

When outlining the Spider's body, don't follow the edge of the cookie precisely—make it a bit rounder by obscuring the corners on the cookie. Try hanging the spider for Halloween. Simply make a hole in it before baking.

GIFT BOX

○ beginner   ● intermediate   ○ advanced

what you need

TO MAKE THE COOKIES
3-inch gift box cookie cutter

Cookie dough of choice (pages 26–33), prepared, chilled, and rolled out

Cooling racks

TO DECORATE
3 cups Royal Icing (pages 40–42)

Pasteurized egg white or water

Gel food colors: turquoise, whitener, super black

4 plastic or parchment paper piping bags (page 53)

4 #1 tips

Assorted paintbrushes

1. **Make the cookies.** Cut out 24 cookies from the dough. Bake and cool as directed.

2. **Make blue lining and flooding icing for the box; outline and paint in.** Mix 1¼ cups royal icing in a bowl with turquoise gel to make Tiffany blue for the box. Thin to lining consistency and spoon ¼ cup into a piping bag fitted with a #1 tip. Thin the remaining icing to flooding consistency and cover with plastic wrap. Using the lining icing, outline the silhouette of the gift box, stopping where it meets the bow. Let set for 5 minutes. Using a paintbrush and the flooding icing, paint in the box, thinning it out where the bow overlaps. Let set until hard, 6 to 8 hours or overnight.

3. **Make white lining and flooding icing for the bow; outline and paint in.** Refresh the royal icing on medium low for 30 seconds. Mix 1¼ cups icing with whitener gel to make white for the ribbon and bow. Thin to lining consistency and spoon ¼ cup into a piping bag fitted with a #1 tip. Thin the remaining icing to flooding consistency, add a little whitener, and cover with plastic wrap. Using the lining icing, outline the silhouette of the ribbon and bow. Let set for 5 minutes. Using a paintbrush and the flooding icing, paint in the bow and ribbon. Let set for 4 to 6 hours.

4. **Make lining icings: light gray to re-outline the bow and dark blue for the box; re-outline.** Refresh the royal icing on medium low for 30 seconds. Spoon ¼ cup icing into each of two bowls. Cover one with plastic wrap. To the

GIFT BOX CONTINUES

remaining bowl, add a toothpick of super black and a drop of whitener gel to make light gray to re-outline the bow. Thin to lining consistency and spoon it all into a piping bag fitted with a #1 tip. To the second bowl, add turquoise gel to make a darker Tiffany blue to re-outline the box. Thin to lining consistency and spoon it all into a piping bag fitted with a #1 tip. Using the gray lining icing, re-outline the bow and ribbon, then make the details in the center. Let set for 5 minutes. Using the darker Tiffany blue, re-outline the box, adding the lines to give it a ¾ perspective.

• MAKES 24 •

SPIDER

● beginner   ○ intermediate   ○ advanced

what you need

TO MAKE THE COOKIES
3-inch gift box cookie cutter

Cookie dough of choice (pages 26–33), prepared, chilled, and rolled out

Cooling racks

TO DECORATE
2 cups Royal Icing (pages 40–42)

Pasteurized egg white or water

Gel food colors: regal purple, whitener, super black, bright red

4 plastic or parchment paper piping bags (page 53)

4 #1 tips

Assorted paintbrushes

1. **Make the cookies.** Cut out 24 cookies from the dough. Bake and cool as directed.

2. **Make purple lining and flooding icing for the spider.** Mix 1½ cups royal icing in a bowl with regal purple and whitener gels to make purple for the spider's body. Thin to lining icing and spoon ¼ cup into a piping bag fitted with a #1 tip. Thin the remaining icing to flooding consistency and cover with plastic wrap.

3. **Outline and paint in the spider.** Position the cookie so that the gift box is upside down. Using the lining icing, outline the spider's body. Let set for 5 minutes. Reserve the lining icing. Using a paintbrush and the flooding icing, paint in the spider. Let set until hard, 6 to 8 hours or overnight.

4. **Make lining icings: black for the pupils and red for the mouth; make white lining and**

flooding icing for the eyes. Refresh the royal icing on medium low for 30 seconds. Spoon 2 tablespoons icing into each of two bowls. Cover one with plastic wrap. To the remaining bowl, add super black gel to make black for the pupils. Thin to lining consistency and spoon all of it into a piping bag fitted with a #1 tip. To the second bowl, add bright red gel to make red for the mouth. Thin to lining consistency and spoon all of it into a piping bag fitted with a #1 tip. Mix ¼ cup royal icing with whitener gel to make white for the eyes. Thin to lining consistency and spoon 2 tablespoons into a piping bag fitted with a #1 tip. Thin the remaining icing to flooding consistency and cover with plastic wrap.

5. **Draw in the spider's hair and legs.** Using the reserved bag of purple lining icing, draw the spider's hair around the rim of the body, beginning just inside the oval and dragging the tip off onto the bare edges of the cookie. Make the spider's eight legs and let set for 5 minutes.

6. **Outline and paint in the eyes. Draw in the mouth and pupils.** Using the white lining icing, outline two circles for the eyes. Let set for 5 minutes. Using a paintbrush and the white flooding icing, paint in the eyes. Using the red lining icing, draw the mouth and fangs. Let set for 2 to 3 hours. Using the black lining icing, make the pupils by holding the piping tip close to the cookie at a 45-degree angle.

····· MAKES 24 ·····

EASTER BUNNY

○ beginner   ○ intermediate   ● advanced

what you need

TO MAKE THE COOKIES
3-inch gift box cookie cutter

Cookie dough of choice (pages 26–33), prepared, chilled, and rolled out

Cooling racks

TO DECORATE
4¼ cups Royal Icing (pages 40–42)

Pasteurized egg white or water

Gel food colors: leaf green, whitener, bright blue, electric pink, lemon yellow, neon green, super black, chocolate brown

8 plastic or parchment paper piping bags (page 53)

8 #1 tips

Assorted paintbrushes

Plate or ceramic mixing palette

EASTER BUNNY CONTINUES

1. **Make the cookies.** Cut out 24 cookies from the dough. Bake and cool as directed.

2. **Make green lining and flooding icing for the grass.** Mix ½ cup royal icing with leaf green and whitener gels to make green for the grass. Thin to lining consistency and spoon ¼ cup into a piping bag fitted with a #1 tip. Thin the remaining icing to flooding consistency and cover with plastic wrap.

3. **Paint in the grass.** Position the cookie so that the top of the gift box is to the right. Using a paintbrush and the green flooding icing, thinly paint the grass, thinning it out where the egg and the bunny overlap it. Let set for 30 minutes.

4. **Make white lining and flooding icing for the bunny and egg; outline and paint in. Make the blades of grass.** Mix 2 cups royal icing in a bowl with whitener gel to make white for the bunny and egg. Thin to lining consistency and spoon ¼ cup into a piping bag fitted with a #1 tip. Thin the remaining icing to flooding consistency and cover with plastic wrap. Using the white lining icing, outline the silhouette of the bunny and the egg. Make the egg as large as possible by drawing it to the top, outer, and bottom edges of the cookie. Let set for 5 minutes. Using a paintbrush and the white flooding icing, paint in the bunny and egg. Let set until hard, 6 to 8 hours or overnight. Using the reserved green lining icing, draw in the grass, making short, vertical lines.

5. **Make watercolors and paint designs on the eggs.** Refresh the royal icing on medium low for 30 seconds. Squeeze dots of bright blue, electric pink, and lemon yellow gels onto a plate or ceramic mixing palette. Using a paintbrush, gradually mix a little water into each gel to make watercolors (see page 66). Using a small watercolor brush and the watercolors, paint patterns, such as stripes, dots, and triangles on the egg. Let set for 5 minutes.

6. **Make green lining and flooding icing for the handle; make lining icing for the decorations and to re-outline the bunny and egg.** Spoon ¼ cup royal icing into each of five bowls. Cover four with plastic wrap. To the remaining bowl, add neon green gel to make pastel green for the handle and the egg decoration. Thin to lining consistency and spoon 2 tablespoons into a piping bag fitted with a #1 tip. Thin the remaining to flooding consistency and cover with plastic wrap. Mix electric pink gel into the second bowl to make pastel pink and spoon all of it into a piping bag fitted with a #1 tip. Mix bright blue gel into the third bowl to make pastel blue and spoon all of it into a piping bag fitted with a #1 tip. Mix lemon yellow gel into the fourth bowl to make pastel yellow and spoon all of it into a piping bag fitted with a #1 tip. Mix super black and whitener gels into the fifth bowl to make light gray and spoon all of it into a piping bag fitted with a #1 tip.

7. **Make decorations on the egg with the lining icings.** Re-outline the bunny, egg, and strap. Using the pastel blue lining icing, re-outline the egg.

Using the pastel green, yellow, pink, and blue lining icings, pipe patterns including dots, stripes, waves, and zigzags on the egg. Using the light gray lining icing, re-outline the bunny and make arms and legs. Using the pastel green lining icing, pipe the outline of the strap around the bunny's arm. Let set for 5 minutes. Using a paintbrush, paint in the strap with the pastel green flooding icing. Using the pastel pink lining icing, pipe the nose and inner ear. Reserve the piping bags of pastel pink, yellow, and green lining icings.

8. **Make brown lining and flooding icing for the basket; outline and paint in. Make the bunny's eye.** Mix ¼ cup royal icing in a bowl with chocolate brown gel to make brown for the basket. Thin to lining consistency and spoon

2 tablespoons into a piping bag fitted with a #1 tip. Thin the remaining icing to flooding consistency, add whitener, and cover with plastic wrap. Using the brown lining icing, outline the silhouette of a basket under the bunny's hand and make a dot for the bunny's eye. Let set for 5 minutes. Using a paintbrush and the brown flooding icing, paint in the basket. Let set for 1 hour.

9. **Re-outline the basket and handle. Make the eggs.** Using the reserved brown lining icing, re-outline the basket and the handle. Let set for 5 minutes. Using the reserved pastel pink, yellow, and green lining icings, make the eggs in the basket. Using the pastel green lining icing, re-outline the green strap.

· MAKES 24 ·

RIBBON AND SCISSORS

○ beginner   ○ intermediate   ● advanced

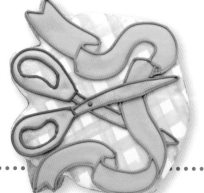

what you need

TO MAKE THE COOKIES
3-inch gift box cookie cutter

Cookie dough of choice (pages 26–33), prepared, chilled, and rolled out

Cooling racks

TO DECORATE
3½ cups Royal Icing (pages 40–42)

Pasteurized egg white or water

Gel food colors: whitener, neon green, super black, royal blue

4 plastic or parchment paper piping bags (page 53)

4 #1 tips

Assorted paintbrushes

Plate or ceramic mixing palette

RIBBON AND SCISSORS CONTINUES

1. **Make the cookies.** Cut out 24 cookies from the dough. Bake and cool as directed.

2. **Make white flooding icing for the background and paint in.** Mix 1¼ cups royal icing in a bowl with whitener gel to make white for the background. Thin to flooding consistency. Paint the surface of the cookie to the edges. Let set until hard, 6 to 8 hours or overnight.

3. **Make watercolor and paint pattern on background.** Squeeze a dot of neon green gel onto the mixing palette. Using a paintbrush, gradually mix in a little water to make a watercolor (see page 66). Paint the pattern on the background, making stripes on the diagonal.

4. **Make green lining and flooding icing for the ribbon.** Refresh the royal icing on medium low for 30 seconds. Mix ½ cup icing in a bowl with neon green gel to make bright green for the ribbon. Thin to lining consistency and spoon ¼ cup into a piping bag fitted with a #1 tip. Thin the remaining icing to flooding consistency, add a little whitener, and cover with plastic wrap.

5. **Outline and paint in the ribbon.** Using the green lining icing, outline the silhouette of the ribbon. Let set for 5 minutes. Using a paintbrush and the green flooding icing, paint in the ribbon. Let set until hard, 6 to 8 hours or overnight.

6. **Make lining and flooding icings: gray for the scissor blades, blue for the handles, and dark green to re-outline the ribbon.** Refresh the royal icing on medium low for 30 seconds. Fill two bowls with ½ cup icing each. Cover one with plastic wrap. To the other bowl, add super black to make medium gray to outline the scissors. Thin to lining consistency and spoon ¼ cup into a piping bag fitted with a #1 tip. Thin the remaining icing to flooding consistency, add whitener to lighten it, and cover with plastic. To the second bowl, add royal blue gel to make blue for the scissor handles. Thin to lining consistency and spoon ¼ cup into a piping bag fitted with a #1 tip. Thin the remaining icing to flooding consistency, add whitener, and cover with plastic wrap. Spoon ¼ cup royal icing into a bowl. Add neon green gel to make darker green to re-outline the ribbon. Thin to lining consistency and spoon it all into a piping bag fitted with a #1 tip.

7. **Outline the blades and handles and paint in.** Using the medium gray lining icing, outline the silhouette of the scissor blades. Skip over the part of the blade that lies under the ribbon. Using the blue icing, outline the silhouette of the handles. Fit the tops of the handles into the two bumps at the top of the cookie. Let set for 5 minutes. Using the light gray and light blue flooding icings, paint in the scissor blades and the handle. Let set for 1 hour.

8. **Re-outline the blades and handles; make the interior details.** Using the medium gray lining icing, re-outline the scissor blades and add detail. Using the blue lining icing, re-outline the scissorhandles. Let set for 5 minutes.

SANTA HEAD CUTTER

The funny thing about this cutter is that when I began to turn it into different cookies, I had no idea I'd get four different holidays out of it. Halloween, Thanksgiving, Christmas, and Easter are covered—but you may find others.

For the turkey, feel free to take liberties with its feathers; you don't have to make them three different colors. They can be all orange or red, too.

SANTA

○ beginner ● intermediate ○ advanced

what you need

TO MAKE THE COOKIES
4¼-inch Santa head cookie cutter

Cookie dough of choice (pages 26–33), prepared, chilled, and rolled out

Cooling racks

TO DECORATE
3½ cups Royal Icing (pages 40–42)

Pasteurized egg white or water

Gel food colors: copper (flesh), whitener, bright red, super black

Pink luster or petal dust

4 plastic or parchment paper piping bags (page 53)

4 #1 tips

Assorted paintbrushes

1. **Make the cookies.** Cut out 16 cookies from the dough. Bake and cool as directed.

2. **Make pink flooding icing for Santa's face and paint in.** Mix 1 cup royal icing in a bowl with copper (flesh) and whitener gels to make pale pink for Santa's face. Thin to flooding consistency. Using a paintbrush and the flooding icing, paint in Santa's face, thinning out the icing into the areas where his hat, mustache, and beard overlap his face. Let set for 4 to 6 hours.

3. **Make lining and flooding icings: white for the fur trim, pom-pom, mustache, and beard; and red for the hat and nose.** Mix 1½ cups royal icing in a bowl with whitener gel to make bright white. Thin to lining consistency and spoon

¼ cup into a piping bag fitted with a #1 tip. Thin the remaining icing to flooding consistency and cover with plastic wrap. Mix ¾ cup royal icing with bright red gel to make red for the hat and nose. Thin to lining consistency and spoon ¼ cup into a piping bag fitted with a #1 tip. Thin the remaining icing to flooding consistency and cover with plastic wrap.

4. **Outline the hat, nose, beard, mustache, and eyebrows.** Using the red lining icing, outline Santa's hat, excluding the parts where the fur and pom-pom overlap. Outline the nose. Let set for 5 minutes. Using the white lining icing, outline the beard and mustache. Do not outline the mustache where it overlaps the beard. Using the

white lining icing, outline the eyebrows. Let set for 5 minutes. Reserve the red and the white lining icings.

5. **Paint in the hat and nose; paint in the beard and eyebrows.** Using a paintbrush and the red flooding icing, paint in the hat, thinning out the icing just beyond where the white fur trim overlaps the hat. Do not bleed the red icing into the pale pink icing. Paint in the nose. Using a paintbrush and the white flooding icing, paint in the beard, thinning out the icing where the white trim over-laps the sideburns. Carefully paint the area where the mustache overlaps the beard. Using a small paintbrush and the white flooding icing, paint in the eyebrows. Let set until hard, 6 to 8 hours or overnight.

6. **Outline the fur trim, pom-pom, and mus-tache. Paint in the pom-pom and mustache.** Using the reserved bag of white lining icing, out-line the fur trim with a scalloped edge beginning at the top left, working across the top of the trim and touching down on the bottom right. Outline the bottom of the fur trim beginning at the top left side and working across the bottom, so that the trim covers half of the eyebrows, and touching down at the bottom right. Outline the pom-pom on the hat. Outline the mustache, butting (see page 64) the top of the mustache to the bottom of the nose; each wing of the mustache should extend over the beard and connect under the nose, leaving a tiny triangle of pale pink above the beard for the lip. Let set for 10 minutes. Using a medium paintbrush and the reserved bowl of white flooding icing, paint in the pom-pom and the mustache. Let set for 4 to 6 hours.

7. **Make gray lining icing to re-outline the beard, mustache, fur, and pom-pom; make black lining icing for the eyes.** Beat the royal icing on medium low for 30 seconds. Spoon ¼ cup royal icing into each of two bowls. Cover one with plastic wrap. To the remaining bowl, add super black and whitener gels to make light gray. Thin to lining consistency and spoon it all into a piping bag fitted with a #1 tip. To the second bowl, add super black to make black. Thin to lin-ing consistency and spoon it all into a piping bag fitted with a #1 tip.

8. **Re-outline the hat, nose, trim, beard, mus-tache, and pom-pom. Draw the eyes. Make blush for the cheeks.** When the white flooding icing is set, use the reserved red lining icing to re-outline the top of the hat and the nose. Using the light gray lining icing, re-outline the white trim, beard, mustache, and pom-pom. Using the black lining icing, draw two half-moons for Santa's eyes. To make blush for the cheeks, gently dip a paintbrush into pink luster or petal dust. Tap the brush over the jar to rid it of excess dust, then brush on the cheeks. Brush or blow off excess dust. Let set for 1 hour.

RABBIT

● beginner   ○ intermediate   ○ advanced

what you need

TO MAKE THE COOKIES
4¼-inch Santa head cookie cutter

Cookie dough of choice (pages 26–33), prepared, chilled, and rolled out

Cooling racks

TO DECORATE
2½ cups Royal Icing (pages 40–42)

Pasteurized egg white or water

Gel food colors: whitener, super black, electric pink

4 plastic or parchment paper piping bags (page 53)

4 #1 tips

Assorted paintbrushes

1. **Make the cookies.** Cut out 16 cookies from the dough. Bake and cool as directed.

2. **Make white lining and flooding icing for the bunny and paint in.** Mix 2 cups royal icing in a bowl with whitener gel to make white for the bunny. Thin to lining consistency and spoon ¼ cup into a piping bag fitted with a #1 tip. Thin the remaining icing to flooding consistency and cover with plastic wrap. Position the cookie so that Santa's pom-pom is at the top. Using the lining icing, outline the silhouette of the bunny's body, making two bumps for the ears and creating a bump for the tail. Let set for 5 minutes. Reserve the white lining icing. Using a paintbrush and the white flooding icing, paint in the bunny. Let set until hard, 6 to 8 hours or overnight.

3. **Make lining icings: gray to re-outline the bunny, black for the eye, and pink for the nose and ear.** Beat the royal icing on medium low for 30 seconds. Mix ¼ cup icing in a bowl with super black and whitener gels to make light gray to re-outline the bunny. Thin to lining consistency and spoon it all into a piping bag fitted with a #1 tip. Spoon 2 tablespoons royal icing into each of two bowls. Cover one with plastic wrap. To the other, add super black gel to make black for the bunny's eye. Thin to lining consistency and spoon into a piping bag fitted with a #1 tip. To the second bowl, add electric pink and whitener to make light pink for the inside of the ear. Thin to lining consistency and spoon into a piping bag fitted with a #1 tip.

4. **Make the nose, inner ear, and eye.** Using the light pink lining icing, make the nose and inner ear. Using the black lining icing, outline the eye and fill in. Let set for 10 minutes.

5. **Re-outline the bunny; make the ears, toes, back leg, whiskers, and pupil.** As the black icing sets, use the light gray lining icing to re-outline the bunny. Make the ears, toes on the feet, and a large slanted "C" for the back leg. Make three lines across the face for whiskers. When the black icing of the eye is set, use the reserved white lining icing to pipe a dot on the eye. Let set for 1 hour.

MAKES 16

TURKEY

○ beginner ● intermediate ○ advanced

what you need

TO MAKE THE COOKIES
4¼-inch Santa head cookie cutter

Cookie dough of choice (pages 26–33), prepared, chilled, and rolled out

Cooling racks

TO DECORATE
4½ cups Royal Icing (pages 40–42)

Pasteurized egg white or water

Gel food colors: chocolate brown, sunset orange, whitener, bright red, buckeye brown, lemon yellow

7 plastic or parchment paper piping bags (page 53)

7 #1 tips

Assorted paintbrushes

1. **Make the cookies.** Cut out 16 cookies from the dough. Bake and cool as directed.

2. **Make lining and flooding icings: brown for the body and orange and white for the feathers.** Mix 2 cups royal icing with chocolate brown gel to make rich brown for the turkey's body. Thin the icing to lining consistency and spoon ¼ cup into a piping bag fitted with a #1 tip. Thin the remaining icing to flooding consistency, add whitener, and cover with plastic wrap. Mix ¾ cup royal icing in a bowl with sunset orange gel to make orange for feathers. Thin to lining consistency and spoon ¼ cup into a piping bag fitted with a #1 tip. Thin the remaining icing to flooding consistency, add whitener, and cover with plastic

TURKEY CONTINUES

wrap. Mix ½ cup royal icing in a bowl with whitener gel to make white for the feathers. Thin to lining consistency and spoon ¼ cup into a piping bag fitted with a #1 tip. Thin the remaining icing to flooding consistency and cover with plastic wrap.

3. **Outline the body and feathers.** Position the cookie so that Santa's pom-pom is at the upper left to become the turkey's head. Using the brown lining icing, outline the silhouette of the turkey, excluding the feathers and making a scalloped edge where the feathers are attached. Using the orange lining icing, outline the orange feathers, butting (see page 64) the line up to the brown outline where the feathers are attached to the turkey's body and leaving a ⅛-inch edge for the white feathers. Using the white lining icing, outline the white feathers, making a scalloped pattern along the edge of the cookie. Let set for 5 minutes.

4. **Paint in the body and feathers.** Using a paintbrush and the brown flooding icing, paint in the body of the turkey. Using a paintbrush and the orange flooding icing, paint in the middle section of the tail feathers, butting the icing up to the piped brown lines. Using another paintbrush and the white flooding icing, paint in the white tail feathers, butting the icing up to the orange line. Let set until hard, 6 to 8 hours or overnight.

5. **Make red lining and flooding icing for the top feathers and the wattle; make lining icings: dark brown for re-outlining the body and feathers and yellow for the beak and feet.** Refresh the royal icing on medium low for 30 seconds. Spoon ½ cup icing into each of two bowls. Cover one with plastic wrap. To the remaining bowl, add bright red gel to make red for the wattle and top feathers. Thin to lining consistency and spoon ¼ cup into a piping bag fitted with a #1 tip. Thin the remaining icing to flooding consistency and cover with plastic wrap. To the second bowl, add chocolate brown and buckeye brown gels to make a darker brown for re-outlining the turkey and the orange feathers. Spoon all of it into a piping bag fitted with a #1 tip. Mix 2 tablespoons royal icing with lemon yellow gel to make golden yellow for the beak and feet. Thin to lining consistency and spoon all of it into a piping bag fitted with a #1 tip.

6. **Outline and paint in the wattle. Re-outline the body and make details; re-outline the orange feathers. Outline and paint in the red feathers.** Using the red lining icing, outline the turkey's wattle. Let set for 5 minutes. Using a paintbrush and the red flooding icing, paint in the wattle, butting the red icing up to the brown lining icing on the head. Using the dark brown lining icing, re-outline the brown parts of the turkey's body, adding the details for the neck, feathers, and wing. Re-outline the scalloped edges of the orange tail feathers. Pipe a brown dot for the eye. Using the red lining icing, outline the red feathers, making a wider scalloped edge on top of the orange feathers so that they cover about half of the orange icing. Let set for 10 minutes. Using

a paintbrush and the red flooding icing, paint in the red feathers, butting up the icing to the dark brown outline. Let set for 4 to 6 hours.

7. **Make the beak and feet. Re-outline the wattle. Make white lining icing and re-outline the tail feathers.** As the red flooding icing sets, make the beak and feet with the yellow lining icing. Using the red lining icing, re-outline the wattle.

Mix ¼ cup royal icing in a bowl with whitener gel to make white for re-outlining the red and white tail feathers. Thin to lining consistency and spoon it all into a piping bag fitted with a #1 tip. When the red flooding icing of the feathers is set, use the white lining icing to re-outline the outer edge of the red feathers and the outer edge of the white tail feathers.

MAKES 16

WITCH

○ beginner   ○ intermediate   ● advanced

what you need

TO MAKE THE COOKIES
4¼-inch Santa head cookie cutter

Cookie dough of choice (pages 26–33), prepared, chilled, and rolled out

Cooling racks

TO DECORATE
4¼ cups Royal Icing (pages 40–42)

Pasteurized egg white or water

Gel food colors: violet, royal blue, chocolate brown, gold, whitener, super black, neon green, lemon yellow, neon orange

8 plastic or parchment paper piping bags (page 53)

8 #1 tips

Assorted paintbrushes

1. **Make the cookies.** Cut out 16 cookies from the dough. Bake and cool as directed.

2. **Make blue flooding icing for the background and paint in.** Mix 1 cup royal icing in a bowl with violet and royal blue gels to make indigo for the background. Thin the icing to loose flooding consistency. Using a paintbrush, paint a thin coat of icing on the entire cookie. Let set for 1 to 2 hours.

WITCH CONTINUES

3. **Make lining and flooding icings: brown for the broom handle and straw yellow for the bristles.** Spoon ¼ cup royal icing into each of two small bowls. Cover one with plastic wrap. To the remaining bowl, add chocolate brown gel to make brown for the broom handle. Thin to lining consistency and spoon 2 tablespoons into a piping bag fitted with a #1 tip. Thin the remaining icing to flooding consistency and cover with plastic wrap. To the second bowl, add gold and whitener gels to make straw yellow for the broom bristles. Thin to lining consistency and spoon 2 tablespoons into a piping bag fitted with a #1 tip. Thin the remaining icing to flooding consistency and cover with plastic wrap.

4. **Outline and paint in the broom. Position the cookie so Santa's pom-pom is at the bottom.** Using the brown lining icing, outline the witch's broom handle. Using the straw yellow lining icing, outline the silhouette of the bristles on the broom. Let set for 5 minutes. Using a paintbrush and the brown flooding icing, paint in the broom handle. Using a paintbrush and the straw flooding icing, paint in the bristles for the broom. Let set for 1 hour.

5. **Make lining and flooding icings for the clothing, face, and hand.** As the straw flooding icing sets, mix 1¼ cups royal icing with super black gel to make black for the hat, cape, body, and shoe. Thin to lining consistency and spoon ¼ cup into a piping bag fitted with a #1 tip. Thin the remaining icing to flooding consistency and cover with plastic wrap. Mix ½ cup royal icing in a bowl with neon green, lemon yellow, and whitener gels to make yellow-green for the witch's face and hand. Thin to lining consistency and spoon ¼ cup into a piping bag fitted with a #1 tip. Thin remaining icing to flooding consistency. Cover with plastic wrap. Mix ¼ cup royal icing in a bowl with neon orange gel to make orange for the stocking. Thin to lining consistency and spoon 2 tablespoons into a piping bag fitted with a #1 tip. Thin the remaining icing to flooding consistency and cover with plastic wrap.

6. **Outline the cape, body, stocking, shoe, face, and hand.** When the broom handle is set, use the black lining icing to outline the witch's cape and body, going over the broom handle to make the arm and leg. Using the orange lining icing, outline the witch's stocking, butting (see page 64) the lines up to the black outline at the bottom of the dress. Using the black lining icing, outline the shoe so that most of it is on top of the straw broom, butting the black lines up to the orange line at the bottom of the stocking. Reserve the bag of black lining icing. Using the yellow-green lining icing, outline the profile of the witch's face with a hooked nose and protruding chin. Do not line the face where the hair overlaps. Outline the hand with the thumb on top of the broom handle, butting the yellow-green line up to the black sleeve of the dress. Let set for 5 minutes. Reserve the bag of yellow-green lining icing.

7. **Paint in the cape, body, shoe, stocking, face, and hand.** Using paintbrushes and the black

flooding icing, paint in the cape, body, and shoe. Cover the black flooding icing and reserve. Using a paintbrush and the orange flooding icing, paint in the stocking, butting the icing up to the bottom of the dress and shoe. Using another paintbrush and the yellow-green flooding icing, paint in the face, butting the icing up to the top of the shoulder and thinning it into the areas where the hair and hat overlap the face. Paint in the hand.

8. **Re-outline the hand. Make gray lining and flooding icing for the hair. Make lining icings: tan for the bristles and yellow for the buckle.** Using the reserved yellow-green lining icing, re-outline the hand. Beat the royal icing on medium low for 30 seconds. Spoon ¼ cup icing into each of three bowls. Cover two with plastic wrap. To the remaining bowl, add super black and whitener gels to make light gray for the hair. Thin to lining consistency and spoon 2 tablespoons into a piping bag fitted with a #1 tip. Thin the remaining icing to flooding consistency and cover with plastic wrap. To the second bowl, add gold and whitener gel to make light tan for the bristles. Thin to lining consistency and spoon it all into a piping bag fitted with a #1 tip. To the third bowl, add gold and lemon yellow gels to make golden yellow for the shoe buckle. Thin to lining consistency and spoon it all into a piping bag fitted with a #1 tip.

9. **Outline and paint in the hat and hair.** Using the reserved black lining icing, outline the hat, following the edge of the cookie for the top of the hat and piping the brim over the face. Using the light gray lining icing, outline the hair, piping across the left side of the face and shoulder and making a zigzag across the top of the cape for the bottom of the hair. Butt the gray piped lines up to the black piped lines at the bottom edge of the hat. Let set for 10 minutes. Using a paintbrush and the reserved black flooding icing, paint in the hat. Using another paintbrush and the gray flooding icing, paint in the hair, butting the icing up to the edge of the hat. Let set for 4 to 6 hours. Reserve the light gray and the black lining icings.

10. **Make the buckle, broom, and hair details; re-outline the hat, cape, body, and shoe; draw in details.** Using the golden yellow lining icing, draw the buckle on the shoe. Using the light tan lining icing, draw lines along the length of the bristles to give texture. When the light gray flooding icing on the hair is set, use the reserved light gray lining icing to draw strands of hair to add texture. When the black flooding icing on the hat is set, use the reserved black lining icing to re-outline the hat. Re-outline the cape and make curved lines on the interior to indicate folds in the cape. Re-outline the body and shoe. Draw black stripes across the orange stocking. Use the tip of the black lining icing to re-outline the profile of the face, adding a mouth and nostril. Pipe a black dot for the eye. Let set for 1 hour.

TEDDY BEAR CUTTER

I experimented widely with the icing colors for all of the cookies in this book and found I was repeatedly drawn to classic shades. I first made the Teddy Bear with baby blue, pink, and yellow, which didn't really resonate for me, quite possibly because the bear I fondly remember was brown and white.

One of my favorite transformations in the book is the XO cookie. By making sharp corners in the arms and legs of the bear, I trick the eye by obscuring the rounded limbs and seeing something else altogether.

TEDDY BEAR

● beginner ○ intermediate ○ advanced

what you need

TO MAKE THE COOKIES
3-inch teddy bear cookie cutter

Cookie dough of choice (pages 26–33), prepared, chilled, and rolled out

Cooling racks

TO DECORATE
3 cups Royal Icing (pages 40–42)

Pasteurized egg white or water

Gel food colors: chocolate brown, buckeye brown, whitener, ivory, electric pink, super black

5 plastic or parchment paper piping bags (page 53)

5 #1 tips

Assorted paintbrushes

---

1. **Make the cookies.** Cut out 24 cookies from the dough. Bake and cool as directed.

2. **Make brown lining and flooding icing for the bear.** Mix 1½ cups royal icing in a small bowl with chocolate brown, buckeye brown, and whitener gels to make brown for the bear. Thin to lining consistency and spoon ¼ cup into a piping bag fitted with a #1 tip. Thin the remaining icing to flooding consistency and cover with plastic wrap.

3. **Outline and paint in the bear.** Using the brown lining icing, outline the silhouette of the bear, following the edge of the cookie to make the ears, arms, and legs. Let set for 5 minutes. Using a paintbrush and the brown flooding icing, paint in the bear. Let icing set 6 to 8 hours or overnight.

4. **Make off-white lining and flooding icing for the bear's paws and snout; make pink lining icing for the inner ears.** Refresh the icing on medium low for 30 seconds. Fill two bowls with ½ cup icing each. Cover one with plastic wrap. To the other bowl, add ivory and whitener gels to make off-white for the paws and snout. Thin to lining consistency and spoon ¼ cup into a piping bag fitted with a #1 tip. Thin the remaining icing to flooding consistency and cover with plastic wrap. To the second bowl, add electric pink and whitener gels to make pale pink for the inner ears. Thin to lining consistency and spoon ¼ cup into a piping bag fitted with a #1 tip. Thin the remaining icing to flooding consistency and cover with plastic wrap.

TEDDY BEAR CONTINUES

5. **Outline the snout, paws, and ears and paint in.** Using the off-white lining icing, outline a large oval at the bottom of the head for the snout. Outline smaller thinner ovals at the ends of the arms and legs for the paws. Using the pale pink lining icing, outline two semicircles for the inner ears. Let set for 5 minutes. Using a paintbrush and the off-white flooding icing, fill in the snout and paws. Using the pale pink flooding icing, fill in the inner ears. Let set for 4 to 6 hours.

6. **Make lining icings: dark brown to re-outline the bear and black to make the eyes, nose, and mouth.** Fill two bowls with ¼ cup icing each. Cover one with plastic wrap. To the other bowl, add chocolate brown and buckeye brown gels to make dark brown. Thin to lining consistency and spoon all of it into a piping bag fitted with a #1 tip. To the second bowl, add super black gel to make black. Thin to lining consistency and spoon all of it into a piping bag fitted with a #1 tip.

7. **Re-outline the bear; make the head and belly; make the nose, mouth, and eyes.** Using the darker brown lining icing, re-outline the silhouette of the teddy bear. Outline the head by piping a curved line from ear to ear, going below the snout. Outline the belly by piping a line starting from below the left cheek, curving down to meet the corners between the arms and legs, and curving back up to below the right cheek. Using the black lining icing, outline a small oval for the nose, and fill it in with the piping tip. Draw the mouth under the nose. Make two black dots for the eyes.

········· MAKES 24 ·········

TOADSTOOLS

○ beginner   ○ intermediate   ● advanced

what you need

TO MAKE THE COOKIES
3-inch teddy bear cookie cutter

Cookie dough of choice (pages 26–33), prepared, chilled, and rolled out

Cooling racks

TO DECORATE
3½ cups Royal Icing (pages 40–42)

Pasteurized egg white or water

Gel food colors: bright blue, whitener, buckeye brown, super black, lemon yellow, egg yellow, bright red, leaf green, neon green

8 plastic or parchment paper piping bags (page 53)

6 #1 tips

1 #1.5 tip

Assorted paintbrushes

1. **Make the cookies.** Cut out 24 cookies from the dough. Bake and cool as directed.

2. **Make blue flooding icing for the sky and paint in.** Mix ½ cup royal icing in a small bowl with bright blue and whitener gels to make pale blue for the sky. Thin to flooding consistency and cover with plastic wrap. Position the cookie so that the bear's feet are at the top. Using a paintbrush and the pale blue flooding icing, thinly paint the whole surface of the cookie. Let set for 1 hour.

3. **Make light brown flooding icing for the underside of the toadstools; make off-white and yellow lining and flooding icings for the dragonfly wings and body.** Fill three bowls with ¼ cup royal icing each. Cover two bowls with plastic wrap. To the remaining bowl, add buckeye brown, super black, and whitener gels to make light brown for the undersides of the toadstools. Thin to flooding consistency and cover with plastic wrap. To the second bowl, add a tiny bit of whitener gel to make translucent off-white for the dragonfly wings. Thin to lining consistency and spoon 3 tablespoons into a piping bag fitted with a #1 tip. Thin the remaining icing to flooding consistency and cover with plastic wrap. To the third bowl, add lemon yellow and egg yellow gels to make yellow for the dragonfly body. Thin to lining consistency and spoon 3 tablespoons into a piping bag fitted with a #1 tip. Thin the remaining icing to flooding consistency and cover with plastic wrap.

4. **Paint in the undersides of the toadstools. Outline the dragonfly body and wings and paint in.** Using a paintbrush and the light brown flooding icing, thinly paint in the areas where the undersides of the toadstools are, thinning out the icing on all sides. Using the yellow lining icing, outline the dragonfly body by piping a small circle for the head, an oval for the middle section of the body, and a long, skinny oval for the end of the body. Using the off-white lining icing, outline the wings, making four long, skinny ovals to the edges of the cookie and connecting them to the yellow body. Let set for 5 minutes. Using a paintbrush and the yellow flooding icing, paint in the dragonfly body. Using the translucent off-white flooding icing, paint in the dragonfly wings.

5. **Make red lining and flooding icing for the toadstools.** Mix ½ cup icing in a small bowl with bright red gel to make red. Thin to lining consistency and spoon ¼ cup into a piping bag fitted with a #1 tip. Thin the remaining icing to flooding consistency and cover with plastic wrap. Mix ¼ cup icing in a small bowl with whitener to make bright white for the polka dots on the toadstools. Thin to a consistency looser than lining consistency and spoon all of it into a piping bag fitted with a #1.5 tip.

6. **Outline and paint in the toadstools; make the dots.** Using the red lining icing, outline the toadstool caps, leaving the areas unlined where

TOADSTOOLS CONTINUES

the white stalks overlap the caps. Outline the insides of the toadstool caps, making a long, skinny oval on top of the light brown icing but leaving the area unlined where the white stalk overlaps. Let set for 5 minutes. Using a paintbrush and the red flooding icing, paint in the toadstool caps, thinning the icing out a little where the stalks overlap. While the icing is still wet, use the looser white lining icing to drop white dots of icing into the red flooding icing. Space the dots apart to make a polka-dot pattern on the toadstool caps. Let set overnight. Wash the #1 piping tips.

7. **Make lining and flooding icing for the stalks; make lining icing to re-outline the dragonfly body.** Refresh the icing on medium low for 30 seconds. Mix ½ cup icing in a small bowl with a little whitener gel to make off-white for the outline of the dragonfly wings. Thin to lining consistency and spoon ¼ cup into a piping bag fitted with a #1 tip. Thin the remaining icing to flooding consistency, add more whitener to make bright white for the toadstool stalks, and cover with plastic wrap. Mix ¼ cup icing in a small bowl with lemon yellow and egg yellow gels to make the same yellow as the dragonfly body for the outline. Thin to lining consistency and spoon all of it into a piping bag fitted with a #1 tip.

8. **Re-outline the dragonfly and wings. Outline and paint in the stalks.** Using the yellow lining icing, re-outline the dragonfly body. Using the off-white lining icing, re-outline the dragonfly wings.

Outline the toadstool stalks, going over the light brown and the red icings of the toadstool caps. Let set for 5 minutes. Using a paintbrush and the white flooding icing, paint in the stalks, butting the icing (see page 64) to the edge of the toadstool caps. Let set for 2 to 3 hours.

9. **Make red lining icing to re-outline the caps; make green lining and flooding icing for the grass.** Mix ¼ cup icing in a small bowl with bright red gel to make red. Thin to lining consistency and spoon all of it into a piping bag fitted with a #1 tip. Mix ½ cup icing in a small bowl with leaf green and neon green gels to make grass green. Thin to lining consistency and spoon ¼ cup into a piping bag fitted with a #1 tip. Thin the remaining icing to flooding consistency and cover with plastic wrap.

10. **Outline and paint in grass. Re-outline the stalks and caps. Make the grass blades and the dragonfly eye.** Using the green lining icing, outline the grass. Starting from the bottom of the cookie, make long points for the blades of grass going over the toadstool stalks. Let set for 5 minutes. Using a paintbrush and the green flooding icing, paint in the grass. Let set for 2 to 3 hours. Meanwhile, using the off-white lining icing, re-outline the toadstool stalks. Using the red lining icing, re-outline the toadstool caps and pipe a dot for the dragonfly eye. Using the green lining icing, pipe vertical lines on the grass to add texture.

XO—HUG AND KISS

● beginner   ○ intermediate   ○ advanced

what you need

TO MAKE THE COOKIES
3-inch teddy bear cookie cutter

Cookie dough of choice (pages 26–33), prepared, chilled, and rolled out

Cooling racks

TO DECORATE
2 cups Royal Icing (pages 40–42)

Pasteurized egg white water

Gel food colors: bright red, whitener, electric pink

5 plastic or parchment paper piping bags (page 53)

5 #1 tips

Assorted paintbrushes

1. **Make the cookies.** Cut out 24 cookies from the dough. Bake and cool as directed.

2. **Make red and white lining and flooding icings for the X and the O.** Fill each of two bowls with ½ cup of icing. Cover one with plastic wrap. To the other bowl, add bright red gel to make red for the X. Thin to lining consistency and spoon ¼ cup into a piping bag fitted with a #1 tip. To the second bowl, add whitener gel to make bright white for the O. Thin to lining consistency and spoon ¼ cup into a piping bag fitted with a #1 tip. Thin the remaining red and white icings to flooding consistency and cover with plastic wrap.

3. **Outline and paint in the X and the O.** Position the cookie so the bear's legs are to the left. Using the red lining icing, outline the X, making the letter fat and blocky and squaring off the ends. Using the white lining icing, outline the letter O, leaving the areas unlined where the hearts overlap. Let set for 5 minutes. Using a paintbrush and the red flooding icing, paint in the X. Using the white flooding icing, paint in the O. Let set for 6 to 8 hours or overnight.

4. **Make red and white linings icing to re-outline the X and the O; make pink lining and flooding icing for the hearts.** Refresh the icing on medium low for 30 seconds. Fill three bowls with ¼ cup icing each. Cover two with plastic wrap. To the remaining bowl, add bright

XO—HUG AND KISS CONTINUES

red gel to make red for the outline of the O and the hearts. Thin to lining consistency and spoon all of it into a piping bag fitted with a #1 tip. To the second bowl, add whitener gel to make bright white for the outline of the X. Thin to lining consistency and spoon all of it into a piping bag fitted with a #1 tip. To the third bowl, add electric pink and whitener gels to make pink for the hearts. Thin to lining consistency and spoon 2 tablespoons into a piping bag fitted with a

#1 tip. Thin the remaining pink icing to flooding consistency and cover with plastic wrap.

5. **Outline and paint in the hearts.** Using the pink lining icing, outline the hearts on the letter O. Let set for 5 minutes. Using a paintbrush and the pink flooding icing, paint in the hearts. Let set for 2 to 3 hours.

6. **Re-outline the X, O, and hearts.** Using the white lining icing, re-outline the letter X. Using the red lining icing, re-outline the letter O and the hearts.

· MAKES 24 ·

RABBIT IN HAT

○ beginner   ● intermediate   ○ advanced

what you need

TO MAKE THE COOKIES
3-inch teddy bear cookie cutter

Cookie dough of choice (pages 26–33), prepared, chilled, and rolled out

Cooling racks

TO DECORATE
3 cups Royal Icing (pages 40–42)

Pasteurized egg white or water

Gel food colors: bright red, super black, whitener, electric pink

Black fine-tipped edible marker (optional)

4 plastic or parchment paper piping bags (page 53)

4 #1 tips

Assorted paintbrushes

1. **Make the cookies.** Cut out 24 cookies from the dough. Bake and cool as directed.

2. **Make red flooding icing for the interior of the hat and paint in.** Mix ¼ cup icing in a

small bowl with bright red gel to make red for the interior of the hat. Thin to flooding consistency and cover with plastic wrap. Position the cookie so the bear's feet are at the top. Using a paintbrush and the red flooding icing, thinly paint in the area where the interior of the hat is, thinning the icing out on all sides. Let set for 1 hour.

3. **Make black lining and flooding icing for the hat.** Mix 1¼ cups icing in a small bowl with super black gel to make black for the hat. Thin to lining consistency and spoon ¼ cup into a piping bag fitted with a #1 tip. Thin the remaining icing to flooding consistency and cover with plastic wrap.

4. **Outline and paint in the hat.** Using the black lining icing, outline the silhouette of the hat, leaving the area unlined where the rabbit's head and ears overlap the brim. Outline the inner edge of the brim (the hole) by piping a flat, thin oval in the middle of the hat, leaving the area unlined where the head overlaps the red and leaving two small gaps where the rabbit's paws rest on the brim. Let set for 5 minutes. Using a paintbrush and the black flooding icing, paint in the hat, thinning out the icing a little where the ears and head overlap. Paint in the rest of the brim, but do not thin out the icing into the red area. Let icing set for 6 to 8 hours or overnight.

5. **Make white lining and flooding icing for the rabbit.** Refresh the icing on medium low for 30 seconds. Mix 1 cup icing in a small bowl with whitener gel to make white for the rabbit. Thin to lining consistency and spoon ¼ cup into a piping bag fitted with a #1 tip. Thin the remaining icing to flooding consistency and cover with plastic wrap.

6. **Outline the rabbit and paint in.** Using the white lining icing, outline the rabbit's head and ears, going over the hat. Outline the paws on top of the brim. Let set for 5 minutes. Using a paintbrush and the white flooding icing, paint in the head, ears, and paws. Let set for 4 to 6 hours.

7. **Make light gray lining icing to re-outline the rabbit; make pink lining and flooding icing for the inner ears.** Fill two bowls with ¼ cup icing each. Cover one with plastic wrap. To the other bowl, add super black and whitener gels to make light gray for the outline of the rabbit. Thin to lining consistency and spoon all of it into a piping bag fitted with a #1 tip. To the second bowl, add electric pink and whitener gels to make pale pink for the inner ears. Thin to lining consistency and spoon 2 tablespoons into a piping bag fitted with a #1 tip. Thin the remaining pale pink icing to flooding consistency and cover with plastic wrap.

8. **Re-outline the rabbit. Outline the inner ears and nose; paint in the inner ears. Make the eyes.** Using the light gray lining icing, re-outline the rabbit and hat, drawing in toes on the paws. Using the pale pink lining icing, pipe the outlines of the inner ears. Make a triangle for the nose. Let set for 5 minutes. Using a paintbrush and the pale pink flooding icing, paint in the inner ears. Using the pale pink lining icing or a black edible marker, draw two dots for the eyes.

GUITAR CUTTER

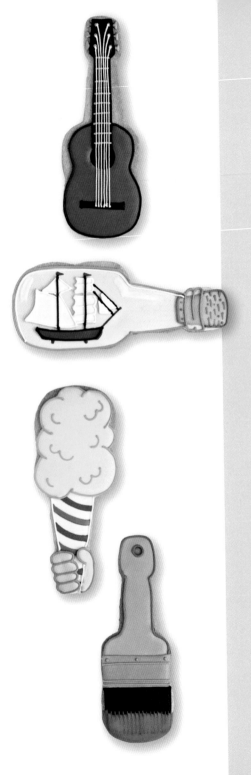

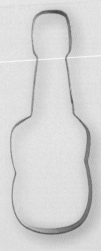

You'll notice I took liberties with this cutter's shape when I outlined the guitar—I just gave it a more realistic-looking silhouette. Do this whenever your vision of a cookie isn't exactly the same as the cutter you find. Putting six strings on the guitar can be tricky; practice before you take the tip to the cookies. Make the lining icing for them slightly tighter—and make only three strings if you're not yet comfortable making tight, straight lines.

The Paintbrush cookie is fun to make because you actually get to dunk the cookie into flooding icing like you would a real paintbrush into a bucket of paint. Try it with a few of your favorite colors.

GUITAR

○ beginner ○ intermediate ● advanced

what you need

TO MAKE THE COOKIES
3-inch guitar cookie cutter

Cookie dough of choice (pages 26–33), prepared, chilled, and rolled out

Cooling racks

TO DECORATE
3½ cups Royal Icing (pages 40–42)

Pasteurized egg white or water

Gel food colors: super black, chocolate brown, sunset orange, whitener, buckeye brown, ivory

7 plastic or parchment paper piping bags (page 53)

6 #1 tips

1 #1.5 tip

Assorted paintbrushes

1. **Make the cookies.** Cut out 24 cookies from the dough. Bake and cool as directed.

2. **Make flooding icing for the black hole and paint in.** Mix 2 tablespoons royal icing in a bowl with super black gel to make black. Thin to loose flooding consistency. Using a paintbrush, thinly paint in the guitar hole, thinning it out to where the body overlaps it. Let set for 1 hour.

3. **Make orange-brown lining and flooding icing for the body of the guitar; outline and paint in.** Mix 1 cup royal icing with sunset orange and chocolate brown to make orange-brown for the body. Thin to lining consistency and spoon ¼ cup into a piping bag fitted with a #1 tip. Thin the remaining icing to flooding consistency, add a

little whitener, and cover with plastic wrap. Using the lining icing, outline the body and a hole in the center of the guitar, making the body narrower at the top and wider at the bottom. Let set for 5 minutes. Using a paintbrush and the flooding icing, paint in the body of the guitar. Let set until hard, 4 to 6 hours.

4. **Make dark brown lining and flooding icing for the neck of the guitar.** Mix ¾ cup royal icing in a bowl with chocolate brown and buckeye brown gels to make dark brown for the neck of the guitar. Thin to lining consistency and spoon into a piping bag fitted with a #1 tip. Thin the remaining icing to flooding consistency and cover with plastic wrap.

GUITAR CONTINUES

5. **Outline the guitar head and neck and paint in. Make the saddle.** When the body is set, use the dark brown lining icing to outline the guitar head (where the strings connect at the top) and the neck, making the neck wide enough to accommodate six strings. Make the thin rectangle for the saddle (where the strings connect at the bottom) by butting (see page 64) up two or three lines next to each other. Let set for 5 minutes. Using a paintbrush and the dark brown flooding icing, paint in the head and neck. Let set until hard, 6 to 8 hours or overnight.

6. **Make lining icings for the tuning pegs, frets, and strings.** Refresh the royal icing on medium low for 30 seconds. Spoon ¼ cup into each of three bowls. Cover two with plastic wrap. To the remaining, add super black and whitener gels to make light gray for the pegs. Thin to lining consistency and spoon it all into a piping bag fitted with a #1.5 tip. To the second bowl, add ivory gel to make tan for the frets. Thin to lining consistency and spoon it all into a piping bag fitted with a #1 tip. To the third bowl, add whitener gel to make white for the strings. Thin to tight lining consistency and spoon all of it into a piping bag fitted with a #1 tip.

7. **Make the pegs, frets, and strings.** Using the light gray lining icing (and the #1.5 tip), make the tuning pegs on either side of the head of the guitar. Make a dot next to each peg where the string is threaded through. Let set for 5 minutes. Using the tan lining icing, make horizontal lines across the neck for the frets. Let set for 5 minutes. Using the white lining icing, make the strings, beginning at the gray dot on the bottom left of the pegs, going over the frets, and touching down on the saddle. Work across the neck; skip the second and fifth strings if you find you can't fit them in.

8. **Make lining icings to re-outline the neck and body; re-outline.** Spoon ¼ cup royal icing into each of two bowls. Cover one with plastic wrap. To the other, add chocolate brown and sunset orange gels to make darker orange-brown to re-outline the neck. Thin to lining consistency and spoon it all into a piping bag fitted with a #1 tip. To the second bowl, add chocolate brown and buckeye brown gels to make dark brown to re-outline the body. Thin to lining consistency and spoon it all into a piping bag fitted with a #1 tip. Using the darker orange-brown lining icing, re-outline the guitar body, excluding the area where the neck overlaps. Using the dark brown lining icing, re-outline the guitar head and neck.

SHIP IN A BOTTLE

○ beginner   ○ intermediate   ● advanced

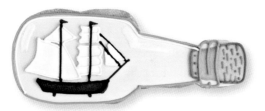

what you need

TO MAKE THE COOKIES
3-inch guitar-shaped cookie cutter

Cookie dough of choice (pages 26–33), prepared, chilled, and rolled out

Cooling racks

TO DECORATE
4 cups Royal Icing (pages 40–42)

Pasteurized egg white or water

Gel food colors: bright blue, whitener, ivory, gold, chocolate brown, bright red, super black

9 plastic or parchment paper piping bags (page 53)

9 #1 tips

Assorted paintbrushes

1. **Make the cookies.** Cut out 24 cookies from the dough. Bake and cool as directed.

2. **Make blue lining and flooding icing for the bottle.** Mix 1 cups royal icing in a bowl with bright blue and whitener gels to make light blue. Thin to lining consistency and spoon cup into a piping bag fitted with a #1 tip. Thin the remaining icing to flooding consistency and cover with plastic wrap.

3. **Outline and paint in the bottle.** Position the cookie so that the bottom of the guitar is the left side of the cookie. Using the blue lining icing, outline the bottle, including the area where the cork will be. Let set for 5 minutes. Using a paintbrush and the flooding icing, paint in the bottle and let set until hard, 6 to 8 hours or overnight.

4. **Make lining and flooding icings: tan for the**

cork, reddish-brown for the boat, and white for the sails. Refresh the royal icing on medium low for 30 seconds. Spoon ½ cup icing into each of three bowls. Cover two with plastic wrap. To the remaining bowl, add ivory and gold gel to make tan for the cork. Thin to lining consistency and spoon ¼ cup into a piping bag fitted with a #1 tip. Thin the remaining icing to flooding consistency and cover with plastic wrap. To the second bowl, add chocolate brown and bright red gels to make reddish-brown for the boat. Thin to lining consistency and spoon ¼ cup into a piping bag fitted with a #1 tip. Thin the remaining icing to flooding consistency and cover with plastic wrap. To the third bowl, add whitener to make white for the sails. Spoon ¼ cup into a piping bag fitted with a #1 tip. Thin the remaining icing to

SHIP IN A BOTTLE CONTINUES

flooding consistency and cover with plastic wrap.

5. **Outline and paint in the cork, hull, and masts.** Using the tan lining icing, outline the cork, going over the light blue flooding icing. Let set for 5 minutes. Using a paintbrush and the tan flooding icing, paint in the cork. Using the reddish-brown lining icing, outline the ship's hull, then make two dots for the hull's stand and a line for the bowsprit (the pole going forward from the stern of a ship). Let set for 5 minutes. Using a paintbrush and the reddish-brown flooding icing, paint in the hull. Using the white lining icing, outline the sails. Let set for 5 minutes. Reserve the white lining icing. Using a paintbrush and the white flooding icing, paint in the sails. Reserve the white flooding icing. Let set until hard, 6 to 8 hours or overnight.

6. **Make lining icing to re-outline the cork, bottle, hull, and masts.** Refresh the royal icing on medium low for 30 seconds. Spoon ¼ cup icing into each of three bowls. Cover two bowls with plastic wrap. To the remaining, add ivory and gold gel to make golden brown to re-outline the cork. Thin to lining consistency and spoon it all into a piping bag fitted with a #1 tip. To the second bowl, add bright blue gel to make a darker blue to re-outline the bottle. Thin to lining consistency and spoon it all into a piping bag fitted with a #1 tip. To the third bowl, add chocolate brown to make dark brown to re-outline the hull and make the masts. Thin to lining consistency and spoon it all into a piping bag fitted with a #1 tip.

7. **Re-outline the bottle, cork, and hull and make details.** Using the darker blue lining icing, re-outline the bottle and make the details for its mouth. Using the golden brown lining icing, re-outline the cork, excluding the part that lies beneath the mouth of the bottle. Holding the tip of the piping bag at a 45-degree angle and touching the cookie, draw short lines and dots on the cork to give it texture. Using the dark brown lining icing, re-outline the hull, then make the masts, going over the sails. Using the reserved white lining icing, outline the bottle within the darker blue outline only on the top and left side. Using a paintbrush and the reserved white flooding icing, swipe the paintbrush along the neck of the bottle and to the top left of the ship for shine marks. Let set for 5 minutes.

8. **Make lining icing for the flags, lines, and details.** Meanwhile, spoon 2 tablespoons royal icing into each of two bowls. Cover one with plastic wrap. To the other, add bright red gel to make red for the flags. Thin to lining consistency and spoon it all into a piping bag fitted with a #1 tip. To the second bowl, add super black gel to make black for the lines connecting the sails to the bowsprit. Thin to lining consistency and spoon all of it into a piping bag fitted with a #1 tip. Using the red lining icing, squeeze a dot on top of each mast, then drag the tip to the right to make a small triangle. Using the black lining icing, make two thin parallel lines from the sails to the bowsprit to connect them.

COTTON CANDY

○ beginner　○ intermediate　● advanced

what you need

TO MAKE THE COOKIES
3-inch guitar cookie cutter

Cookie dough of choice (pages 26–33), prepared, chilled, and rolled out

Cooling racks

TO DECORATE
3¼ cups Royal Icing (pages 40–42)

Pasteurized egg white or water

Gel food colors: electric pink, whitener, bright red, royal blue, copper (flesh)

7 plastic or parchment paper piping bags (page 53)

7 #1 tips

Assorted paintbrushes

1. **Make the cookies.** Cut out 24 cookies from the dough. Bake and cool as directed.

2. **Make pink lining and flooding icing for the cotton candy.** Mix 1 cup royal icing with electric pink and whitener gels to make pink for the cotton candy. Thin to lining consistency and spoon ¼ cup into a piping bag fitted with a #1 tip. Thin the remaining icing to flooding consistency and cover with plastic wrap.

3. **Make white lining and flooding icing for the cone.** Mix ¾ cup royal icing with whitener gel to make white for the cone. Thin to lining consistency and spoon ¼ cup into a piping bag fitted with a #1 tip. Thin the remaining icing to flooding consistency and cover with plastic wrap.

4. **Outline the cotton candy and the cone and paint in.** Position the cookie so the guitar head is the bottom. Using the pink lining icing, outline the silhouette of the cotton candy, exaggerating the curves along the edge of the cookie. Let set for 5 minutes. Using the white lining icing, outline the paper cone, making sure the white lines are touching the outline of the cotton candy and leaving the areas where the hand overlaps the cone unlined. Let set for 5 minutes. Reserve the white lining icing. Using a paintbrush and the pink flooding icing, paint in the cotton candy. Using a paintbrush and the white flooding icing, paint in the cone, thinning out the icing where the

COTTON CANDY CONTINUES

fingers overlap. Let set until hard, 6 to 8 hours or overnight.

5. **Make red and blue lining and flooding icings for the stripes.** Refresh the royal icing on medium low for 30 seconds. Spoon ¼ cup icing into each of two bowls. Cover one with plastic wrap. To the other, add bright red gel to make red for the stripes on the cone. Thin to lining consistency and spoon 2 tablespoons into a piping bag fitted with a #1 tip. Thin the remaining icing to flooding consistency and cover with plastic wrap. To the second bowl, add royal blue gel to make blue for the stripes on the cone. Thin to lining consistency and spoon 2 tablespoons into a piping bag fitted with a #1 tip. Thin the remaining icing to flooding consistency and cover with plastic wrap.

6. **Outline and paint in the stripes.** Using the red lining icing, outline the red stripes on the cone. Using the blue lining icing, outline the blue stripes on the cone. Let set for 5 minutes. Using paintbrushes and the red and blue flooding icings, thinly paint in the red and blue stripes. Let set for 4 to 6 hours.

7. **Make dark pink lining icing to re-outline the cotton candy and make interior details.** Refresh the royal icing on medium low for 30 seconds. Mix ¼ cup icing in a bowl with electric pink and whitener gels to make darker pink to outline the cotton candy. Thin to lining consistency and spoon it all into a piping bag fitted with a #1 tip. Re-outline the cotton candy, extending the lines at the bumps to give the cotton candy a fluffy look. Draw small scallops in the interior.

8. **Make lining and flooding icing for the hand; outline and paint in.** Mix ½ cup royal icing in a bowl with copper (flesh) and whitener gels to make desired skin tone. Thin to lining consistency and spoon ¼ cup into a piping bag fitted with a #1 tip. Thin the remaining icing to flooding consistency and cover with plastic wrap. Using the lining icing, draw the silhouette of the four fingers on the left side of the cone and the thumb and palm on the right side of the cone. Do not draw in the lines that go over the cone. Let set for 5 minutes. Using a paintbrush and the skin tone flooding icing, paint in the fingers and thumb. Let set for 4 to 6 hours.

9. **Make lining icing to re-outline the hand and re-outline. Re-outline the cone.** When the skin-tone flooding icing is set, mix ¼ cup royal icing in a bowl with copper (flesh) and whitener gels to make a darker shade of the skin tone to re-outline the hand. Thin to lining consistency and spoon it all into a piping bag fitted with a #1 tip. Re-outline the fingers and thumb, delineating the fingers and thumb that sit on top of the cone. Using the reserved white lining icing, re-outline the cone, skipping the areas where the fingers overlap it. Let set for 1 hour.

PAINTBRUSH

○ beginner ● intermediate ○ advanced

what you need

TO MAKE THE COOKIES
3-inch guitar-shaped cookie cutter

Cookie dough of choice (pages 26–33), prepared, chilled, and rolled out

Cooling racks

TO DECORATE
3½ cups Royal Icing (pages 40–42)

Pasteurized egg white or water

Gel food colors: lemon yellow, ivory, whitener, buckeye brown, gold, super black, bright red

4 plastic or parchment paper piping bags (page 53)

4 #1 tips

Assorted paintbrushes

Parchment paper

1. **Make the cookies.** Cut out 24 cookies from the dough. Bake and cool as directed.

2. **Make tan and dark brown lining and flooding icings for the paintbrush.** Spoon ¾ cup royal icing into each of two bowls. Cover one with plastic wrap. To the remaining, add lemon yellow and ivory gels to make tan for the handle. Thin to lining consistency and spoon ¼ cup into a piping bag fitted with a #1 tip. Thin the remaining icing to flooding consistency, add a little whitener, and cover with plastic wrap. To the second bowl, add buckeye brown to make dark brown for the bristles. Thin to lining consistency and spoon ¼ cup into a piping bag fitted with a #1 tip. Thin the remaining icing to flooding consistency and cover with plastic wrap.

3. **Outline and paint in the handle and the bristles.** Using the tan lining icing, outline the brush handle, stopping at the metal fastener and thinning out the icing where the metal part of the brush overlaps the handle. Outline a small circle at the top of the handle. Let set for 5 minutes. Using a paintbrush and the tan flooding icing, paint in the handle, thinning out the icing where the metal part overlaps. Using the dark brown lining icing, outline the bristles along the sides and tips, skipping the area where the metal piece meets the bristles. Let set for 5 minutes. Reserve the dark brown lining icing. Using a paintbrush and dark brown flooding icing, paint in the bristles, thinning out the icing where the metal piece overlaps. Let set until hard, 6 to 8 hours or overnight.

PAINTBRUSH CONTINUES

4. **Make golden brown lining icing to re-outline the handle; make light gray lining and flooding icing for the metal fastener.** Mix ¼ cup royal icing with gold gel to make dark golden brown to outline the handle. Thin to lining consistency and spoon it all into a piping bag fitted with a #1 tip. Mix ¾ cup royal icing in a bowl with super black and whitener gels to make light gray to outline the metal. Thin to lining consistency and spoon ¼ cup into a piping bag fitted with a #1 tip. Thin the remaining icing to flooding consistency and cover with plastic wrap.

5. **Outline and paint in the fastener.** Using the light gray lining icing, outline the metal piece of the brush, going over the handle and the bristles. Let set for 5 minutes. Using a paintbrush and the light gray flooding icing, paint in the metal piece. Let set for 2 to 3 hours. Reserve the gray lining icing.

6. **Re-outline the handle, draw in the bristles, and make the details.** As the light gray flooding icing sets, use the golden brown lining icing to re-outline the brush handle and the hole in it. Using the reserved dark brown lining icing, make bristles over the brown area of the brush, making the lines as straight as possible and spacing them evenly apart. When the light gray flooding icing is set, use the reserved light gray lining icing to make the details on the metal piece.

7. **Make the "paint" and dip the cookie.** Place a piece of parchment paper on a clean work surface. Mix 1 cup royal icing in a mug with bright red and whitener gels to make red for the paint. Thin it to flooding consistency. Holding the handle of the paintbrush cookie, dip it into the red icing, holding the cookie straight up and down, so that the "paint" goes halfway up the bristles. Pull the cookie out of the icing, hold the cookie over the mug to let excess icing drip off, and lay the cookie down on parchment until the icing sets, 4 to 6 hours.

BALLOON CUTTER

This group of cookies is all about celebration. The wreath and balloon are pretty self-explanatory, but the beauty of the balloon is that you can embellish it with a name, a salutation, or a number for a special birthday. The money bag works great for someone who just got that big promotion. It looks just as easy to make as the balloon, but the dollar sign can be somewhat challenging. Practice making it on parchment first, or use an edible pen to draw it on. You might be wondering what type of celebration the target would work for. I once made it for a friend who had enjoyed a big success—she hit the bull's-eye!

BALLOON

● beginner ○ intermediate ○ advanced

what you need

TO MAKE THE COOKIES
3-inch balloon cookie cutter

Cookie dough of choice (pages 26–33), prepared, chilled, and rolled out

Cooling racks

TO DECORATE
2 cups Royal Icing (pages 40–42)

Pasteurized egg white or water

Gel food colors: royal blue, whitener

3 plastic or parchment paper piping bags (page 53)

3 #1 tips

Assorted paintbrushes

1. **Make the cookies.** Cut out 24 cookies from the dough. Bake and cool as directed.

2. **Make lining and flooding icing for the balloon.** Mix 1½ cups royal icing in a small bowl with royal blue gel to make blue. Thin to lining consistency and spoon ¼ cup into a piping bag fitted with a #1 tip. Thin the remaining icing to flooding consistency and cover with plastic wrap.

3. **Outline and paint in the balloon.** Using the blue lining icing, outline the silhouette of the balloon, following the edge of the cookie and creating a knot at the bottom; let the edges of the cookie show at the knot. Let set for 5 minutes. Using a paintbrush and the flooding icing, paint in the balloon. Let set for 6 to 8 hours or overnight.

4. **Make white lining and flooding icing for the shine mark; outline and paint in.** Refresh the royal icing on medium low for 30 seconds. Mix ¼ cup icing in a small bowl with whitener gel to make bright white for the shine mark. Thin to lining consistency. Spoon 3 tablespoons into a piping bag fitted with a #1 tip. Thin the remaining icing to flooding consistency and cover with plastic wrap. Using the white lining icing, outline the shine mark on the balloon. Let set for 5 minutes. Using a paintbrush and the flooding icing, fill in the shine mark.

5. **Make lining icing and re-outline the balloon.** Meanwhile, mix ¼ cup royal icing with the royal blue gel paste to make darker blue for the outline of the balloon. Thin to lining consistency and spoon it all into a piping bag fitted with a #1 tip. Re-outline the balloon and draw the knot. Let set for 4 to 6 hours.

WREATH

○ beginner ● intermediate ○ advanced

what you need

TO MAKE THE COOKIES
3-inch balloon cookie cutter

Cookie dough of choice (pages 26–33), prepared, chilled, and rolled out

Cooling racks

TO DECORATE
2 cups Royal Icing (pages 40–42)

Pasteurized egg white or water

Gel food colors: leaf green, whitener, bright red

3 plastic or parchment paper piping bags (page 53)

3 #1 tips

Assorted paintbrushes

1. **Make the cookies.** Cut out 24 cookies from the dough. Bake and cool as directed.

2. **Make green lining and flooding icing for the wreath.** Mix 1 cup royal icing in a small bowl with the leaf green gel to make the green for the wreath. Thin to lining consistency and spoon ¼ cup into a piping bag fitted with a #1 tip. Thin the remaining icing to flooding consistency, add a little whitener, and cover with plastic wrap.

3. **Outline and paint in the wreath; make details.** Using the lining icing, outline the wreath, drawing a jagged line along the edge of the cookie to make the wreath look bushy. Outline the inner circle, drawing it in the same manner to make the hole in the middle of the wreath.

Let set for 5 minutes. Using a paintbrush and the green flooding icing, paint in the wreath. Let set for 6 to 8 hours or overnight.

4. **Make red lining and flooding icing for the bow.** Refresh the royal icing on medium low for 30 seconds. Mix ½ cup royal icing in a small bowl with bright red gel to make red for the bow. Thin to lining consistency and spoon ¼ cup into a piping bag fitted with a #1 tip. Thin the remaining icing to flooding consistency, add a little whitener, and cover with plastic wrap.

5. **Outline and paint in the bow; make the holly berries and re-outline the bow.** Using the red lining icing, outline the silhouette of the bow with the tip hovering close to the cookie. Let set for

WREATH CONTINUES

5 minutes. Reserve the red lining icing. Using a paintbrush and the red flooding icing, paint in the bow. Using some of the reserved lining icing, make the holly berries on the wreath and re-outline the bow. Let set for 2 hours.

6. **Make dark green lining icing for the holly leaves; make the leaves and re-outline the wreath.** In a small bowl, mix ½ cup royal icing with leaf green gel to make a darker green for the holly leaves. Thin to lining consistency and spoon all of it into a piping bag fitted with a #1 tip. Re-outline the wreath, following the jagged edges. Draw holly leaves near the clusters of berries.

7. **Re-outline the ribbon.** Using the reserved red lining icing, re-outline the ribbon with the tip hovering close to the cookie.

· MAKES 24 ·

MONEY BAG

○ beginner   ● intermediate   ○ advanced

what you need

TO MAKE THE COOKIES
3-inch balloon cookie cutter

Cookie dough of choice (pages 26–33), prepared, chilled, and rolled out

Cooling racks

TO DECORATE
2 cups Royal Icing (pages 40–42)

Pasteurized egg white or water

Gel food colors: ivory, gold, whitener, leaf green, chocolate brown

3 plastic or parchment paper piping bags (page 53)

3 #1 tips

Assorted paintbrushes

1. **Make the cookies.** Cut out 24 cookies from the dough. Bake and cool as directed.

2. **Make tan lining and flooding icing for the bag; outline and paint in.** Mix 1½ cups royal icing in a small bowl with ivory, gold, and whitener gels to make tan for the bag. Thin to lining consistency, then spoon ¼ cup into a piping bag fitted with a #1 tip. Thin the remaining icing to flooding consistency, add a little whitener, and cover with plastic wrap. Using the lining icing, outline the

silhouette of the money bag, making it narrow along the sides near the top. To give a gathered look at the top, draw a jagged edge. Let set for 5 minutes. Using a paintbrush and the tan flooding icing, paint in the bag and let set until hard, 6 to 8 hours or overnight.

3. **Make green lining and flooding icing for the dollar sign; outline and paint in.** Refresh the royal icing on medium low for 30 seconds. Mix ¼ cup icing in a small bowl with leaf green gel and one toothpick of ivory gel paste to make green for the dollar sign. Spoon 2 tablespoons icing into a piping bag fitted with a #1 tip. Thin the remaining icing to flooding consistency and cover with plastic wrap. Using the lining icing, outline an S in the center of the bag. Let set for 5 minutes. Reserve the green lining icing. Using a paintbrush and the green flooding icing, paint in the S in a very thin layer. Let set until hard, about 1 hour.

4. **Make caramel brown lining icing to re-outline the bag and make details. Draw a line through the money symbol.** Meanwhile, mix a scant ¼ cup royal icing in a bowl with gold and chocolate brown gels to make caramel brown to re-outline the bag. Spoon all of the icing into a piping bag fitted with a #1 tip. Re-outline the money bag, then draw the band where the bag is cinched and a few vertical lines for the folds. Using the reserved green lining icing, make a vertical line through the center of the S. Let set until hard, 4 to 6 hours.

TARGET

○ beginner ○ intermediate ● advanced

what you need

TO MAKE THE COOKIES
3-inch balloon cookie cutter

Cookie dough of choice (pages 26–33), prepared, chilled, and rolled out

Cooling racks

TO DECORATE
3 cups Royal Icing (pages 40–42)

Pasteurized egg white or water

Gel food colors: whitener, bright red, super black, royal blue, chocolate brown

5 plastic or parchment paper piping bags (page 53)

5 #1 tips

Assorted paintbrushes

1. **Make the cookies.** Cut out 24 cookies from the dough. Bake and cool as directed.

2. **Make lining and flooding icing for the white circles; outline and paint in.** Mix 1¼ cups royal icing in a small bowl with the whitener gel to make bright white for the circles. Thin to lining consistency, then spoon ¼ cup into a piping bag fitted with a #1 tip. Thin the remaining icing to flooding consistency and cover with plastic wrap. Using the lining icing, outline a circle for the target, following the edge of the cookie except at the arrow feathers. Let set for 5 minutes. Using a paintbrush and the white flooding icing, paint in the entire circle. Let set for 6 to 8 hours or overnight.

3. **Make lining and flooding icing for the red stripes; outline and paint in.** Refresh the royal icing on medium low for 30 seconds. Mix ½ cup icing in a small bowl with the bright red gel to make bright red. Thin to lining consistency and spoon ¼ cup into a piping bag fitted with a #1 tip. Thin the remaining icing to thin flooding consistency and cover with plastic wrap. Using the red lining icing, outline the rings of the target by making five concentric circles, beginning at the edge and making them approximately ¼ inch apart. Let set for 5 minutes. Using a paintbrush and the red flooding icing, paint in every other ring, beginning with the outermost ring and ending in the center bull's-eye. Paint them thinly so that the red rings don't rise too far above the white background. Let set until hard, 2 to 3 hours.

4. **Make lining and flooding icing for the**

arrowhead. Refresh the royal icing on medium low for 30 seconds. Mix ¼ cup icing in a small bowl with super black gel to make black for the arrowhead. Thin to lining consistency and spoon 2 tablespoons into a piping bag fitted with a #1 tip. Thin the remaining icing to flooding consistency and cover with plastic wrap.

5. **Make lining icing and flooding icing for the feathers.** Mix ½ cup royal icing in a small bowl with royal blue gel paste to make dark blue for the feathers. Spoon ¼ cup of this into a second bowl. Thin one bowl to lining consistency and spoon all of it into a piping bag fitted with a #1 tip. Add whitener gel to the other bowl to make a lighter blue, then thin to flooding consistency and cover with plastic wrap.

6. **Outline the arrowhead; outline the feathers and paint them in.** Using the black lining icing, outline the arrowhead by putting its point halfway into the bull's-eye. Reserve the black lining icing. Using the dark blue lining icing, outline the arrow feathers by making a heart shape with the bottom point piercing the outer ring of the target. Let set for 5 minutes. Reserve the blue lining icing. Using a small paintbrush and the black flooding icing, paint in the arrowhead. Using the lighter blue flooding icing, paint in the heart. Let set until hard, 1 to 2 hours.

7. **Make brown lining and flooding icing for the shaft; outline and paint in.** Mix ¼ cup royal icing in a small bowl with chocolate brown to make brown for the arrow shaft. Thin to lining

consistency and spoon 2 tablespoons into a piping bag fitted with a #1 tip. Add a drop of whitener to the remaining icing, thin to flooding consistency, and cover with plastic wrap. Using the brown lining icing, outline the shaft of the arrow from the bottom of the arrowhead and going on top of the feathers. Let set for 5 minutes. Using a paintbrush and the brown flooding icing, carefully paint in the shaft. Let set for 10 minutes.

8. **Re-outline the arrowhead, shaft, and feathers. Draw in the feathers' details.** Using the reserved black lining icing, re-outline the arrowhead. Using the reserved brown lining icing, re-outline the shaft. Using the reserved blue lining icing, re-outline the feathers without lining over the shaft. Draw the feather details. Let set until completely hard, 1 hour.

BASEBALL MITT CUTTER

Each of these cookies features an example of how to give a flat cookie dimension. The baseball looks like its popping off the glove, an illusion I achieved by piling on the icing; the swan's beak is outlined and painted in on top of the white flooding icing; the placement, size, and scale of the sesame seeds on the hamburger bun make the bun look curved; re-outlining just the underside of the handle on the cookie jar makes it look like you can actually grasp it.

BASEBALL MITT

○ beginner ● intermediate ○ advanced

what you need

TO MAKE THE COOKIES
3¾-inch baseball mitt cutter

Cookie dough of choice (pages 26–33), prepared, chilled, and rolled out

Cooling racks

TO DECORATE
3 cups Royal Icing (pages 40–42)

Pasteurized egg white or water

Gel food colors: chocolate brown, sunset orange, super black, whitener, bright red

5 plastic or parchment paper piping bags (page 53)

4 #1 tips

1 #1.5 tip

Assorted paintbrushes

1. **Make the cookies.** Cut out 18 cookies from the dough. Bake and cool as directed.

2. **Make brown lining and flooding icing for the mitt; outline and paint in.** Mix 1¾ cups royal icing in a bowl with chocolate brown and sunset orange gels to make leather brown. Thin to lining consistency and spoon ¼ cup into a piping bag fitted with a #1 tip. Thin the remaining icing to flooding consistency and cover with plastic wrap. Using the lining icing, outline the silhouette of the mitt, making the hand first, followed by the web between the thumb and first finger. Let set for 5 minutes. Using a paintbrush and the flooding icing, paint in the mitt. Let set until hard, 6 to 8 hours or overnight.

3. **Make dark brown lining icing to re-outline the mitt; re-outline and make details.** Refresh the royal icing on medium low for 30 seconds. Mix ¼ cup icing in a small bowl with chocolate brown gel to make dark brown for the outline. Thin to lining consistency and spoon all of it into a piping bag fitted with a #1 tip. Re-outline the silhouette of the mitt, then make a second line running along the bottom from the pinkie to the thumb. Outline the fingers of the mitt.

4. **Make black lining icing for the stitching and lacing; draw in the details.** Mix ¼ cup royal icing in a bowl with super black gel to make black. Thin to lining consistency and spoon it all into a piping bag fitted with a #1.5 tip. Draw the stitching and lacing on the mitt, squeezing hard and moving slowly to make fatter lines.

BASEBALL MITT CONTINUES

5. **Make white lining and flooding icing for the baseball; outline and paint in.** Mix ½ cup royal icing in a bowl with whitener gel to make white for the baseball. Thin to lining consistency and spoon ¼ cup into a piping bag fitted with a #1 tip. Thin the remaining icing to thicker flooding consistency and cover with plastic wrap. Using the lining icing, outline a circle in the center of the mitt. Let set for 5 minutes. Using a paintbrush and the flooding icing, paint in the baseball, using ample icing so that it is rounded. Let set until hard, 6 to 8 hours or overnight.

6. **Make red lining icing for the stitching; draw in.** Refresh the royal icing on medium low for 30 seconds. Mix ¼ cup icing in a bowl with the bright red gel to make bright red. Thin to lining consistency and spoon all of it into a piping bag fitted with a #1 tip. Draw the stitching on the baseball. Let set for 5 minutes.

· MAKES 18 ·

SWAN

○ beginner ● intermediate ○ advanced

what you need

TO MAKE THE COOKIES
3¾-inch baseball mitt cutter

Cookie dough of choice (pages 26–33), prepared, chilled, and rolled out

Cooling racks

TO DECORATE
2½ cups Royal Icing (pages 40–42)

Pasteurized egg white or water

Gel food colors: whitener, sunset orange, super black

4 plastic or parchment paper piping bags (page 53)

4 #1 tips

Assorted paintbrushes

· ·

1. **Make the cookies.** Cut out 18 cookies from the dough. Bake and cool as directed.

2. **Make white lining and flooding icing for the swan, reserving about 2 tablespoons** for the eyes; outline and paint in. Mix 1¾ cups royal icing in a bowl with whitener gel to make bright white. Thin to lining consistency and spoon ¼ cup into a piping bag fitted with

a #1 tip. Thin the remaining icing to lining consistency and cover with plastic wrap. Using the lining icing, outline the silhouette of the swan, making bumps for the feathers along the top and left edge of the cookie. Outline the tiny triangular space below the head and along the neck as well as the petal shape beneath where the two wings overlap. Let set for 5 minutes. Using a paintbrush and the white flooding icing, paint in the swan. Let set until hard, 6 to 8 hours or overnight.

3. **Make lining and flooding icings: orange for the beak and black for the face.** Refresh the royal icing on medium low for 30 seconds. Spoon ¼ cup into each of two bowls. Cover one with plastic wrap. To the remaining, add sunset orange gel to make orange for the beak. Thin to lining consistency and spoon 2 tablespoons into a piping bag fitted with a #1 tip. Thin the remaining to flooding consistency, add whitener, and cover with plastic wrap. To the second bowl, mix in super black gel to make black for the face. Spoon 2 tablespoons into a piping bag fitted with a #1 tip. Thin the remaining icing to flooding consistency and cover with plastic wrap.

4. **Outline and paint in the beak and face.** Using the orange lining icing, outline the beak, using the photo as a guide for positioning it. Using the black lining icing, outline the black part of the swan's face. Reserve the black lining icing. Let set for 5 minutes. Using a paintbrush and the orange flooding icing, paint in the beak. Using another paintbrush and the black flooding icing, paint in the black part of the face. Let set until hard, 4 to 6 hours or overnight.

5. **Make gray lining icing and re-outline the swan and make the feathers and eye.** Refresh the royal icing at medium low for 30 seconds. Mix ¼ cup icing in a bowl with super black and whitener gels to make light gray to outline the feathers. Thin to lining consistency and spoon it all into a piping bag fitted with a #1 tip. Re-outline the swan, then draw the feathers, working in sections, beginning with the head and neck, then making the center wing and finishing with the outer feathers. Make a small dot on the black part of the face for the swan's eye.

6. **Make the nostril.** Using the reserved black lining icing, draw a small dash on the beak for a nostril. Let set until hard, about 2 hours.

CHEESEBURGER

○ beginner   ○ intermediate   ● advanced

what you need

TO MAKE THE COOKIES
3¾-inch baseball mitt cutter

Cookie dough of choice (pages 26–33), prepared, chilled, and rolled out

Cooling racks

TO DECORATE
4½ cups Royal Icing (pages 40–42)

Pasteurized egg white or water

Gel food colors: chocolate brown, egg yellow, sunset orange, gold, ivory, whitener, lemon yellow, super black, buckeye brown, bright red, leaf green, neon green, red red

10 plastic or parchment paper piping bags (page 53)

9 #1 tips

1 #1.5 tip

Assorted paintbrushes

1. **Make the cookies.** Cut out 18 cookies from the dough. Bake and cool as directed.

2. **Make golden brown lining and flooding icing for the bottom bun; make beige flooding icing for the cut side of the bottom bun.** Mix 1½ cups royal icing in a bowl with chocolate brown, egg yellow, sunset orange, and gold gels to make golden brown for the bun. Thin to lining consistency and spoon ¼ cup into a piping bag fitted with a #1 tip. Thin the remaining icing to flooding consistency and cover with plastic wrap. Mix ½ cup royal icing in a bowl with ivory, gold, and whitener gels to make beige for the cut side of the bottom bun. Thin to flooding consistency and cover with plastic wrap.

3. **Outline and paint in the bottom bun,** **including the cut side.** Turn the cookie on its side so that the tip of the mitt's thumb is at 12 o'clock. Using the golden brown lining icing, outline the side of the bottom bun, including the line that defines the cut side. Let set for 5 minutes. Using a paintbrush and the golden brown flooding icing, paint in the side of the bottom bun. Using another paintbrush and the beige flooding icing, thinly paint in the cut side of the bun, as in the photo, butting the icing up (see page 64) to the brown outline and thinning it out into the area where the onion and top bun overlap. Let set until dry to the touch, about 2 hours.

4. **Make lining and flooding icings: white for the onion, dark brown for the patty, and**

red for the tomato. Refresh the royal icing on medium low for 30 minutes. Fill each of three bowls with a generous ½ cup icing each. Cover two with plastic wrap. To the remaining bowl, add ivory and lemon yellow gels to make off-white for the onion. Thin to lining consistency and spoon 2 tablespoons into a piping bag fitted with a #1 tip. Thin the remaining icing to flooding consistency, add a little whitener, and cover with plastic wrap. To the second bowl, add chocolate brown, super black, and buckeye gels to make dark brown for the patty. Thin to lining consistency and spoon 2 tablespoons into a piping bag fitted with a #1 tip. Thin the remaining icing to flooding consistency, add a little whitener, and cover with plastic wrap. To the third bowl, add bright red and sunset orange gels to make tomato red. Thin to lining consistency and spoon 2 tablespoons into a piping bag fitted with a #1 tip. Thin the remaining icing to flooding consistency, add a little whitener, and cover with plastic wrap.

5. **Outline the onion, patty, and tomato.** Using the off-white lining icing, outline the onion, going over the bottom bun and leaving the top of the onion unlined where the patty overlaps it. Reserve the off-white lining icing. Using the dark brown lining icing, outline the patty with a jagged line, stopping where the tomato overlaps the patty on the top and the top of the bun overlaps on the right. Using the red lining icing, outline

the tomato, thinning out where it overlaps with the bun. Let set for 5 minutes.

6. **Paint in the onion, patty, and tomato.** Using a paintbrush and the off-white flooding icing, paint in the onion, butting the icing up to the brown line of the patty. Using another paintbrush and the dark brown flooding icing, paint in the patty, butting the icing up to the red line of the tomato. Using another paintbrush and the red flooding icing, paint in the tomato, thinning it into the area where the bun overlaps it. Let set until hard, 6 to 8 hours or overnight.

7. **Make more golden brown lining and flooding icing for the top bun; outline and paint in.** Refresh the remaining royal icing on medium low for 30 seconds. Mix ¾ cup icing in a small bowl with chocolate brown, egg yellow, sunset orange, and gold gels to make the same golden brown as above. Thin to lining consistency and spoon ¼ cup into a piping bag fitted with a #1 tip. Thin the remaining icing to flooding consistency and cover with plastic wrap. Using the golden brown lining icing, outline the top bun, going on top of the right edges of the tomato, patty, and onion. Let set for 5 minutes. Using a paintbrush and the golden brown flooding icing, thickly paint in the top bun so that it is slightly puffy.

8. **Make lining and flooding icings: green for the pickles and yellow for the cheese. Make lining icings: dark brown to re-outline the patty and dark red for the tomato.** Fill four

CHEESEBURGER CONTINUES

bowls with ¼ cup royal icing each. Cover three with plastic wrap. To the remaining, add leaf green, neon green, and chocolate brown gels to make pickle green. Thin to lining consistency and spoon 2 tablespoons into a piping bag fitted with a #1 tip. Thin the remaining icing to flooding consistency, add a little whitener, and cover with plastic wrap. To the second bowl, add lemon yellow and egg yellow gels to make orange-yellow for the cheese. Thin to lining consistency and spoon 2 tablespoons into a piping bag fitted with a #1 tip. Thin the remaining icing to flooding consistency, add a little whitener, and cover with plastic wrap. To the third bowl, add buckeye brown and super black gels to make dark brown to re-outline the patty. Thin to lining consistency and spoon all of it into a piping bag fitted with a #1 tip. To the fourth bowl, add bright red and red red gels to make dark red. Thin to lining consistency and spoon all of it into a piping bag fitted with a #1 tip.

9. **Outline and paint in the pickle and cheese. Re-outline the onion, patty, and tomato and make details.** Using the green lining icing, outline the pickles on the bun. Reserve the green lining icing. Using the reserved off-white lining icing, re-outline the onion then draw concentric exaggerated ovals within it for the rings. Using the orange-yellow lining icing, outline the slice of cheese including the edges along the tomato. Using the dark brown lining icing, re-outline the

patty, drawing jagged lines to make it look three-dimensional. Using the dark red lining icing, re-outline the tomato, then draw a second dark line just inside it to make the side of the slice. Draw the cross section of the tomato within that. Let set for 5 minutes. Using a paintbrush and the orange-yellow flooding icing, thinly paint in the cheese slice. Using another paintbrush and the green flooding icing, thinly paint in the pickles. Let set until hard, 3 to 4 hours.

10. **Re-outline the pickles; make lining icing for and draw on the sesame seeds.** Using the reserved pickle green lining icing, re-outline the pickles. Refresh the royal icing on medium low for 30 seconds. Mix ¼ cup royal icing in a bowl with ivory and whitener gels to make off-white for the sesame seeds. Thin to slightly looser than lining consistency. Spoon the icing into a piping bag fitted with a #1.5 tip and draw the sesame seeds on the top of the bun by holding the tip close to the cookie, squeezing very gently, and then pulling away quickly. Let set for 5 minutes.

COOKIE JAR

○ beginner ○ intermediate ● advanced

what you need

TO MAKE THE COOKIES
3¾-inch baseball mitt cutter

Cookie dough of choice (pages 26–33), prepared, chilled, and rolled out

Cooling racks

TO DECORATE
3 cups Royal Icing (pages 40–42)

Pasteurized egg white or water

Gel food colors: chocolate brown, gold, whitener, bright red, super black

6 plastic or parchment paper piping bags (see page 53)

6 #1 tips

Assorted paintbrushes

1. **Make the cookies.** Cut out 18 cookies from the dough. Bake and cool as directed.

2. **Make golden brown lining and flooding icing for the cookies; outline and paint in.** Mix ½ cup royal icing in a bowl with chocolate brown and gold gels to make golden brown for the cookies. Thin to lining consistency and spoon ¼ cup into a piping bag fitted with a #1 tip. Thin the remaining icing to flooding consistency, add a little whitener, and cover with plastic wrap. Using the lining icing, outline the silhouette of the cookies, using the fingers of the glove as a guide to make four cookies. Do not outline the cookies where the jar overlaps. Let set for 5 minutes. Using a paintbrush and the golden brown flooding icing, thinly paint in the cookies, thinning the icing where the jar overlaps. Let set until hard, 3 to 4 hours.

3. **Make red lining and flooding icing for the jar and stripes; outline and paint in.** Refresh the royal icing on medium low for 30 seconds. Mix ½ cup icing in a bowl with bright red gel to make bright red. Thin to lining consistency and spoon ¼ cup into a piping bag fitted with a #1 tip. Thin the remaining icing to flooding consistency, add a little whitener, and cover with plastic wrap. Using the red lining icing, outline the cookie jar, leaving the right side of the jar unlined where the lid overlaps it. Outline the stripes on the jar with four lines equidistant from one another and stopping where the lid overlaps the jar. Let set for 5 minutes. Using a paintbrush and the red flooding icing, paint in the red stripes on the jar, thinning them out where the lid overlaps the jar. Let set until hard, 4 to 6 hours.

COOKIE JAR CONTINUES

4. **Make dark brown lining icing to re-outline the cookies and make the chocolate chips.** Refresh the royal icing on medium low for 30 seconds. Mix ¼ cup icing in a bowl with chocolate brown gel to make dark brown for the chocolate chips and to re-outline the cookies. Thin to lining consistency and spoon all of it into a piping bag fitted with a #1 tip. Re-outline the cookies. Draw the chocolate chips by touching the cookie with the piping tip, squeezing the bag, and moving the tip slightly to make an irregular chip shape.

5. **Make white lining and flooding icing for the stripes and lid; paint in stripes only.** Mix 1¼ cups royal icing in a bowl with whitener gel to make bright white. Thin to lining consistency and spoon ¼ cup into a piping bag fitted with a #1 tip; set aside. Thin the remaining icing to flooding consistency and, using a paintbrush, use it to paint in the white stripes on the jar, thinning out the icing where the lid overlaps. Reserve the white flooding icing. Let set until hard, about 2 hours.

6. **Make red lining icing to re-outline the red stripes and jar. Outline and paint in the lid with white icing, re-outline the jar.** Refresh the royal icing on medium low for 30 seconds. Spoon ¼ cup into a bowl and mix with bright red gel to make bright red to re-outline the stripes. Thin to lining consistency and spoon all of it into a piping bag fitted with a #1 tip. Using the reserved white lining icing, outline the lid, going over the stripes of the jar. Using the red lining icing, re-outline the cookie jar. Let set for 5 minutes. Using a paintbrush, paint in the lid with the white flooding icing. Let set until hard, 6 to 8 hours or overnight. Reserve the white flooding icing.

7. **Make gray lining icing and re-outline the lid and make details. Outline and paint in the handle.** Refresh the royal icing on medium low for 30 seconds. Mix ¼ cup icing with super black and whitener gels to make medium gray to re-outline the lid. Thin to lining consistency and spoon all of it into a piping bag fitted with a #1 tip. Re-outline the lid, then draw a second line just inside it to make the side of the lid. Outline an oval for a handle. Let set for 5 minutes. Stir the reserved white flooding icing well to refresh it. Using it and a paintbrush, paint in the handle. Use the gray lining icing to make a slightly thicker line on the underside of the handle. Let set for 2 to 4 hours.

FOOTBALL HELMET CUTTER

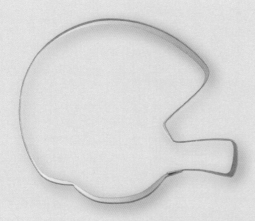

It was fun to figure out how to use the mouth-guard part of this cutter in other cookie designs. The leaves of the pineapple, the trunk of the elephant, the bird's tail . . . there are endless possibilities. My elephant is tusk-less, but you can easily add a tusk to yours with some white icing. And of course the bird can be iced in any color.

When you're putting the cutouts on the baking sheet, be sure to gently nudge the dough out of the mouth-guard part of the cutter: Thin appendages like this tend to stay behind in the cutter and break off.

FOOTBALL HELMET

○ beginner ● intermediate ○ advanced

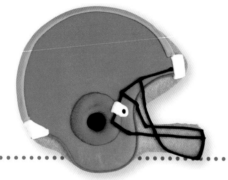

what you need

TO MAKE THE COOKIES
3½-inch football helmet cookie cutter

Cookie dough of choice (pages 26–33), prepared, chilled, and rolled out

Cooling racks

TO DECORATE
3 cups Royal Icing (pages 40–42)

Pasteurized egg white or water

Gel food colors: super black, neon orange, sunset orange, whitener, bright blue

4 plastic or parchment paper piping bags (page 53)

4 #1 tips

Assorted paintbrushes

1. **Make the dough.** Cut out 20 cookies from the dough. Bake and cool as directed.

2. **Make flooding icing for the ear hole and paint on.** Mix 1 tablespoon royal icing in a bowl with super black gel to make black for the ear hole on the helmet. Thin to slightly looser than flooding consistency. Using a paintbrush, thinly paint the black ear hole on the cookie, making it slightly larger than the actual ear hole will be, and let set for 30 minutes.

3. **Make orange lining and flooding icing for the helmet; outline and paint in.** Mix 1¼ cups royal icing in a bowl with neon orange and sunset orange gels to make orange for the helmet. Thin to lining consistency and spoon ¼ cup into a piping bag fitted with a #1 tip. Thin the remaining icing to flooding consistency, add a little whitener, and

cover with plastic wrap. Using the lining icing, outline the helmet, taking care to make the curves in the front and lower back. Outline the ear hole. Let set for 10 minutes. Reserve the orange lining icing. Using a paintbrush and the orange flooding icing, paint in the helmet. Let set until hard, 6 to 8 hours or overnight. Reserve the orange flooding icing.

4. **Make blue lining and flooding icing for the stripe; outline and paint in.** Refresh the royal icing on medium low for 30 seconds. Mix ½ cup icing in a bowl with bright blue gel to make bright blue for the stripe. Thin to lining consistency and spoon ¼ cup into a piping bag fitted with a #1 tip. Thin the remaining icing to flooding consistency, add a little whitener, and cover with plastic wrap. Using the lining icing, outline the blue stripe that runs along the body of the

helmet. Let set for 10 minutes. Using a paintbrush and the blue flooding icing, paint in the stripe. Let set for 2 hours.

5. **Re-outline the ear hole and outline the ring around it; paint in.** Using the reserved orange lining icing, re-outline the black hole and make another circle around that one about ¼ inch wide. Let set for 5 minutes. Using another paintbrush and the reserved orange flooding icing, paint in the ring around the black ear hole. Let set for 4 to 6 hours or overnight.

6. **Make black lining icing for the face guard; make white lining and flooding icing for the details.** Refresh the royal icing on medium low for 30 seconds. Mix ¼ cup icing with super black gel to make black for the face guard. Thin to lining consistency and spoon all of it into a piping bag fitted with a #1 tip. Mix ½ cup icing in a bowl with whitener gel to make bright white. Thin to lining consistency and spoon ¼ cup into a piping bag fitted with a #1 tip. Thin the remaining icing to flooding consistency and cover with plastic wrap.

7. **Draw in the face guard. Make white helmet details and paint in.** Using the black lining icing, outline the face guard, moving slowly to achieve a thicker than normal line and going over the painted orange ring. Let set for 10 minutes. Reserve the black lining icing. Using the white lining icing, outline the helmet details, going over the black lines where necessary. Let set for 10 minutes. Using a paintbrush and the white flooding icing, paint in the details. Let set for 4 to 6 hours.

8. **Make the screw detail.** Using the reserved black lining icing, pipe a dot on the middle white detail for a screw.

· MAKES 20 ·

ELEPHANT

● beginner   ○ intermediate   ○ advanced

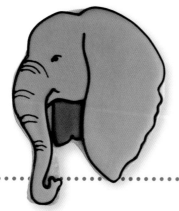

what you need

TO MAKE THE COOKIES
3½-inch football helmet cookie cutter

Cookie dough of choice (pages 26–33), prepared, chilled, and rolled out

Cooling racks

TO DECORATE
2 cups Royal Icing (pages 40–42)

Pasteurized egg white or water

Gel food colors: super black, chocolate brown, whitener

2 plastic or parchment paper piping bags (page 53)

2 #1 tips

Assorted paintbrushes

ELEPHANT CONTINUES

1. **Make the cookies.** Cut out 20 cookies from the dough. Bake and cool as directed.

2. **Make dark gray lining and flooding icing for underside of back ear.** Spoon ½ cup royal icing into a bowl and mix with super black and chocolate brown gels to make dark gray for the underside of the back ear. Thin to lining consistency and spoon ¼ cup into a piping bag fitted with a #1 tip. Thin the remaining icing to flooding consistency, add a little whitener, and cover with plastic wrap.

3. **Outline the back ear and paint in.** Position the cookie so the helmet's mouth guard is pointing down. Using the lining icing, outline the left and bottom sides of the back ear. Let set for 5 minutes. Reserve the dark gray lining icing. Using a paintbrush and the flooding icing, paint in the back ear, thinning it out where the chin and front ear overlap it. Let set until hard, 3 to 4 hours.

4. **Make light gray lining and flooding icing for the elephant; outline and paint in.** Refresh the royal icing on medium low for 30 seconds. Spoon 1¼ cups into a bowl and mix with super black, chocolate brown, and whitener gels to make light gray for the elephant's head. Thin to flooding consistency and cover with plastic wrap. Using the reserved dark gray lining icing, outline the silhouette of the elephant. Let set for 5 minutes. Using a large paintbrush and the light gray flooding icing, paint in the elephant. Let set until hard, 6 to 8 hours or overnight.

5. **Make dark gray lining icing to re-outline the elephant and make details.** Refresh the royal icing on medium low for 30 seconds. Mix ¼ cup icing with super black gel to make dark gray to re-outline the elephant and make the details. Thin to lining consistency and spoon it all into a piping bag fitted with a #1 tip. Re-outline the elephant's silhouette and make the head and ear details. Draw lines on the trunk. Make a dot for the eye by holding the piping tip on the cookie at a 45-degree angle and squeezing. Draw the eyebrow over the eye. Let set for 5 minutes.

BIRD IN NEST

○ beginner ● intermediate ○ advanced

what you need

TO MAKE THE COOKIES
3½-inch football helmet cookie cutter

Cookie dough of choice (pages 26–33), prepared, chilled, and rolled out

Cooling racks

TO DECORATE
3 cups Royal Icing (pages 40–42)

Pasteurized egg white or water

Gel food colors: super black, chocolate brown, whitener, bright red, bright blue, lemon yellow

6 plastic or parchment paper piping bags (page 53)

6 #1 tips

Assorted paintbrushes

Plate or ceramic mixing palette

1. **Make the cookies.** Cut out 20 cookies from the dough. Bake and cool as directed.

2. **Make black flooding icing for the interior of the nest and paint in.** Mix 2 tablespoons royal icing in a bowl with super black gel to make black for the interior of the nest. Thin to slightly looser than flooding consistency. Position the cookie so the helmet's mouth guard is at 10 o'clock. Using a paintbrush, thinly paint an oval for the inside of the nest, thinning it out where the rim and front of the nest overlap it. Let set for 30 minutes.

3. **Make brown lining and flooding icing for the nest; outline and paint in.** Mix ¾ cup royal icing with chocolate brown gel to make brown for the nest. Thin to lining consistency and spoon ¼ cup into a piping bag fitted with a #1 tip.

Thin the remaining icing to flooding consistency, add a little whitener, and cover with plastic wrap. Using the lining icing, outline the silhouette of the nest, skipping the part where the bird overlaps. Outline the black oval, again skipping where the bird overlaps. Let set for 10 minutes. Using a paintbrush and the brown flooding icing, paint in the nest, thinning the icing where the bird overlaps. Let set until hard, 6 to 8 hours or overnight.

4. **Make lining and flooding icings: red for the bird and blue for the eggs.** Refresh the royal icing on medium low for 30 seconds. Spoon ¾ cup icing into each of two bowls. Cover one with plastic wrap. To the remaining, add bright red gel to make red for the bird. Thin to lining

BIRD IN NEST CONTINUES

consistency and spoon ¼ cup into a piping bag fitted with a #1 tip. Thin the remaining icing to flooding consistency, add a little whitener, and cover with plastic wrap. To the other bowl, mix in a toothpick of bright blue and even less chocolate brown gel to make pale blue for the eggs. Thin to lining consistency and spoon ¼ cup into a piping bag fitted with a #1 tip. Thin the remaining icing to flooding consistency, add a little whitener, and cover with plastic wrap.

5. **Outline and paint in the bird and eggs.** Using the red lining icing, outline the silhouette of the bird, following the edge of the cookie along the top and tail and going over the top right corner of the nest. Let set for 5 minutes. Reserve the red lining icing. Using the blue lining icing, outline the silhouette of the eggs. Let set for 5 minutes. Using a paintbrush and the red flooding icing, paint in the bird. Using a small paintbrush and the pale blue flooding icing, paint in the eggs. Let set until hard, 6 to 8 hours or overnight.

6. **Make lining icings: dark brown to re-outline and make details on the nest and yellow for the beak and feet.** Refresh the royal icing on medium low for 30 seconds. Spoon ¼ cup into each of two bowls. Cover one with plastic wrap. To the other, add chocolate brown and super black gels to make dark brown to re-outline and make details on the nest. Thin to lining consistency and

spoon all of it into a piping bag fitted with a #1 tip. To the second bowl, add lemon yellow gel to make chrome yellow for the beak and feet. Thin to lining consistency and spoon it all into a piping bag fitted with a #1 tip.

7. **Outline and draw in the beak and legs. Re-outline the bird and make details. Re-outline the nest and make details.** Using the yellow lining icing, outline the bird's beak and fill it in with the tip. Make the legs. Let set for 5 minutes. Using the reserved red lining icing, re-outline the bird and make the wing and tail details. Using the dark brown lining icing, re-outline the nest and make the woven pattern on it. Squeeze a tiny dot on the bird's head for its eye. Let set until hard, about 1 hour.

8. **Make watercolor to speckle the eggs.** Meanwhile, squeeze a dot of chocolate brown gel onto a plate or ceramic mixing palette. Using a paintbrush, mix in a little water to make a watercolor (see page 66). Paint speckles on the eggs.

9. **Make the pupil for the eye.** Spoon 2 tablespoons of royal icing into a bowl. Add a drop of whitener and thin to lining consistency. Spoon into a piping bag fitted with a #1 tip, and pipe a dot on the eye.

BOWL OF FRUIT

○ beginner   ○ intermediate   ● advanced

what you need

TO MAKE THE COOKIES
3½-inch football helmet cutter

Cookie dough of choice (pages 26–33), prepared, chilled, and rolled out

Cooling racks

TO DECORATE
5 cups Royal Icing (pages 40–42)

Pasteurized egg white or water

Gel food colors: bright blue, whitener, sunset orange, lemon yellow, egg yellow, bright red, leaf green, teal green, gold, chocolate brown

10 plastic or parchment paper piping bags (page 53)

10 #1 tips

Assorted paintbrushes

1. **Make the cookies.** Cut out 20 cookies from the dough. Bake and cool as directed.

2. **Make medium blue lining and flooding icing for the inside of bowl; outline and paint in.** Mix ½ cup royal icing in a bowl with bright blue gel to make medium blue. Thin to lining consistency and spoon 2 tablespoons into a piping bag fitted with a #1 tip. Thin the remaining icing to flooding consistency, add a little whitener, and cover with plastic wrap. Position the cookie so the helmet's mouth guard is at 10 o'clock. Using the lining icing, outline the interior of the bowl on the top left and far right edges, skipping the space where the pineapple overlaps. Let set for 5 minutes. Reserve the medium blue lining icing. Using a paintbrush and the flooding icing, thinly paint in the left and right corners of the inside of the bowl, thinning it out where the fruit overlaps. Let set until dry, 2 to 3 hours.

3. **Make light blue flooding icing for outside of bowl; outline and paint in.** Refresh the remaining royal icing on medium-low speed for 30 seconds. Mix ½ cup icing in a bowl with bright blue and whitener gels to make lighter blue for the exterior of the bowl. Thin to flooding consistency and cover with plastic wrap. Using the reserved medium blue lining icing, outline the bowl and let set for 5 minutes. Using a paintbrush and the light blue flooding icing, paint in the bowl. Let set until dry, 3 to 4 hours.

BOWL OF FRUIT CONTINUES

4. **Make lining and flooding icings for the fruit: orange, yellow, gold, red, green.** Meanwhile, spoon ½ cup royal icing into each of five bowls. Cover four with plastic wrap. To the remaining, add sunset orange gel to make the orange for the orange. Thin to lining consistency and spoon ¼ cup into a piping bag fitted with a #1 tip. Thin the remaining to flooding consistency and cover with plastic wrap. To the second bowl, add lemon yellow gel to make yellow for the bananas. Thin to lining consistency and spoon ¼ cup into a piping bag fitted with a #1 tip. Thin the remaining icing to flooding consistency and cover with plastic wrap. To the third bowl, add lemon yellow and egg yellow gels to make gold for the pineapple. Thin to lining consistency and spoon ¼ cup into a piping bag fitted with a #1 tip. Thin the remaining icing to flooding consistency and cover with plastic wrap. To the fourth bowl, add bright red to make red for the apple. Thin to lining consistency and spoon ¼ cup into a piping bag fitted with a #1 tip. Thin the remaining icing to flooding consistency and cover with plastic wrap. To the fifth bowl, add leaf green and teal green to make the green for the leaves of the pineapple. Thin to lining consistency and spoon ¼ cup into a piping bag fitted with a #1 tip. Thin the remaining to flooding consistency and cover with plastic wrap.

5. **Outline the fruits.** Using the yellow lining icing, outline the silhouette of the bananas. Using the orange lining icing, outline the curve of the orange. Using the red lining icing, outline the curve of the apple. Using the gold lining icing, outline the silhouette of the pineapple. Using the green lining icing, outline the silhouette of the pineapple leaves. Let set for 5 minutes. Reserve the red, orange, and yellow lining icings.

6. **Paint in the fruits.** Using a paintbrush, paint in each piece of fruit and the pineapple leaves with the respective flooding icing, butting up (see page 64) each color to the outlines on the adjacent piece(s) of fruit and the edge of the bowl. Let set until hard, 6 to 8 hours or overnight.

7. **Make lining icing to re-outline the fruits and bowl and to make details.** Refresh the royal icing on medium low for 30 seconds. Spoon ¼ cup icing into each of four bowls. Cover three with plastic wrap. To the remaining bowl, add gold gel to make golden brown for re-outlining and making the details on the pineapple. Thin to lining consistency and spoon all of it into a piping bag fitted with a #1 tip. To the second bowl, add chocolate brown gel to make dark brown for the banana stem, apple stem, and dots on the orange. Thin to lining consistency and spoon all of it into a piping bag

fitted with a #1 tip. To the third bowl, add leaf green and teal green gels to make dark green for re-outlining the leaves of the pineapple. Thin to lining consistency and spoon all of it into a piping bag fitted with a #1 tip. To the fourth bowl, add bright blue gel to make medium blue to re-outline the bowl. Thin to lining consistency and spoon it all into a piping bag fitted with a #1 tip.

8. **Re-outline the fruits and bowl and make details.** Use the reserved red, orange, and yellow lining icings or spoon 2 tablespoons of refreshed royal icing into each of three bowls and color as in step 4. Spoon into each of three piping bags fitted with #1 tips and re-outline the apple, orange, and bananas. Make the interior lines on the bananas to define the two. Using the golden brown lining icing, re-outline the pineapple and draw in the details. Using the dark brown lining icing, draw in the banana stems, apple stem, and dots on the orange. Using the dark green lining icing, re-outline the pineapple leaves and draw in the details. Using the medium blue lining icing, re-outline the bowl. Let set for 10 minutes.

TEXAS CUTTER

To be honest, sometimes I have to remind myself which cutter I used to make a particular cookie after it is decorated. That's certainly true of the Chinese Takeout box. By squaring off some of the rounded edges, I found shapes that mimicked the flaps and front of a traditional container. This cutter is also a good example of how it isn't necessary to use every square inch of a cookie to make the design you want: The Turtle and her baby was such an irresistible idea that I insisted on figuring out a way to make it work—in Texas! It's a great cookie to make for a baby shower or Mother's or Father's Day.

TEXAS

● beginner ○ intermediate ○ advanced

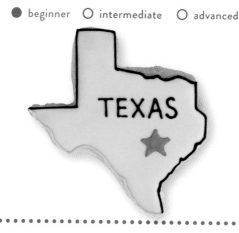

what you need

TO MAKE THE COOKIES
3-inch Texas cookie cutter

Cookie dough of choice (pages 26–33), prepared, chilled, and rolled out

Cooling racks

TO DECORATE
2 cups Royal Icing (pages 40–42)

Pasteurized egg white or water

Gel food colors: lemon yellow, egg yellow, whitener, super black, bright blue, bright red

4 plastic or parchment paper piping bags (page 53)

4 #1 tips

Assorted paintbrushes

1. **Make the cookies.** Cut out 24 cookies from the dough. Bake and cool as directed.

2. **Make yellow lining and flooding icing for Texas.** Mix 1¼ cups royal icing in a small bowl with lemon yellow, egg yellow, and whitener gels to make yellow for Texas. Thin to lining consistency and spoon ¼ cup into a piping bag fitted with a #1 tip. Thin the remaining icing to flooding consistency and cover with plastic wrap.

3. **Outline and paint in Texas.** Using the yellow lining icing, outline Texas, making the lines on the top left corner straight and squared off. Draw squiggly lines for the rest of the outline, following the edge of the cookie. Let set for 5 minutes. Using a paintbrush and yellow flooding icing, paint in Texas. Let set until hard, 6 to 8 hours or overnight.

4. **Make lining icings: black to re-outline Texas and blue to outline the Rio Grande; make red lining and flooding icing for the star.** Refresh the royal icing on medium low for 30 seconds. Fill three bowls with ¼ cup icing each. Cover two with plastic wrap. To the remaining bowl, add super black gel to make black. Thin to lining consistency and spoon all of it into a piping bag fitted with a #1 tip. To the second bowl, add bright blue and whitener gels to make light blue for the Rio Grande. Thin to lining consistency and spoon all of it into a piping bag fitted with a #1 tip. To the third bowl, add bright red gel to make red for the star. Thin to lining consistency and spoon 2 tablespoons into a piping bag fitted with a #1 tip. Thin the remaining

TEXAS CONTINUES

red icing to flooding consistency and cover with plastic wrap.

5. **Outline the Rio Grande, re-outline the entire state, and write the word TEXAS; outline and paint in the star.** Using the light blue lining icing, re-outline the bottom left edge of Texas for the Rio Grande. Using the black lining icing, re-outline the rest of Texas and write the word TEXAS across the cookie. Using the red lining icing, outline a star at the bottom right corner of Texas for the capital. Let set for 5 minutes. Using a paintbrush and the red flooding icing, fill in the star. Let set for 1 hour.

BIRDHOUSE

○ beginner ● intermediate ○ advanced

what you need

TO MAKE THE COOKIES
3-inch Texas cookie cutter

Cookie dough of choice (pages 26–33), prepared, chilled, and rolled out

Cooling racks

TO DECORATE
2½ cups Royal Icing (pages 40–42)

Pasteurized egg white or water

Gel food colors: bright red, buckeye brown, chocolate brown, bright blue, whitener, lemon yellow, super black, electric pink

Black fine-tipped edible marker (optional)

7 plastic or parchment paper piping bags (page 53)

6 #1 tips

1 #1.5 tip

Assorted paintbrushes

1. **Make the cookies.** Cut out 24 cookies from the dough. Bake and cool as directed.

2. **Make lining and flooding icings: red for the birdhouse and brown for the post.** Mix ¾ cup royal icing in a small bowl with bright red gel to make red for the birdhouse. Thin to lining consistency and spoon ¼ cup into a piping bag fitted with a #1 tip. Thin the remaining to flooding consistency and cover with plastic wrap. Mix ¼ cup icing in a small bowl with buckeye brown and chocolate brown gels to make brown for the wood post. Thin to lining consistency and spoon 2 tablespoons into a piping bag fitted with a #1 tip. Thin the remaining brown icing to flooding consistency and cover with plastic wrap.

3. **Outline and paint in the birdhouse and post.** Position the cookie so the bottom point of Texas is at the top. Using the red lining icing, outline the birdhouse, leaving the top right area unlined where the bird overlaps the birdhouse. Using the brown lining icing, outline the wood post at the bottom right corner of the cookie, butting (see page 64) the brown line to the bottom edge of the birdhouse. Let set for 5 minutes. Using a paintbrush and the red flooding icing, paint in the birdhouse, thinning the icing out in the area where the bird overlaps. Using a paintbrush and the brown flooding icing, paint in the post. Let set for 6 to 8 hours or overnight.

BIRDHOUSE CONTINUES

4. **Make lining and flooding icings: light blue for the bird and yellow for the beak.** Refresh the royal icing on medium low for 30 seconds. Mix ½ cup icing in a small bowl with bright blue and whitener gels to make light blue for the bird. Thin to lining consistency and spoon ¼ cup into a piping bag fitted with a #1 tip. Thin the remaining icing to flooding consistency and cover with plastic wrap. Mix ¼ cup icing in a small bowl with lemon yellow gel to make yellow for the beak. Thin to lining consistency and spoon 2 tablespoons into a piping bag fitted with a #1 tip. Thin the remaining icing to flooding consistency and cover with plastic wrap.

5. **Outline and paint in the bird and the beak; make details.** Using the light blue lining icing, outline the bird on top of the birdhouse. Pipe the wing so that the top edge of the wing follows the top right edge of the cookie, and draw bumps for feathers. Leave room at the right side of the cookie for the beak and worm. Using the yellow lining icing, outline the beak, butting (see page 64) the yellow line up to the head. Make the legs and feet. Let set for 5 minutes. Using a paintbrush and the light blue flooding icing, paint in the bird. Using a paintbrush and the yellow flooding icing, paint in the beak. Let set for 4 to 6 hours.

6. **Make lining icing to re-outline the bird, birdhouse, and post; make details.** Mix ¼ cup royal icing in a small bowl with super black gel to make black for the outline of the bird and birdhouse. Thin to lining consistency and spoon all of it into a piping bag fitted with a #1 tip. Using the black lining icing, re-outline the bird, including the beak, exaggerating the scallops on the wing and tail to make the feathers. Make a black dot for the eye. Re-outline the birdhouse and wood post. Pipe a line just within the top left outline of the birdhouse to make the roof.

7. **Make lining icings: pink for the worm and dark brown for the wood grain.** Fill two bowls with ¼ cup royal icing each. Cover one with plastic wrap. To the other bowl, add electric pink, buckeye brown, and whitener gels to make pink for the worm. Thin to lining consistency and spoon all of it into a piping bag fitted with a #1.5 tip. To the second bowl, add buckeye brown and chocolate brown gels to make dark brown for the wood grain. Thin to lining consistency and spoon all of it into a piping bag fitted with a #1 tip.

8. **Make the worm, wood grain, and hole in the birdhouse.** Using the pink lining icing, squeeze firmly to pipe a fat worm around the beak. Using the dark brown lining icing, pipe short vertical lines across the wood post for wood grain. Using the black lining icing, outline the part of the hole visible behind the bird, and fill in the hole with the piping tip. Or, if you have a black fine-tipped edible marker, draw the hole behind the bird, and color it in with the marker. Let set for 15 minutes.

CHINESE TAKEOUT

○ beginner   ○ intermediate   ● advanced

what you need

TO MAKE THE COOKIES
3-inch Texas cookie cutter

Cookie dough of choice (pages 26–33), prepared, chilled, and rolled out

Cooling racks

TO DECORATE
2 cups Royal Icing (pages 40–42)

Pasteurized egg white or water

Gel food colors: gold, lemon yellow, whitener, ivory, bright red

6 plastic or parchment paper piping bags (page 53)

5 #1 tips

1 #1.5 tip

Assorted paintbrushes

1. **Make the cookies.** Cut out 24 cookies from the dough. Bake and cool as directed.

2. **Make golden brown flooding icing for the background of the noodles and paint in.** Mix ¼ cup royal icing in a small bowl with gold, lemon yellow, and whitener gels to make golden brown for the noodle background. Thin to flooding consistency and cover with plastic wrap. Using a paintbrush, thinly paint in the area where the noodles are, thinning the icing out on left, right, and bottom where the box overlaps. Do not thin out the icing on the top where the chopsticks will go. This should remain bare. Let set for 4 to 6 hours.

3. **Make lining and flooding icings: white for the box and light tan for the chopsticks.** Mix

½ cup royal icing in a small bowl with whitener gel to make bright white for the box. Thin to lining consistency and spoon ¼ cup into a piping bag fitted with a #1 tip. Thin the remaining to flooding consistency and cover with plastic wrap. Mix ¼ cup icing in a small bowl with ivory and whitener gels to make light tan for the chopsticks. Thin to lining consistency and spoon 2 tablespoons into a piping bag fitted with a #1 tip. Thin the remaining to flooding consistency and cover with plastic wrap.

4. **Outline and paint in the box and chopsticks.** Position the cookie so the bottom point of Texas is at 9 o'clock. Using the white lining icing, outline the takeout box, going over the golden brown icing and making the lines straight. Using the light

CHINESE TAKEOUT CONTINUES

tan lining icing, outline the chopsticks so that they cross each other, making an X shape. Leave the bottoms of the chopsticks unlined where they stick into the noodles. Let set for 5 minutes. Using a paintbrush and the white flooding icing, paint in the takeout box. Using a paintbrush and the light tan flooding icing, paint in the chopsticks. Do not thin the icing out into the noodles. Let set for 6 to 8 hours or overnight.

5. **Make lining icings: light gold for the noodles, white to re-outline the box, and tan to re-outline the chopsticks.** Refresh the royal icing on medium low for 30 seconds. Fill three bowls with ¼ cup icing each. Cover two with plastic wrap. To the remaining bowl, add gold, lemon yellow, and whitener gels to make light golden brown for the noodles. Thin to lining consistency and spoon all of it into a piping bag fitted with a #1.5 tip. To the second bowl, add whitener gel to make bright white for the re-outline of the box. Thin to lining consistency and spoon all of it into a piping bag fitted with a #1 tip. To the third bowl, add ivory and whitener gels to make tan for the outline of the chopsticks. Thin to lining consistency and spoon all of it into a piping bag fitted with a #1 tip.

6. **Make the noodles; re-outline the box and chopsticks.** Using the light golden brown lining icing, pipe squiggly lines all over the darker golden brown icing for the noodles, making sure to cover the bottoms of the chopsticks so that they look like they are stuck into the noodles. Don't be afraid to build up the squiggles and cover up the golden brown background. Using the white lining icing, re-outline the takeout box. Using the tan lining icing, re-outline the chopsticks so that one crosses in front of the other.

7. **Make lining icing for the pagoda and draw it in.** Mix ¼ cup royal icing in a small bowl with bright red gel to make red for the pagoda. Thin to lining consistency and spoon all of it into a piping bag fitted with a #1 tip. Using the red lining icing, draw the pagoda on the takeout box by dragging the tip on the icing to make thin lines.

TURTLE

○ beginner ● intermediate ○ advanced

what you need

TO MAKE THE COOKIES
3-inch Texas cookie cutter

Cookie dough of choice (pages 26–33), prepared, chilled, and rolled out

Cooling racks

TO DECORATE
3 cups Royal Icing (pages 40–42)

Pasteurized egg white or water

Gel food colors: leaf green, neon green, chocolate brown, lemon yellow, whitener, super black

4 plastic or parchment paper piping bags (page 53)

4 #1 tips

Assorted paintbrushes

1. **Make the cookies.** Cut out 24 cookies from the dough. Bake and cool as directed.

2. **Make green lining and flooding icing for the turtle's head; make chartreuse flooding icing for the belly.** Fill two bowls with ½ cup royal icing each. Cover one with plastic wrap. To the other bowl, add leaf green, neon green, and chocolate brown gels to make green for the head. Thin to lining consistency and spoon ¼ cup into a piping bag fitted with a #1 tip. Thin the remaining icing to flooding consistency and cover with plastic wrap. To the second bowl, add neon green and lemon yellow gels to make chartreuse for the turtle's belly. Thin the icing to flooding consistency and cover with plastic wrap.

3. **Outline the head, neck, and belly and paint in.** Position the cookie so the bottom point of Texas is at 4 o'clock. Using the green lining icing, outline the head and neck, leaving the area unlined where the shell overlaps the neck. Outline the turtle's belly, starting at the bottom of the neck and stopping on the bottom right edge where the shell meets the belly. Leave the top of the belly unlined where the shell overlaps. Let set for 5 minutes. Using a paintbrush and the green flooding icing, paint in the head and neck, thinning the icing out

TURTLE CONTINUES

to the right where the shell overlaps. Using the chartreuse flooding icing, paint in the belly, butting (see page 64) the icing up to the piped green line of the bottom of the neck and thinning it out where the shell overlaps. Let set for 4 to 6 hours.

4. **Make dark green lining and flooding icing for the shell.** Mix 1 cup royal icing in a small bowl with leaf green and chocolate brown gels to make dark green for the turtle shell. Thin to lining consistency and spoon ¼ cup into a piping bag fitted with a #1 tip. Thin the remaining icing to flooding consistency and cover with plastic wrap.

5. **Outline and paint in the shell.** Using the dark green lining icing, outline the shell, going over the neck and belly. Leave enough space above the shell for the baby turtle and leave a gap unlined where the baby overlaps the shell. Let set for 5 minutes. Using a paintbrush and the dark green flooding icing, paint in the shell, thinning out the icing slightly where the baby turtle overlaps the shell. Let set for 6 to 8 hours or overnight.

6. **Make green lining and flooding icing for the legs; make light green flooding icing for the baby turtle.** Refresh the royal icing on medium low for 30 seconds. Mix ½ cup icing in a small bowl with leaf green, neon green, and chocolate brown gels to make the same green as the turtle's head for the legs.

Thin to lining consistency and spoon ¼ cup into a piping bag fitted with a #1 tip. Thin the remaining icing to flooding consistency and cover with plastic wrap. Mix ¼ cup icing in a small bowl with leaf green, chocolate brown, and whitener gels to make light green for the baby turtle. Thin to flooding consistency and cover with plastic wrap.

7. **Outline the legs, feet, and baby turtle and paint in.** Using the green lining icing, outline the legs and feet, going over the chartreuse belly and butting (see page 64) the line up to the bottom edge of the shell. Outline the baby turtle on top of the shell. Let set for 5 minutes. Using a paintbrush and the green flooding icing, paint in the legs and feet. Using the light green flooding icing, paint in the baby turtle. Let set for 2 to 3 hours.

8. **Make black lining icing to re-outline the turtles; re-outline the turtles and make the eyes, mouth, and shell pattern.** Mix ¼ cup royal icing in a small bowl with super black gel to make black for the outline of the turtles. Thin to lining consistency and spoon all of it into a piping bag fitted with a #1 tip. Using the black lining icing, re-outline both turtles. Pipe black dots for the eyes and a curved line for the mouth on the bigger turtle. Make the pattern on the turtles' backs. Let dry for 1 hour.

CIRCLE CUTTER

If for some reason your cookies don't turn out perfectly round, you can use a similar size circle cutter and trace a perfect circle onto the cookie using an edible marker. At first I found the circle shape a little uninspiring because it was so easy to come up with ideas for it. But actually the pizza and vintage copper penny are two of my favorites! Challenge yourself to see how many ideas you can come up with.

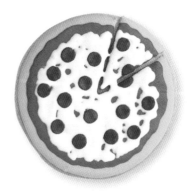

COPPER PENNY

○ beginner   ● intermediate   ○ advanced

what you need

TO MAKE THE COOKIES
3-inch circle cookie cutter

Cookie dough of choice (pages 26–33), prepared, chilled, and rolled out

Cooling racks

TO DECORATE
1¾ cups Royal Icing (pages 40–42)

Pasteurized egg white or water

Gel food colors: chocolate brown, bright red, sunset orange, whitener, super black

2 plastic or parchment paper piping bags (page 53)

1 #1 tip

1 #1.5 tip

Large paintbrush

1. **Make the cookies.** Cut out 22 cookies from the dough. Bake and cool as directed.

2. **Make the lining and flooding icing for the penny; outline and paint in.** Mix 1¼ cups royal icing in a small bowl with sunset orange, bright red, chocolate brown, and whitener gels to make copper brown for the penny. Thin to lining consistency and spoon ¼ cup into a piping bag fitted with a #1 tip. Thin the remaining icing to flooding consistency and cover with plastic wrap. Using the lining icing, outline the penny. Let set for 5 minutes. Using a large paintbrush and the flooding icing, paint in the penny. Let set until hard, 6 to 8 hours or overnight.

3. **Make lining icing and re-outline the penny, make the wheat, and write the words.** Refresh the royal icing on medium low for 30 seconds. Mix ½ cup icing in a small bowl with chocolate brown and super black gels to make dark brown for the outline, words, and wheat. Thin to lining consistency and spoon ¼ cup into a piping bag fitted with a #1.5 tip. Cover the bowl with plastic wrap and reserve in case you want to practice "writing" letters before you make them on the cookie. Using the lining icing, re-outline the penny. Write "CENT" in the middle of the cookie, then write "ONE" above it and a smaller "USA" below it, making sure to leave room on either side for the wheat stalks. Make two stalks of wheat curved around the words, drawing the long stalks first, then adding the kernels from the top down. Let set for 1 hour.

GLOBE

● beginner   ○ intermediate   ○ advanced

what you need

TO MAKE THE COOKIES

3-inch circle cookie cutter

Cookie dough of choice (pages 26–33), prepared, chilled, and rolled out

Cooling racks

TO DECORATE

1¾ cups Royal Icing (pages 40–42)

Pasteurized egg white or water

Gel food colors: bright blue, neon green, whitener, leaf green

2 plastic or parchment paper piping bags (page 53)

2 #1 tips

Assorted paintbrushes

1. **Make the cookies.** Cut out 22 cookies from the dough. Bake and cool as directed.

2. **Make the lining and flooding icing for the oceans; outline and paint in.** Mix 1¼ cups royal icing in a bowl with the bright blue and neon green gels to make blue for the ocean. Thin to lining consistency and spoon ¼ cup into a piping bag fitted with a #1 tip. Thin the remaining icing to flooding consistency, add whitener, and cover with plastic wrap. Using the lining icing, outline the globe along the edge of the cookie. Let set for 5 minutes. Using a large paintbrush and the flooding icing, paint in the globe. Let set until hard, 6 to 8 hours or overnight.

3. **Make the green lining and flooding icing for the continents; outline and paint in.** Refresh the royal icing on medium low for 30 seconds. Mix ½ cup icing with neon green and leaf green gels to make green for the continents. Thin to lining consistency and spoon ¼ cup into a piping bag fitted with a #1 tip. Thin the remaining icing to flooding consistency, add a little whitener, and cover with plastic wrap. Using the green lining icing, loosely outline the shapes of the continents (do not try to make them perfectly). Let set for 5 minutes. Reserve the lining icing if you want to re-outline the continents. Using a small paintbrush and the flooding icing, paint in the continents. Let set until hard, 4 to 6 hours. When the icing has set, re-outline the continents, if desired, with the reserved lining icing. Let set for 10 minutes.

GRAPEFRUIT

○ beginner ● intermediate ○ advanced

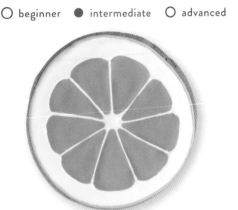

what you need

TO MAKE THE COOKIES
3-inch circle cookie cutter

Cookie dough of choice (pages 26–33), prepared, chilled, and rolled out

Cooling racks

TO DECORATE
1½ cups Royal Icing (pages 40–42)

Pasteurized egg white or water

Gel food colors: egg yellow, whitener, electric pink

2 plastic or parchment paper piping bags (page 53)

2 #1.5 tips

Assorted paintbrushes

1. **Make the cookies.** Cut out 22 cookies from the dough. Bake and cool as directed.
2. **Make yellow lining icing for the grapefruit peel and outline it.** Mix ¼ cup royal icing in a bowl with egg yellow and whitener gels to make yellow for the grapefruit peel. Thin to lining consistency and spoon all of it into a piping bag fitted with a #1.5 tip. Outline the skin of the grapefruit along the edge of the cookie. Let set for 5 minutes.
3. **Make white lining and flooding icing for the pith; outline and paint in.** Mix ¾ cup royal icing in a small bowl with whitener gel to make white for the pith. Spoon ¼ cup into a piping bag fitted with a #1.5 tip. Thin the remaining icing to flooding consistency and cover with plastic wrap. Using the white lining

icing, outline the segments of the grapefruit by first making a scallop pattern around the circle about ¼ inch from the yellow outline. You should be able to make nine scallops. Outline the sides of each segment by making a line from the low point of each scallop to the center of the cookie, allowing the lines to run together in the center. Let set for 10 minutes. Using a small paintbrush and the white flooding icing, paint in the border between the peel and the pink segments, carefully butting the icing up (see page 64) to the edge of the peel. Let set until hard, 6 to 8 hours or overnight.

4. **Make pink flooding icing for the segments and paint in.** Refresh the remaining royal icing on medium low for 30 seconds. Mix ½ cup icing

in a small bowl with electric pink, egg yellow, and whitener gels to make pink for the segments. Thin to flooding consistency. Using a small paintbrush, paint in the segments, butting the icing up to the white lines without covering them. Let set until hard, 6 to 8 hours or overnight.

PEPPERONI
PIZZA

○ beginner   ○ intermediate   ● advanced

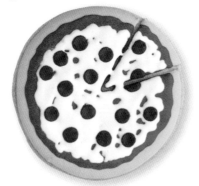

what you need

TO MAKE THE COOKIES
3-inch circle cookie cutter

Cookie dough of choice (pages 26–33), prepared, chilled, and rolled out

Cooling racks

TO DECORATE
2½ cups Royal Icing (pages 40–42)

Pasteurized egg white or water

Gel food colors: egg yellow, chocolate brown, whitener, bright red, sunset orange, red red, super black

4 plastic or parchment paper piping bags (page 53)

3 #1 tips

1 #1.5 tip

Assorted paintbrushes

1. **Make the cookies.** Cut out 22 cookies from the dough. Bake and cool as directed.

2. **Make yellow lining and flooding icing for the crust; outline and paint in.** Mix 1¼ cups royal icing in a small bowl with egg yellow, chocolate brown, and whitener gels to make golden yellow for the crust. Thin to lining consistency and spoon ¼ cup into a piping bag fitted with a #1 tip. Thin the remaining icing to flooding consistency, add a little whitener, and cover with plastic wrap.

Using the lining icing, outline the pizza crust just inside the edge of the cookie (this will give you room to make the slice look as if it is pulled away), making a V into the center of the cookie for the slice. Outline the pizza slice, lining the very edge of the cookie for the crust and leaving a space between the slice and the rest of the pizza. Let set for 5 minutes. Using a large paintbrush and the golden yellow flooding icing, paint in the pizza

PEPPERONI PIZZA CONTINUES

and the pizza slice. Let set until hard, 6 to 8 hours or overnight.

3. **Make red lining and flooding icing for the tomato sauce; outline and paint in.** Refresh the royal icing on medium low for 30 seconds. Mix ½ cup icing in a small bowl with bright red and sunset orange gels to make orangey red for the sauce. Thin to lining consistency and spoon ¼ cup into a piping bag fitted with a #1 tip. Thin the remaining icing to flooding consistency and cover with plastic wrap. Using the lining icing, outline the edge of the pizza sauce, making a wiggly circle inside the edge of the crust to leave enough of it exposed so that it reads as crust. Outline the slice in the same way. Let set for 5 minutes. Using a large paintbrush and the orangey red flooding icing, thinly paint in the tomato sauce on the pizza and the slice. Let set until hard, 4 to 6 hours or overnight.

4. **Make white icing for the mozzarella; pipe on pizza.** Refresh the royal icing on medium low for 30 seconds. Mix ½ cup icing in a small bowl with a toothpick of egg yellow gel paste to make off-white. Thin to between lining and flooding consistency. Spoon all of it into a piping bag fitted with a #1.5 tip. Cover the pizza by dragging the tip all over the tomato sauce, making imperfect edges within the edges of the tomato sauce. Allow small, irregular spots of the sauce to show through the cheese. Drag the tip in two or three places between the edges of the pizza and the pizza slice to make it look like the cheese is stretching between the slice and the pie. Let set until hard, 6 to 8 hours or overnight.

5. **Make burnt red lining and flooding icing for the pepperoni; outline and paint in.** Refresh the royal icing on medium low for 30 seconds. Mix ¼ cup icing in a small bowl with bright red, red red, and a teeny tiny toothpick of super black gel paste to make burnt red for the pepperoni. (Vegetarians, you can make bell-pepper green with leaf green and a toothpick of chocolate brown; thin to lining consistency and spoon 2 tablespoons into a piping bag fitted with a #1 tip.) Thin the remaining icing to flooding consistency and cover with plastic wrap. Using the lining icing, draw pepperoni (or pepper) slices randomly over the cheese. Let set for 5 minutes. Using a small paintbrush and the burnt red flooding icing, very thinly paint in the pepperoni slices (you don't want them to be puffy). Let set until hard, 4 to 6 hours or overnight.

GHOST CUTTER

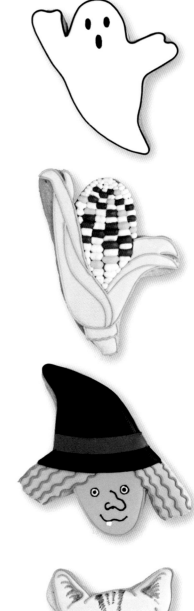

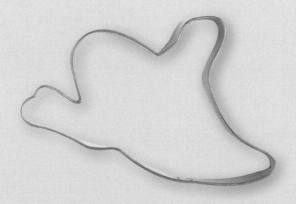

This cutter produced four fall-themed cookies (if you consider the gray cat a Halloween cat, as I do).

Black lining icing has a tendency to bleed when applied to white icing that is not thoroughly dry, so make sure the Ghost's cloak has hardened properly before re-outlining. You can also use the black icing to write "BOO" on the ghost's body.

To make the Witch's hair appropriately frizzy, hold the piping tip close to the cookie as you squeeze the icing out of the bag, making wiggly lines.

I'm especially glad that I saw the Kitty in the ghost cutter because good cat cutters are hard to find.

GHOST

● beginner ○ intermediate ○ advanced

what you need

TO MAKE THE COOKIES
3½-inch ghost cookie cutter

Cookie dough of choice (pages 26–33), prepared, chilled, and rolled out

Cooling racks

TO DECORATE
1½ cups Royal Icing (pages 40–42)

Pasteurized egg white or water

Gel food colors: whitener, super black

2 plastic or parchment paper piping bags (page 53)

2 #1 tips

Large paintbrush

1. **Make the cookies.** Cut out 24 cookies from the dough. Bake and cool as directed.

2. **Make the lining and flooding icing for the ghost. Outline and paint in.** Mix 1¼ cups royal icing in a bowl with whitener gel to make white for the ghost. Thin to lining consistency and spoon ¼ cup into a piping bag fitted with a #1 tip. Thin the remaining icing to flooding consistency and cover with plastic wrap. Using the lining icing, outline the ghost, following the edge of the cookie and exaggerating the contours of the fingers. Let set for 5 minutes. Using a large paintbrush, paint in the ghost. Let set until hard, 6 to 8 hours or overnight.

3. **Make black lining icing to re-outline the ghost; draw the eyes and mouth.** Beat the royal icing on medium low for 30 seconds. Spoon ¼ cup into a small bowl and mix with super black gel to make black for outlining the ghost. Spoon all of it into a piping bag fitted with a #1 tip. Re-outline the ghost. Draw in the eyes and mouth by holding the tip on the cookie at a 45-degree angle and squeezing the bag. Let set for 15 minutes.

INDIAN CORN

○ beginner   ● intermediate   ○ advanced

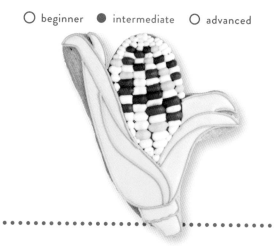

what you need

TO MAKE THE COOKIES
3½-inch ghost cookie cutter

Cookie dough of choice (pages 26–33), prepared, chilled, and rolled out

Cooling racks

TO DECORATE
2 cups Royal Icing (pages 40–42)

Pasteurized egg white or water

Gel food colors: ivory, gold, whitener, lemon yellow, bright red, super black, buckeye brown, regal purple, violet

6 plastic or parchment paper piping bags (page 53)

2 #1 tips

4 #1.5 tips

Large paintbrush

1. **Make the cookies.** Cut out 24 cookies from the dough. Bake and cool as directed.

2. **Make beige lining and flooding icing for the husk.** Mix ¾ cup royal icing in a bowl with the ivory and gold gels to make warm beige for the husk. Thin to lining consistency and spoon ¼ cup into a piping bag fitted with a #1 tip. Thin the remaining icing to flooding consistency, add a little whitener, and cover with plastic wrap.

3. **Outline the husk and paint in.** Position the cookie so that the ghost's head is the top. Using the lining icing, outline the silhouette of the corn husk including the stem at the bottom. Let set for 5 minutes. Using a large paintbrush and the warm beige flooding icing, paint in the corn husk. Let set until hard, 4 to 6 hours.

4. **Make icings for the kernels.** Refresh the royal icing on medium low for 30 seconds. Spoon ¼ cup icing into each of four bowls. Cover three with plastic wrap. To the remaining, add ivory and whitener gels to make off-white for some of the corn kernels. Thin to a little looser than lining consistency and spoon into a piping bag fitted with a #1.5 tip. To the second bowl, mix in lemon yellow and whitener gels to make yellow. Thin and spoon into a piping bag as above. To the third bowl, mix in bright red, super black,

INDIAN CORN CONTINUES

buckeye brown, and whitener gels to make maroon. Thin and spoon into a piping bag as above. To the fourth bowl, mix in regal purple, violet, and super black gels to make dark purple. Thin and spoon into a piping bag as above.

5. **Make the kernels.** Using the off-white icing, make a few fat kernels of corn by squeezing the bag while moving it very slowly so that the icing builds up enough to make the size kernel you want. Make the kernels different sizes, smaller at the top and gradually larger toward the bottom. Allow the icing to set for about 3 minutes to avoid the kernels' running into one another, then make more kernels next to them. Let set for 4 to 6 hours. Use the yellow, maroon, and dark purple icings in the same manner, making the kernels fat enough to fill the spaces so that no bare cookie shows through and allowing the kernels to set before using a new color.

6. **Make dark beige lining icing to re-outline the husk; re-outline and make the details.** Mix ¼ cup royal icing in a bowl with ivory and gold gels to make dark beige for re-outlining the husk. Thin to lining consistency and spoon it all into a piping bag fitted with a #1 tip. Re-outline the corn husk, adding the details on the husk.

· MAKES 24 ·

WITCH'S HEAD

○ beginner ● intermediate ○ advanced

what you need

TO MAKE THE COOKIES

3½-inch ghost cookie cutter

Cookie dough of choice (pages 26–33), prepared, chilled, and rolled out

Cooling racks

TO DECORATE

3½ cups Royal Icing (pages 40–42)

Pasteurized egg white or water

Gel food colors: neon green, super black, whitener, regal purple

6 plastic or parchment paper piping bags (page 53)

6 #1 tips

Assorted paintbrushes

1. **Make the cookies.** Cut out 24 cookies from the dough. Bake and cool as directed.

2. **Make green lining and flooding icing for the witch's face.** Mix ¾ cup royal icing in a bowl with the neon green gel to make bright green for the face. Thin to lining consistency and spoon ¼ cup into a piping bag fitted with a #1 tip. Thin the remaining icing to flooding consistency and cover with plastic wrap.

3. **Outline and paint in the face.** Position the cookie so that the ghost's head is the bottom. Using the green lining icing, outline the witch's face, stopping where it meets the hair. Let set for 5 minutes. Reserve the green lining icing. Using a medium paintbrush and the flooding icing, paint in the face, thinning it out where the hair and hat overlap the face. Let set for 4 to 6 hours.

4. **Make the gray lining and flooding icing for the hair; outline and paint in.** Refresh the remaining icing on low for 30 seconds. Mix ¾ cup icing in a bowl with super black and whitener gels to make gray for the hair. Thin to lining consistency and spoon ¼ cup icing into a piping bag fitted with a #1 tip. Thin the remaining icing to flooding consistency and cover with plastic wrap. Using the lining icing, outline the silhouette of the hair, making squiggly lines and going over the face, stopping where the hair meets the hat. Let set for 5 minutes. Using a medium paintbrush and the gray flooding icing, paint in the hair, thinning it out where the hat overlaps it. Let set for 4 to 6 hours.

5. **Make black lining and flooding icing for the hat; outline and paint in.** Refresh the royal icing on medium low for 30 seconds. Mix 1¼ cups icing with super black gel to make black for the witch's hat. Thin to lining consistency and spoon ¼ cup icing into a piping bag fitted with a #1 tip. Thin the remaining icing to flooding consistency and cover with plastic wrap. Using the black lining icing, outline the hat, going over the hair and face. Let set for 5 minutes. Reserve the black lining icing. Using a large paintbrush and the black flooding icing, paint in the hat. Let set until hard, 6 to 8 hours or overnight.

6. **Make white and gray lining icings for the witch's eyes and strands of hair. Make purple lining and flooding icing for the hatband.** Refresh the royal icing on medium low for 30 seconds. Spoon ¼ cup icing into each of three bowls. Cover two with plastic wrap. To the remaining, add whitener to make white for the witch's eyes. Thin to lining consistency and spoon all of it into a piping bag fitted with a #1 tip. To the second bowl, add super black and whitener gels to make darker gray for the strands of hair. Thin to lining consistency and spoon all of it into a piping bag fitted with a #1 tip. To

WITCH'S HEAD CONTINUES

the third bowl, add regal purple to make purple for the hatband. Thin to lining consistency and spoon 2 tablespoons into a piping bag fitted with a #1 tip. Thin the remaining icing to flooding consistency, add a little whitener, and cover with plastic wrap.

7. **Re-outline the face, draw details; re-outline the hair; outline and paint in the band.** Using the reserved green lining icing, re-outline the face. Using the reserved black lining icing, draw the nose, mouth, and two circles for the eyes. Reserve the icing again. Using the darker gray lining icing, re-outline the hair and make additional squiggly lines on the interior. Using the purple lining icing, outline the band on the hat. Let set for 5 minutes. Using a small paintbrush and the purple flooding icing, paint in the band. Using the white lining icing, squeeze two small dots in the black circles for the eyes. Make one tooth coming out of the mouth. Using the reserved black lining icing, squeeze a tiny dot in each eye for the pupils. Let set for 15 minutes.

· · · · · · · · · · · · · · · · MAKES 24 · · · · · · · · · · · · · · · ·

KITTY

○ beginner   ● intermediate   ○ advanced

what you need

TO MAKE THE COOKIES
3½-inch ghost cookie cutter

Cookie dough of choice (pages 26–33), prepared, chilled, and rolled out

Cooling racks

TO DECORATE
2 cups Royal Icing (pages 40–42)

Pasteurized egg white or water

Gel food colors: super black, whitener, chocolate brown

4 plastic or parchment paper piping bags (page 53)

4 #1 tips

Assorted paintbrushes

Plate or ceramic mixing palette

1. **Make the cookies.** Cut out 24 cookies from the dough. Bake and cool as directed.

2. **Make gray lining and flooding icing for the cat.** Mix 1¼ cups royal icing in a bowl with super

black, whitener, and chocolate brown gels to make light gray for the cat. Thin to lining consistency and spoon ¼ cup into a piping bag fitted with a #1 tip. Thin the remaining icing to flooding consistency and cover with plastic wrap.

3. **Outline and paint in the cat.** Position the cookie so that the ghost's head is at 8 o'clock. Using the lining icing, outline the silhouette of the cat, making small bumps for the toes on the paws. Let set for 5 minutes. Using a large paintbrush and the flooding icing, paint in the cat. Let set until hard, 6 to 8 hours or overnight.

4. **Make lining icings: dark gray to re-outline the cat, black to make the eyes, and brown for the nose.** Spoon ¼ cup royal icing into each of three bowls. Cover two with plastic wrap. To the remaining, add super black, whitener, and chocolate brown gels to make darker gray to outline the cat and define its legs. Spoon it all into a piping bag fitted with a #1 tip. To the second bowl, add super black gel to make black for the eyes. Spoon

it all into a piping bag fitted with a #1 tip. To the third bowl, add chocolate brown to make brown for the nose. Thin to lining consistency and spoon into a piping bag fitted with a #1 tip.

5. **Re-outline the cat and make details.** Using the darker gray lining icing, re-outline the cat, including the interior lines for the head, legs, and toes. Using the black lining icing, draw two curvy lines for the eyes. Using the dark brown lining icing, draw in the nose and fill it in by holding the tip on the cookie at a 45-degree angle and squeezing the piping bag. Draw a small vertical line under the nose.

6. **Make gray watercolor and paint on the cat's stripes.** Squeeze a dot of super black gel onto a plate or ceramic mixing palette. Using a small paintbrush, mix with water to make black watercolor (see page 66). Paint the stripes and inner ear details onto the cat. Let set for 5 minutes.

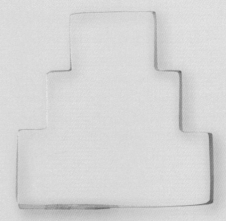

WEDDING CAKE CUTTER

You'll notice that all of the cookies in this group are oriented the same way. Challenge yourself to see if you can turn the cutter one way or another and find a different design in it.

The Typewriter is one of my favorites. Think of it as an all-occasion card and write a short message on the "paper" with edible marker.

The wedding cake also has so many possibilities. Embellish it with flowers or even a monogram.

WEDDING CAKE

● beginner ○ intermediate ○ advanced

what you need

TO MAKE THE COOKIES
4-inch wedding cake cookie cutter

Cookie dough of choice (pages 26–33), prepared, chilled, and rolled out

Cooling racks

TO DECORATE
2½ cups Royal Icing (pages 40–42)

Pasteurized egg white or water

Gel food colors: whitener, neon green, bright blue, royal blue

Edible gold luster dust

Vodka or lemon extract

3 plastic or parchment paper piping bags (page 53)

3 #1 tips

Assorted paintbrushes

1. **Make the cookies.** Cut out 12 cookies from the dough. Bake and cool as directed.

2. **Make white lining and flooding icings.** Mix 1½ cups royal icing in a small bowl with whitener gel to make bright white. Thin to lining consistency and spoon ¼ cup into a piping bag fitted with a #1 tip. Thin the remaining icing to flooding consistency and cover with plastic wrap.

3. **Outline the cake and paint in.** Using the white lining icing, outline the silhouette of the cake. To make sure that the tiers look level, pipe the rectangular outline of each tier, beginning with the bottom tier. Keep the lines and corners as straight and squared off as possible. Let set for 5 minutes. Paint in the tiers with the white flooding icing, painting over the horizontal outlines on the interior of the cookie. Let set dor 6 to 8 hours or overnight.

4. **Make blue lining and flooding icing.** Refresh the royal icing on medium low for 30 seconds. Mix ¾ cup icing in a bowl with neon green, bright blue, royal blue, and whitener gels to make robin's egg blue. Thin to lining consistency and spoon ¼ cup into a piping bag fitted with a #1 tip. Thin the remaining icing to flooding consistency and cover with plastic wrap.

5. **Re-outline the tiers and make the bands.** Using the robin's egg blue lining icing, re-outline the tiers, then make a horizontal line ¼ inch above the bottom of each tier to make three rectangular bands. Let set for 5 minutes. Paint in the bands with the robin's egg blue flooding icing.

WEDDING CAKE CONTINUES

Make blue dots along the top edge of the bands, spacing them evenly apart.

6. **Make white lining icing for the ribbon. Make gold ribbons and white dots.** Mix ¼ cup royal icing in a bowl with whitener gel to make bright white. Thin to lining consistency and spoon all of it into a piping bag fitted with a #1 tip. Using the white lining icing, make a wavy line across the middle of each tier. Make white dots above the wavy line on the top half of each tier. Let set for 5 minutes. Mix a little gold luster dust with vodka or lemon extract in a bowl with a paintbrush. Paint a band of gold just under each wavy line, butting it up (see page 64) to the white line and making the band thinner and thicker with each curve. Let set for 30 minutes.

• MAKES 12 •

STACKED LUGGAGE

○ beginner ○ intermediate ● advanced

what you need

TO MAKE THE COOKIES
4-inch wedding cake cookie cutter

Cookie dough of choice (pages 26–33), prepared, chilled, and rolled out

Cooling racks

TO DECORATE
4½ cups Royal Icing, (pages 40–42)

Pasteurized egg white or water

Gels: lemon yellow, gold, ivory, whitener, chocolate brown, royal blue, bright blue, neon green, super black, bright red

Edible gold and silver luster dust

Vodka or lemon extract

10 plastic or parchment paper piping bags (page 53)

10 #1 tips

Assorted paintbrushes

1. **Make the cookies.** Cut out 12 cookies from the dough. Bake and cool as directed.
2. **Make the lining and flooding icings for the suitcases.** Fill three bowls with ¾ cup each of icing. Cover two with plastic wrap. To the first bowl, add the bright blue, royal blue, and whitener gels to make blue for the suitcase. Thin to lining consistency and spoon ¼ cup into a piping bag fitted with a #1 tip. Thin the remainder to flooding consistency and cover with plastic wrap. To the second bowl, add the lemon yellow, gold, ivory, and whitener gels to make yellow for the suitcase. Thin to lining consistency and spoon ¼ cup into a piping bag fitted with a #1 tip. Thin the remainder to flooding consistency and cover with plastic wrap. To the third bowl, add the lemon yellow, neon green, ivory, and whitener gels to make green for the suitcase. Thin to lining consistency and spoon ¼ cup into a piping bag fitted with a #1 tip. Thin to flooding consistency and cover with plastic wrap.
3. **Outline and paint in the suitcases.** Using the blue lining icing, outline the bottom suitcase, rounding the corners. Using the green lining icing, outline the middle suitcase, rounding the corners and butting the green line (see page 64) to the top of the blue suitcase. Using the yellow lining icing, outline the top suitcase, rounding the corners and butting the yellow line to the top of the green suitcase. Let set for 5 minutes. Using a paintbrush and the blue, green, and yellow flooding icings, paint in the suitcases. Let set for 6 to 8 hours or overnight.
4. **Make lining and flooding icings for the details.** Refresh the remaining icing on medium low for 30 seconds. Fill two bowls with ¼ cup each of icing. Cover one with plastic wrap. To the first bowl, add a toothpick each of super black and whitener gels to make gray for the metal parts. Thin to lining consistency and spoon 2 tablespoons into a piping bag fitted with a #1 tip. Thin the remainder to flooding consistency and cover with plastic wrap. To the second bowl, add ¼ cup of the chocolate brown gel to make leather brown. Thin to lining consistency and spoon 2 tablespoons into a piping bag fitted with a #1 tip. Thin the remainder to flooding consistency and cover with plastic wrap.
5. **Outline and paint in the details.** Using the gray lining icing, outline the metal corners on the blue suitcase and two semicircles that the blue handle attaches to. Using the brown lining icing, outline the leather trim on the green suitcase and two small rectangles where the green handle attaches. Reserve the brown lining icing. Outline the leather belts and the tag on the blue suitcase. Let set for 5 minutes. Using a small paintbrush and the gray flooding icing, fill in all the metal parts on the blue suitcase. Using the brown flooding icing, paint in all the leather parts on the blue and green suitcases. Let set for 1 hour.
6. **Make the lining icings to re-outline the suitcases.** Fill three bowls with ½ cup each of icing. Cover two with plastic wrap. To the first bowl, add the bright blue, royal blue, and whitener

STACKED LUGGAGE CONTINUES

gels to make dark blue for the outline of the blue suitcase. Thin to lining consistency and spoon ¼ cup into a piping bag fitted with a #1 tip. Thin the remainder to flooding consistency and cover with plastic wrap. To the second bowl, add a toothpick each of lemon yellow, gold, ivory, and whitener gels to make dark yellow for the outline of the yellow suitcase. Thin to lining consistency and spoon ¼ cup into a piping bag fitted with a #1 tip. Thin the remainder to flooding consistency and cover with plastic wrap. To the third bowl, add the lemon yellow, neon green, ivory, and whitener gels to make dark green for the outline of the green suitcase. Thin to lining consistency and spoon ¼ cup into a piping bag fitted with a #1 tip. Thin the remaining icing to flooding consistency and cover with plastic wrap.

7. **Re-outline the blue suitcase and make details.** Using the dark blue lining icing, re-outline the blue suitcase. Pipe a horizontal line across the top of the suitcase to show where it opens, going around the leather belts. Outline the blue handle. Outline a small rectangle on the yellow suitcase for a sticker. Let set for 5 minutes. Using a small paintbrush and the dark blue flooding icing, fill in the blue handle.

8. **Re-outline the yellow suitcase and make more details.** Using the dark yellow lining icing, re-outline the yellow suitcase. Make a horizontal line across the middle of the suitcase to show where it opens, and pipe two vertical lines just within the left and right edges of the yellow suitcase. Make

two small ovals for where the brown handle attaches and a small circle in the middle for the lock. Make two ovals for the latches on top of the horizontal line on the yellow suitcase. Make two bigger ovals on top of the horizontal line on the green suitcase for the latches. Outline two rectangles just under the horizontal line on the blue suitcase. Then make two ovals just above the two rectangles. Outline a square around each belt for the buckle. Let set for 5 minutes. Using the reserved brown lining icing, make two lines butted up to each other for the handle on the yellow suitcase. Using a small paintbrush and the dark yellow flooding icing, fill in the rectangles on the blue suitcase. Let set for 15 minutes. Using the dark yellow lining icing, pipe two smaller ovals on top of the rectangles to complete the latches.

9. **Re-outline the green suitcase and paint in details.** Using the dark green lining icing, re-outline the green suitcase. Pipe a horizontal line across the top of the suitcase to show where it opens. Outline the green handle on top of the brown rectangles. Let set for 5 minutes. Using the small paintbrush and the dark green flooding icing, fill in the green handle.

10. **Make lining and flooding icing for metal details and stickers. Make details.** Fill two bowls with 2 generous tablespoons each of icing. Cover one with plastic wrap. To the other, add super black and whitener gels to make dark gray. Thin to lining consistency and spoon all of it into a

piping bag fitted with a #1 tip. To the second bowl, add bright red gel to make red for the outline of the stickers. Thin to lining consistency and spoon all of it into a piping bag fitted with a #1 tip. Using the dark gray lining icing, make two dots on each metal corner of the blue suitcase for screws. Make dots on the leather belts and a line connecting the blue handle to the leather tag. Using the red lining icing, outline a triangle and small rectangle on the yellow suitcase and a rectangle on the green suitcase for the stickers. Let set for 15 minutes.

Mix 2 tablespoons of icing in a small bowl with whitener gel to make bright white. Thin to flooding consistency. Using a small paintbrush and the white flooding icing, paint in all the stickers.

11. **Make metallic paint with luster dust and paint on.** Using a small paintbrush, mix a little gold and silver luster dust with vodka or lemon extract, each in a separate bowl. Paint all the latches and the buckles gold. Paint the metal parts on the blue suitcase silver. Let set for 1 hour, until dry.

·················· MAKES 12 ··················

TYPEWRITER

○ beginner ○ intermediate ● advanced

what you need

TO MAKE THE COOKIES
4-inch wedding cake cookie cutter

Cookie dough of choice (pages 26–33), prepared, chilled, and rolled out

Cooling racks

TO DECORATE
5 cups Royal Icing (pages 40–42)

Pasteurized egg white or water

Gel food colors: royal blue, bright blue, neon green, whitener, super black, sunset orange, bright red, gold, lemon yellow, electric pink

10 plastic or parchment paper piping bags (page 53)

10 #1 tips

Assorted paintbrushes

1. **Make the cookies.** Cut out 12 cookies from the dough. Bake and cool as directed.
2. **Make green lining and flooding icing for the desk.** Mix ¾ cup royal icing in a small bowl with royal blue, bright blue, neon green, and whitener gels to make light green. Thin to lining consistency and spoon ¼ cup into a piping bag fitted

TYPEWRITER CONTINUES

with a #1 tip. Thin the remaining icing to flooding consistency and cover with plastic wrap.

3. **Outline and paint in the desk.** Using the light green lining icing, outline the desk, leaving the top unlined where the typewriter overlaps the desk. Let set for 5 minutes. Using a large paintbrush and the light green flooding icing, paint in the desk, thinning the icing where the typewriter overlaps. Let set until hard, 6 to 8 hours or overnight.

4. **Make black flooding icing for the area behind the keys.** Refresh the royal icing on medium low for 30 seconds to 1 minute. Mix 2 generous tablespoons of icing in a small bowl with the super black gel to make black. Thin the icing to a very loose flooding consistency. Using a medium paintbrush and the very loose black flooding icing, thinly paint in the dark area behind the typewriter keys. Let set for 1 hour. The black should be completely dry or it will bleed through the red.

5. **Make lining and flooding icings: orange-red for the typewriter and white for the paper.** Meanwhile, fill two bowls with 1 cup royal icing each. Cover one with plastic wrap. To the first bowl, add sunset orange and bright red gels to make orange-red. Thin to lining consistency and spoon ¼ cup into a piping bag fitted with a #1 tip. Thin the remaining icing to flooding consistency and cover with plastic wrap. To the second bowl, add the whitener gel to make bright white. Thin to lining consistency and spoon ¼ cup into a piping

bag fitted with a #1 tip. Thin the remaining icing to flooding consistency and cover with plastic wrap.

6. **Outline and paint in the typewriter and paper.** Using the orange-red lining icing, outline the typewriter, making sure to go completely around the painted black area. Leave space above the typewriter for the black cylinder. Outline the inner edge of the typewriter on top of the black painted area. Using the white lining icing, outline the piece of paper above the typewriter, butting (see page 64) the white line to the top of the typewriter. Let set for 5 minutes. Reserve the white lining icing. Using a medium paintbrush and the orange-red flooding icing, paint in the typewriter. Using a medium paintbrush and the white flooding icing, paint in the piece of paper. Let set for 4 to 6 hours or until dry. Reserve the white flooding icing.

7. **Re-outline the paper; make the keys and space bar.** Using the reserved white lining icing, re-outline the piece of paper. Make fat ovals on the black icing for the typewriter keys. Outline a long thin rectangle on the bottom for the space bar. Let set for 5 minutes. Using a small paintbrush and the reserved white flooding icing, paint in the space bar and paint in the white keys.

8. **Make black lining and flooding icing for the cylinder and spool outline and paint in.** Mix ¼ cup royal icing in a small bowl with the super black gel to make black. Thin to lining consistency and spoon 2 tablespoons into a piping bag fitted with a #1 tip. Thin the remaining icing to flooding

consistency and cover with plastic wrap. Using the black lining icing, outline the right and left sides of the cylinder that sits above the typewriter. Outline each side so that the black line butts up to the edge of the paper and the edge of the typewriter. Outline a thin rectangle on each end of the cylinder so that it sticks out from the sides of the typewriter. Let set for 5 minutes. Using a small paintbrush and the black flooding icing, fill in the right and left sides of the cylinder. Let set for 1 hour. Using the black lining icing, outline the spools on the right and left sides of the typewriter just below the black cylinder. Using a small paintbrush and the black flooding icing, fill in the spools.

9. **Make gray lining and flooding icing for the bail and metal part; make lining icings: orange-red to re-outline the typewriter and dark gray to make the type keys.** Fill three bowls with ¼ cup royal icing each. Cover two with plastic wrap. To the first bowl, add super black and whitener gels to make light gray. Thin to lining consistency and spoon 2 tablespoons into a piping bag fitted with a #1 tip. Thin the remaining light gray icing to flooding consistency and cover with plastic wrap. To the second bowl, add sunset orange and bright red gels to make dark orange-red to re-outline the typewriter. Thin to lining consistency and spoon all of it into a piping bag fitted with a #1 tip. To the third bowl, add super black and whitener gels to make dark gray for the type keys. Thin to lining consistency and spoon all of it into a piping bag fitted with a #1 tip.

10. **Outline and paint in the metal part and make the details.** Using the light gray lining icing, outline the metal part on the front of the typewriter. Pipe a dot in the middle of the top edge of the metal part. Pipe a horizontal line across the length of the black cylinder and the piece of paper for the bail. Let set for 5 minutes. Using the black lining icing, pipe two short lines just above the light gray bail. Using a small paintbrush and the light gray flooding icing, paint in the metal part. Reserve the lining icing. Let icing set for 2 to 3 hours.

11. **Re-outline the typewriter and cylinder and make the details.** Using the dark orange-red lining icing, re-outline the typewriter and pipe horizontal lines across it. Using the dark gray lining icing, re-outline each end of the black cylinder. Pipe a curve across the metal shape and lines fanning down from the curve for the type keys. Reserve the dark gray lining icing.

12. **Make lining icings for the pencil.** Fill three bowls with ¼ cup royal icing each. Cover two with plastic wrap. To the first bowl, add gold gel to make dark brown for the pencil tip. Thin to lining consistency and spoon all of it into a piping bag fitted with a #1 tip. To the second bowl, add gold, lemon yellow, and whitener gels to make light yellow for the pencil. Thin to lining consistency and spoon all of it into a piping bag fitted with a #1 tip. To the third bowl, add electric

TYPEWRITER CONTINUES

pink gel to make pink for the eraser. Thin to lining consistency and spoon all of it into a piping bag fitted with a #1 tip.

13. **Make the pencil.** Using the light yellow lining icing, pipe the length of the pencil on top of the desk, slowly squeezing the bag to make fat lines.

Using the dark brown lining icing, pipe a triangle at the front of the pencil. Using the dark gray lining icing, squeeze a dot at the tip for the graphite. Using the light gray lining icing, pipe the metal band at the end of the pencil. Using the pink lining icing, pipe the eraser. Let set for 2 hours.

·········· MAKES 12 ··········

WITCH'S FEET

○ beginner ● intermediate ○ advanced

what you need

TO MAKE THE COOKIES
4-inch wedding cake cookie cutter

Cookie dough of choice (pages 26–33), prepared, chilled, and rolled out

Cooling racks

TO DECORATE
3 cups Royal Icing (pages 40–42)

Pasteurized egg white or water

Gel food colors: neon green, super black, gold, lemon yellow, whitener

4 plastic or parchment paper piping bags (page 53)

4 #1 tips

Assorted paintbrushes

1. **Make the cookies.** Cut out 12 cookies from the dough. Bake and cool as directed.

2. **Make green lining and flooding icing for the stockings.** Mix 1 cup royal icing in a small bowl with neon green gel to make neon green for the stockings. Thin to lining consistency and spoon ¼ cup into a piping bag fitted with a #1 tip. Thin

the remaining icing to flooding consistency and cover with plastic wrap.

3. **Outline and paint in the stockings.** Using the green lining icing, outline each leg. Leave the areas unlined where the shoe overlaps the leg. Let set for 5 minutes. Using a medium paintbrush and the neon green flooding icing, paint in the legs,

thinning the icing where the shoe overlaps the legs. Let set for 4 to 6 hours.

4. **Make black lining and flooding icing for the shoes.** Mix 1¼ cups royal icing in a small bowl with super black gel to make black for the shoes. Thin to lining consistency and spoon ¼ cup into a piping bag fitted with a #1 tip. Thin the remaining icing to flooding consistency and cover with plastic wrap.

5. **Outline and paint in the shoes and stripes.** Using the black lining icing, outline each shoe, leaving the area unlined where the buckle overlaps the edge of each shoe. Make the toe of each shoe curl up. Outline horizontal stripes on the stockings. Let set for 5 minutes. Using a large paintbrush and the black flooding icing, paint in the shoes. Using a small paintbrush, paint in the stripes. Let set for 6 to 8 hours or overnight.

6. **Make yellow lining and flooding icing for the buckles; outline and paint in.** Refresh the royal icing on medium low for 30 seconds. Mix ½ cup icing in a small bowl with gold, lemon yellow, and whitener gels to make golden yellow for the buckles. Thin to lining consistency and spoon ¼ cup into a piping bag fitted with a #1 tip.

Thin the remaining icing to flooding consistency and cover with plastic wrap. Using the golden yellow lining icing, outline each buckle. Outline a smaller rectangle inside each buckle. Let set for 5 minutes. Using a medium paintbrush and the golden yellow flooding icing, paint in the buckles.

7. **Make black lining icing to re-outline the shoes.** Mix ¼ cup royal icing in a small bowl with super black gel to make black for the outline of the shoes. Thin to lining consistency and spoon all of it into a piping bag fitted with a #1 tip. Using the black lining icing, re-outline the shoes. Let set for 1 hour.

SEASHELL CUTTER

This cutter presented the possibility to make a pie with a slice out of it without having to trick the eye with icing as on the Pepperoni Pizza (page 155). The lattice crust can be tricky; practice making it on parchment before putting it on your cookie. Be sure to make the stripes far enough apart so that the fruit filling can show through. Of course, you can skip the lattice altogether and make a full crust on top.

I've given the shell a pastel ombré effect here, but you can make it a solid pastel in any color you like.

The car is my favorite in this group; I created it with an exaggerated perspective to accommodate the shape of the cookie.

SEASHELL

● beginner   ○ intermediate   ○ advanced

what you need

TO MAKE THE COOKIES
3-inch seashell cookie cutter

Cookie dough of choice (pages 26–33), prepared, chilled, and rolled out

Cooling racks

TO DECORATE
2 cups Royal Icing (pages 40–42)

Pasteurized egg white or water

Gel food colors: ivory, whitener, electric pink, regal purple, lemon yellow, gold

Pink luster or petal dust

2 plastic or parchment paper piping bags (page 53)

2 #1 tips

Assorted paintbrushes

Plate or ceramic mixing palette

1. **Make the cookies.** Cut out 24 cookies from the dough. Bake and cool as directed.

2. **Make beige lining and flooding icing for the shell; outline and paint in.** Mix 1½ cups royal icing in a bowl with ivory and whitener gels to make beige. Thin to lining consistency and spoon ¼ cup into a piping bag fitted with a #1 tip. Thin the remaining icing to flooding consistency and cover with plastic wrap. Using the lining icing, outline the silhouette of the shell, rounding the corners at the bottom of the shell. Let set for 5 minutes. Using a paintbrush and the flooding icing, paint in the shell. Let set until hard, 6 to 8 hours or overnight.

3. **Make watercolors and paint onto shell.** Squeeze dots of electric pink, regal purple, and lemon yellow gel onto a plate or ceramic mixing palette. Using a paintbrush, mix a little water into the electric pink gel to make a watercolor (see page 66). Paint the top edge of the shell a very light pink. Rinse the brush in water and pat dry slightly. Using the damp brush, blend the pink watercolor you applied gradually down the top third of the shell so that the pink fades into the beige icing, creating an ombré effect. Thoroughly rinse the paintbrush. Mix a little water into the regal purple gel to make a watercolor. Paint an arc of light purple across the middle of the shell. Rinse the brush in water and pat dry slightly. Using the damp brush, blend the top and bottom of the purple watercolor you applied so that it

SEASHELL CONTINUES

gradually fades into the beige icing. Thoroughly rinse the brush and use it to mix a little water into the lemon yellow gel to make a watercolor. Paint the bottom of the shell a light yellow, using the same technique as above to blend the yellow gel. Let the watercolors set for 30 minutes.

4. **Make pink lining icing to re-outline the shell and make the ridges.** Beat the royal icing on medium low for 30 seconds. Mix ½ cup royal icing in a bowl with electric pink, gold, and whitener gels to make peachy pink to re-outline the shell and make the interior ridges. Thin to lining consistency and spoon all of it into a piping bag fitted with a #1 tip. Using the lining icing, re-outline the shell. At each dip in the outline, draw the piping bag down to the bottom center of the shell to make the ridges along its surface. Re-outline the corners at the bottom left and right of the shell. Let set for 1 hour.

· MAKES 24 ·

CAR

○ beginner ○ intermediate ● advanced

what you need

TO MAKE THE COOKIES
3-inch seashell cookie cutter

Cookie dough of choice (pages 26–33), prepared, chilled, and rolled out

Cooling racks

TO DECORATE
3½ cups Royal Icing (pages 40–42)

Pasteurized egg white or water

Gel food colors: super black, whitener, violet, royal blue, lemon yellow

7 plastic or parchment paper piping bags (page 53)

5 #1 tips

2 #1.5 tips

Assorted paintbrushes

· ·

1. **Make the cookies.** Cut out 24 cookies from the dough. Bake and cool as directed.

2. **Make flooding icings: gray for the road and white for the windshield; paint in.** Mix ½ cup royal icing in a bowl with super black and whitener gels to make dark gray for the road. Thin to flooding consistency and cover with plastic wrap. Mix 2 tablespoons royal icing with whitener gel to make

white for the windshield. Thin to flooding consistency and cover with plastic wrap. Position the cookie so that the scalloped edge is the bottom and the hinge of the shell is the top. Using a paintbrush and the white flooding icing, thinly paint the windshield of the car, thinning the icing where the car overlaps it. Using a paintbrush and the dark gray flooding icing, paint the road at the bottom of the cookie, thinning the icing where the wheels and bumper overlap with the road. Let set for 1 hour.

3. **Make lining and flooding icings: indigo for the car and black for the tires.** Mix 1 cup royal icing in a bowl with violet and royal blue gels to make indigo. Thin to lining consistency and spoon ¼ cup into a piping bag fitted with a #1 tip. Thin the remaining icing to flooding consistency, add a little whitener, and cover with plastic wrap. Mix ½ cup royal icing in a bowl with super black gel to make black for the tires and grille. Spoon ¼ cup into a piping bag fitted with a #1 tip. Thin the remaining icing to flooding consistency and cover with plastic wrap.

4. **Outline and paint in the tires and car.** Using the black lining icing, outline the tires, piping over the road at the bottom left and right halves of the tires. Do not line the tops of the tires where they meet the bumper. Let set for 5 minutes. Reserve the bag of black lining icing. Using a paintbrush and the black flooding icing, paint in the tires, thinning out the icing slightly where the bumper overlaps. Using the indigo lining icing, outline the silhouette of the car, including underneath the bumper and a rectangle around the icing where the windshield is. Let set for 5 minutes. Using a paintbrush and the indigo flooding icing, paint in the car. Let set until hard, 6 to 8 hours or overnight.

5. **Make lining and flooding icings: gray for the bumper and grille and yellow for the headlights and road line. Make white lining icing to re-outline the windshield and hood ornament.** Refresh the royal icing on medium low for 30 seconds. Mix ½ cup icing in a bowl with super black and whitener gels to make light gray. Thin to lining consistency and spoon ¼ cup into a piping bag fitted with a #1.5 tip. Thin the remaining to flooding consistency and cover with plastic wrap. Mix ¼ cup royal icing in a bowl with lemon yellow and whitener gels to make yellow. Thin to lining consistency and spoon 2 tablespoons into a piping bag fitted with a #1.5 tip. Thin the remaining to flooding consistency and cover with plastic wrap. Mix 2 tablespoons royal icing with whitener gel. Thin to lining consistency and spoon it all into a piping bag fitted with a #1 tip.

6. **Outline and paint in the grille, bumper, and headlights. Make the lines on the road.** Using the light gray lining icing, outline the bumper, piping over the car and the tires. Outline the grille, centering it on top of the bumper. Using the yellow lining icing, make vertical dashes down the center of the road. Outline the headlights. Let set for 5 minutes. Using a

CAR CONTINUES

paintbrush and the gray flooding icing, paint in the bumper and grille. Using a paintbrush and the light yellow flooding icing, paint in the headlights. Let set for 4 to 6 hours.

7. **Make the steering wheel and re-outline the tires and windshield.** While the flooding icing sets, use the reserved black lining icing to make the top of the steering wheel in the far right of the windshield. Re-outline the tires and reserve the black piping icing. Using the white lining icing, re-outline the windshield and make an inverted triangle above the center of the grille.

8. **Make lining icings to re-outline the car, bumper, grille, and headlights. Make the details.** Once the flooding icing has set, spoon ¼ cup royal icing into each of two bowls. Cover one with plastic wrap. To the remaining, add violet and royal blue gels to make dark blue to re-outline the car. Thin to lining consistency and spoon it all into a piping bag fitted with a #1 tip. To the second bowl, add super black and whitener gels to make darker gray to re-outline the bumper. Thin to lining consistency and spoon it all into a piping bag fitted with a #1 tip. Using the dark blue lining icing, re-outline the body of the car and add the fenders. Using the dark gray lining icing, re-outline the bumper and grille. Follow the outline of the grille with another piped line just inside it. Re-outline the headlights. Using the reserved black lining icing, make vertical lines along the width of the grille. Let set until hard, about 3 hours.

· **MAKES 24** ·

FISHBOWL

○ beginner　● intermediate　○ advanced

what you need

TO MAKE THE COOKIES
3-inch seashell cookie cutter

Cookie dough of choice (pages 26–33), prepared, chilled, and rolled out

Cooling racks

TO DECORATE
3¼ cups Royal Icing (pages 40–42)

Pasteurized egg white or water

Gel food colors: whitener, bright blue, gold, lemon yellow, ivory, sunset orange, leaf green, super black

8 plastic or parchment paper piping bags (page 53)

8 #1 tips

Assorted paintbrushes

1. **Make the cookies.** Cut out 24 cookies from the dough. Bake and cool as directed.

2. **Make lining and flooding icings: pale blue for the glass and light blue for the water.** Mix ¾ cup royal icing in a bowl with whitener and bright blue gels to make super pale blue for the glass. Spoon ¼ cup icing into a piping bag fitted with a #1 tip. Thin the remaining icing to flooding consistency and cover with plastic wrap. Mix 1 cup royal icing in a bowl with bright blue and whitener gels to make light blue for the water. Thin to lining consistency and spoon ¼ cup into a piping bag fitted with a #1 tip. Thin the remaining icing to flooding consistency and cover with plastic wrap.

3. **Outline and paint in the fishbowl.** Using the super pale blue lining icing, outline the entire fishbowl, obscuring the scalloped edges of the cookie with a smooth line. Let set for 5 minutes. Using the light blue lining icing, make a scalloped line across the neck of the bowl, just below its narrowest part. Using a paintbrush and the super pale blue flooding icing, paint in the section above the scallop, butting up the icing (see page 64) to the water line. Using a paintbrush and the light blue flooding icing, paint in the remaining part of the fishbowl, butting the icing up to the water line. Let set until hard, 6 to 8 hours or overnight.

4. **Make sand lining and flooding icing for the castle; make lining icings: orange for the fish and green for the seaweed.** Refresh the royal icing on medium low for 30 seconds. Mix ½ cup icing in a bowl with gold, lemon yellow, ivory, and whitener gels to make sand color. Thin to lining consistency and spoon ¼ cup into a piping bag fitted with a #1 tip. Thin the remaining icing to flooding consistency and cover with plastic wrap. Spoon ¼ cup royal icing into each of two bowls. Cover one with plastic wrap. To the other, add sunset orange gel to make orange for the fish. Thin to lining consistency and spoon all of it into a piping bag fitted with a #1 tip. To the second bowl, add leaf green gel to make seaweed green. Thin to lining consistency and spoon all of it into a piping bag fitted with a #1 tip.

5. **Outline and paint in the sand and castle. Make the seaweed and fish.** Using the sand-colored lining icing, outline the sand along the bottom of the bowl. Outline the top of the sand as well as the silhouette of the castle. Let set for 5 minutes. Reserve the sand lining icing. Using a paintbrush and the sand flooding icing, paint in the sand and the sand castle. Let set for 4 to 6 hours. Using the orange lining icing, make two fish in the water, using the tip of the piping bag to draw each body, fin, and tail. Let set for 5 minutes. Make the side fin on top of the body of each fish. Using the green lining icing, outline the seaweed and fill it in, holding the tip close to the cookie.

6. **Make lining icings: dark blue to re-outline the bowl, white for the bubbles, and black for the castle details.** While the sand flooding icing sets,

mix ¼ cup royal icing with bright blue gel to make darker blue to re-outline the bowl. Thin to lining consistency and spoon it all into a piping bag fitted with a #1 tip. Mix 2 tablespoons royal icing with whitener gel to make bright white for the bubbles. Thin to lining consistency and spoon it all into a piping bag fitted with a #1 tip. Mix 2 tablespoons icing with super black gel to make black for the castle details. Thin to lining consistency and spoon it all into a piping bag fitted with a #1 tip.

7. **Re-outline the sand, castle, and bowl. Make details.** Using the reserved sand lining icing, re-outline the sand and the castle. Pipe small dots all over the sand and castle to give them texture. Using the super black lining icing, pipe a black dot on each fish for the eye, then draw the arched door and pair of windows on the castle. Using the darker blue lining icing, re-outline the bowl, excluding the bottom where the sand is. Re-outline the waterline. Using the white lining icing, pipe a few small white dots for bubbles above each fish. Let set until dry, 4 to 6 hours.

· MAKES 24 ·

BLUEBERRY PIE

○ beginner   ○ intermediate   ● advanced

what you need

TO MAKE THE COOKIES
3-inch seashell cookie cutter

Cookie dough of choice (pages 26–33), prepared, chilled, and rolled out

Cooling racks

TO DECORATE
2¼ cups Royal Icing (pages 40–42)

Pasteurized egg white or water

Gel food colors: violet, regal purple, gold, lemon yellow, whitener, chocolate brown

3 plastic or parchment paper piping bags (page 53)

3 #1 tips

Assorted paintbrushes

1. **Make the cookies.** Cut out 24 cookies from the dough. Bake and cool as directed.
2. **Make purple flooding icing for the berries and paint in.** Mix ¾ cup royal icing with violet and regal purple gels to make dark purple for the berries. Thin to flooding consistency. Using a

paintbrush and the flooding icing, paint in a thin layer to cover the cookie, stopping just short of the edge. Let set for 4 hours.

3. **Make yellow lining and flooding icing for the crust.** Mix 1 cup royal icing with gold, lemon yellow, and whitener gels to make golden yellow. Thin to lining consistency and spoon ¼ cup into a piping bag fitted with a #1 tip. Thin the remaining icing to flooding consistency, add whitener, and cover with plastic wrap.

4. **Outline the rim of the crust.** Position the cookie with the scalloped edge on the bottom and the shell hinge at the top. Using the golden yellow lining icing, outline the silhouette of the pie, giving it a scalloped crust and making a deep V into the center of the pie where the slice is cut out. Outline the cut slice of pie, using the deep V as a guide and piping a scalloped crust along the top of the cookie. Outline the inside rim of the crust on both the pie and the slice. Let set for 5 minutes.

5. **Outline the lattice crust and paint in.** To make the lattice top, first outline an overlapping grid with golden yellow lining icing. Later, you will use golden brown lining icing to pipe lines on the grid to give it the woven effect. Outline evenly spaced vertical lines across the width of the pie (excluding slice), wide enough to paint the interior and allow the blueberries to show through. Next pipe evenly spaced horizontal lines across the pie in the same manner, piping over the vertical lines, working around the slice. Make

the same pattern on the slice, aligning the lattice so that if you replaced the slice in the pie, the lattice would line up. Using a paintbrush and the golden yellow flooding icing, paint in the crust and the lattice. Let set until hard, 6 to 8 hours or overnight.

6. **Make lining icings: bluish purple for the berries and golden brown to re-outline the crust.** Refresh the royal icing on medium low for 30 seconds. Spoon 2 tablespoons royal icing into a small bowl. Add violet, regal purple, and whitener gels to make bluish purple. Thin to lining consistency and spoon all of it into a piping bag fitted with a #1 tip. Spoon ¼ cup royal icing into a second bowl. Mix in gold, lemon yellow, chocolate brown, and whitener gels to make golden brown. Thin to lining consistency and spoon all of it into a piping bag fitted with a #1 tip. Using the bluish-purple lining icing, pipe dots for blueberries on top of the dark purple icing in between the lattice strips. Pipe additional dots within the V that separates the slice from the pie. Using the golden brown lining icing, re-outline the scalloped crust and inside rim around the pie and the slice. Re-outline the triangular slice. To outline the woven lattice, begin with the horizontal strips, piping lines around each section of the strip that will rest on top and leaving gaps in between where the vertical strips will overlap. Next, pipe lines around each section of vertical strips that overlap the horizontal strips. Let set for 2 hours.

JACK-O'-LANTERN CUTTER

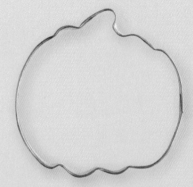

A presidential profile, a stack of pancakes, a bunch of bananas—this cutter allowed me to make all three in addition to the Jack-o'-Lantern. You'll notice I make very conscious choices when it comes to decorating these cookies—by forgoing re-outlining George Washington's profile, you draw attention straight to his hair, which instantly tells everyone who he is.

The way the syrup flows down the stack of pancakes makes it seem as if it has just been poured. And re-outlining the bananas just so makes them look as if they are in a bunch.

JACK-O'-LANTERN

● beginner   ○ intermediate   ○ advanced

what you need

TO MAKE THE COOKIES
3-inch jack-o'-lantern cookie cutter

Cookie dough of choice (pages 26–33), prepared, chilled, and rolled out

Cooling racks

TO DECORATE
3 cups Royal Icing (pages 40–42)

Pasteurized egg white or water

Gel food colors: chocolate brown, whitener, sunset orange, lemon yellow

4 plastic or parchment paper piping bags (page 53)

4 #1 tips

Assorted paintbrushes

1. **Make the cookies.** Cut out 24 cookies from the dough. Bake and cool as directed.

2. **Make the brown lining and flooding icing for the stem; outline and paint in.** Mix ¼ cup royal icing in a bowl with chocolate brown gel to make brown for the stem. Thin to lining consistency and spoon 2 tablespoons into a piping bag fitted with a #1 tip. Thin the remaining icing to flooding consistency, add a little whitener, and cover with plastic wrap. Using the lining icing, outline the stem, leaving the bottom where it meets the pumpkin unlined. Let set for 5 minutes. Using a paintbrush and the brown flooding icing, paint in the stem, thinning out the icing where the pumpkin overlaps the stem. Let set for 1 hour.

3. **Make the orange lining and flooding icing for the pumpkin; outline and paint in.** Mix 1½ cups royal icing in a bowl with sunset orange gel to make orange for the pumpkin. Thin to lining consistency and spoon ¼ cup into a piping bag fitted with a #1 tip. Thin the remaining icing to flooding consistency and cover with plastic wrap. Using the lining icing, outline the silhouette of the pumpkin, going over the stem and making four bumps at the top of the cookie and four coordinating bumps at the bottom of the cookie. Using a paintbrush and the orange flooding icing, paint in the pumpkin. Let set until hard, 6 to 8 hours or overnight.

4. **Make lining icings: dark orange for the facial features and to re-outline the pumpkin and**

JACK-O'-LANTERN CONTINUES

brown for the stem. Refresh the royal icing on medium low for 30 seconds. Spoon ¼ cup icing into each of two bowls. Cover one with plastic wrap. To the other, add sunset orange and chocolate brown gels to make dark orange for the facial features and re-outlining the pumpkin. Thin to lining consistency and spoon it all into a piping bag fitted with a #1 tip. To the second bowl, add chocolate brown to make darker brown for outlining the stem. Thin to lining consistency and spoon it all into a piping bag fitted with a #1 tip.

5. **Outline the facial features and re-outline the pumpkin and stem; make the ribs.** Using the dark orange lining icing, outline the eyes, nose, and mouth (you can make any face you like, as if carving a pumpkin). Let set for 5 minutes. Using the same icing, re-outline the pumpkin and make the ribs, drawing curved horizontal lines to connect the tips of the top bumps with the tips of the bottom bumps, going around the eyes and avoiding the nose and mouth. Using the darker brown lining icing, re-outline the stem and draw in the ribs. Let set for 5 minutes.

6. **Make yellow flooding icing for the face.** Mix ¼ cup royal icing in a bowl with lemon yellow gel to make yellow for the face. Add whitener. Thin to flooding consistency and paint in the eyes, nose, and mouth carefully, butting the yellow up to the outlines. Let set until hard, 6 to 8 hours.

· · · · · · · · · · · · · · · · · · · MAKES 24 ·

PANCAKES

○ beginner ○ intermediate ● advanced

what you need

TO MAKE THE COOKIES
3-inch jack-o'-lantern cookie cutter

Cookie dough of choice (pages 26–33), prepared, chilled, and rolled out

Cooling racks

TO DECORATE
3 cups Royal Icing (pages 40–42)

Pasteurized egg white or water

Gel food colors: whitener, gold, lemon yellow, chocolate brown, buckeye brown, super black

5 plastic or parchment paper piping bags (page 53)

5 #1 tips

Assorted paintbrushes

Plate or ceramic mixing palette

1. **Make the cookies.** Cut out 24 cookies from the dough. Bake and cool as directed.

2. **Make white lining and flooding icing for the plate; outline and paint in.** Mix ½ cup royal icing in a bowl with whitener gel to make white for the plate and fork. Thin to lining consistency and spoon ¼ cup into a piping bag fitted with a #1 tip. Thin the remaining to flooding consistency and cover with plastic wrap. Position the cookie so that the pumpkin stem is the left side. Using the lining icing, outline the silhouette of the plate and the parts of the fork that don't overlap it, leaving the top edge of the plate unlined where the pancakes overlap. Let set for 5 minutes. Using a paintbrush and the white flooding icing, paint in the plate and fork, thinning out the icing where the pancakes will overlap. Let set until hard, 4 to 6 hours or overnight.

3. **Make yellow lining and flooding icing for the pancakes; outline and paint in.** Mix 1½ cups royal icing with gold, lemon yellow, and whitener gels to make golden yellow for the pancakes. Thin to lining consistency and spoon ¼ cup into a piping bag fitted with a #1 tip. Thin the remaining to flooding consistency and cover with plastic wrap. Using the lining icing, outline the silhouette of the stack of pancakes, starting above the fork handle and making small bumps for each pancake edge along the left edge of the cookie. Round out the top of the cookie and continue to make small bumps along the right edge of the cookie. Pipe the bottom edge of the pancake stack on top of the white icing and stop where the fork meets the pancakes. Let set for 5 minutes. Using a paintbrush and the flooding icing, paint in the stack of pancakes, butting up the icing (see page 64) to the fork. Let set until hard, 6 to 8 hours or overnight.

4. **Make brown lining and flooding icing for the maple syrup; make gray lining icing to re-outline the fork and plate.** Refresh the royal icing on medium low for 30 seconds. Mix ½ cup icing with chocolate brown and buckeye brown gels to make dark brown for the syrup. Thin to lining consistency and spoon ¼ cup into a piping bag fitted with a #1 tip. Thin the remaining icing to flooding consistency and cover with plastic wrap. Mix ¼ cup royal icing with super black and whitener gels to make light gray for re-outlining the fork and plate. Thin to lining consistency and spoon all of it into a piping bag fitted with a #1 tip.

5. **Outline the maple syrup and paint in. Re-outline the fork and outline the tines.** Using the dark brown lining icing, outline the maple syrup, drawing drips going down the stack of pancakes. Let set for 5 minutes. Reserve the brown lining icing. Using a paintbrush and the dark brown flooding icing, paint in the maple syrup. Let set for 4 to 6 hours. While the dark brown flooding icing sets, use the light gray lining icing to re-outline the plate and fork, including the top of the fork and the tines. Do not worry if you can squeeze in only three tines.

PANCAKES CONTINUES

6. **Re-outline the pancakes.** Using the reserved dark brown lining icing, re-outline the silhouette of the stack and outline each pancake by connecting the points on the left side to the points on the right. Draw a few pancakes in between the lines if you need to fill empty space. Let set for 5 minutes.

7. **Make yellow lining and flooding icing for the butter; outline and paint in.** After the flooding icing for the syrup sets, mix ¼ cup royal icing with lemon yellow and whitener gels to make yellow for the butter. Thin to lining consistency and spoon 2 tablespoons into a piping bag fitted with a #1 tip. Thin the remaining icing to flooding consistency and cover with plastic wrap. Using the lining icing, outline the butter pat on top of the maple syrup. Let set for 5 minutes. Using a paintbrush and the yellow flooding icing, paint in the butter pat.

8. **Make watercolor to paint the top half of each pancake.** Squeeze a dot of chocolate brown gel onto a plate or ceramic mixing palette. Using a paintbrush, mix in a little water to make a watercolor (see page 66). Paint the top half of each pancake in the stack, filling in the top of the very top one and working around the maple syrup. Let set for a few minutes.

● **MAKES 24** ● ● ● ● ● ● ● ● ● ● ● ● ● ● ● ● ●

GEORGE WASHINGTON

○ beginner ● intermediate ○ advanced

what you need

TO MAKE THE COOKIES
3-inch jack-o'-lantern cookie cutter

Cookie dough of choice (pages 26–33), prepared, chilled, and rolled out

Cooling racks

TO DECORATE
4½ cups Royal Icing (pages 40–42)

Pasteurized egg white or water

Gel food colors: ivory, whitener, super black, buckeye brown, sunset orange

5 plastic or parchment paper piping bags (page 53)

5 #1 tips

Assorted paintbrushes

1. **Make the cookies.** Cut out 24 cookies from the dough. Bake and cool as directed.

2. **Make skin tone lining and flooding icing for the face; outline and paint in.** Mix 1¼ cups royal icing with ivory and whitener gels to make skin tone color for the face. Thin to lining consistency and spoon ¼ cup into a piping bag fitted with a #1 tip. Thin the remaining icing to flooding consistency and cover with plastic wrap. Position the cookie so that the stem of the pumpkin is the nose of George Washington. Using the lining icing, outline the silhouette of the face, stopping where the chin meets the collar. Let set for 5 minutes. Using a paintbrush and the flooding icing, paint in the face, thinning out the icing where the hair overlaps the face and where the collar overlaps the neck. Let set until hard, 6 to 8 hours or overnight.

3. **Make gray lining and flooding icing for the hair and brown lining icing for the facial details.** Refresh the royal icing on medium low for 30 seconds. Mix 1¼ cups icing in a bowl with super black and whitener gels to make light gray for the hair. Thin to lining consistency and spoon ¼ cup into a piping bag fitted with a #1 tip. Thin the remaining icing to flooding consistency and cover with plastic wrap. Mix ¼ cup royal icing with buckeye brown gel to make brown for the face details. Thin to lining consistency and spoon all of it into a piping bag fitted with a #1 tip.

4. **Outline and paint in the hair and eyebrows. Make facial details.** Using the light gray lining icing, outline the silhouette of the hair, making big bumps along the edge for the curls. Outline the eyebrow. Let set for 5 minutes. Using a paintbrush and the light gray flooding icing, paint in the hair and the eyebrow. Let set for 4 to 6 hours. Using the brown lining icing, outline the eye. Draw a C shape to indicate the nostril and a short line in between the lips to indicate the mouth. Reserve the brown lining icing.

5. **Make lining and flooding icings: white for the collar and orange for the jacket.** While the light gray flooding icing sets, mix 1 cup royal icing with whitener gel to make bright white. Thin to lining consistency and spoon ½ cup into a piping bag fitted with a #1 tip. Thin the remaining icing to flooding consistency and cover with plastic wrap. Mix ½ cup royal icing with sunset orange gel to make orange for the jacket. Thin to lining consistency and spoon ¼ cup into a piping bag fitted with a #1 tip. Thin the remaining icing to flooding consistency and cover with plastic wrap.

6. **Outline and paint in the collar, jacket, and eye. Draw in the curls.** Using the white lining icing, outline the collar across the neck and under the chin, butting up (see page 64) the line to the bottom of the hair. Draw in the curls. Using the orange lining icing, outline the jacket, butting the orange line of the jacket up to the white line of the collar. Let set for 5 minutes. Using a

GEORGE WASHINGTON CONTINUES

paintbrush and the white flooding icing, paint in the collar and eye. Using another paintbrush and the orange flooding icing, paint in the jacket. Let set for 4 to 6 hours.

7. **Re-outline the hair. Outline and paint in the pupil.** When the light gray flooding icing is set, use the reserved white lining icing to re-outline the hair and draw in the curls. Draw a few short white lines on the eyebrow. Reserve the white lining icing. Let set for 5 minutes. When the white flooding icing for the eye is set, use the reserved brown lining icing to outline and fill in the pupil of the eye. Let set for 15 minutes. Using the reserved white lining icing, squeeze a small dot on the pupil for a highlight.

••••••••••••••••••••••••••••••••••• **MAKES 24** •••••••••••••••••••••••••••••••••••

BANANAS

○ beginner ● intermediate ○ advanced

what you need

TO MAKE THE COOKIES
3-inch jack-o'-lantern cookie cutter

Cookie dough of choice (pages 26–33), prepared, chilled, and rolled out

Cooling racks

TO DECORATE
2 cups Royal Icing (pages 40–42)

Pasteurized egg white or water

Gel food colors: lemon yellow, chocolate brown, whitener, gold

2 plastic or parchment paper piping bags (page 53)

2 #1 tips

Assorted paintbrushes

Plate or ceramic mixing palette

1. **Make the cookies.** Cut out 24 cookies from the dough. Bake and cool as directed.
2. **Make yellow lining and flooding icing for the bananas; outline and paint in.** Mix 1½ cups royal icing with lemon yellow and chocolate brown gels to make yellow. Thin to lining consistency and spoon ¼ cup into a piping bag fitted with a #1 tip. Thin the remaining icing to flooding consistency, add a little whitener, and cover with plastic wrap.

Using the lining icing, outline the silhouette of the bunch of bananas, making the top of the stem square. Let set for 5 minutes. Using a paintbrush and the flooding icing, paint in the bananas. Let set until hard, 6 to 8 hours or overnight.

3. **Make brown lining icing and re-outline the bananas and make details.** Refresh the royal icing on medium low for 30 seconds. Mix ¼ cup icing in a bowl with chocolate brown gel to make dark brown for outlining the bananas and adding details. Thin to lining consistency and spoon all of it into a piping bag fitted with a #1 tip. Using the brown lining icing, re-outline the silhouette of the bananas, then make the curved lines to delineate each banana. Let set for 5 minutes.

4. **Make watercolors and paint in details.** Squeeze dots of gold and chocolate brown gels onto a plate or ceramic mixing palette. With two paintbrushes, mix a little water into each to make watercolors (see page 66). Using the gold watercolor, lightly paint streaks along the length of each banana. Using the chocolate brown watercolor, paint in the stem and the ends of the bananas, then paint a few dots on each one. Let set for a few minutes.

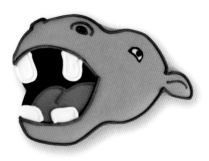

PEAR CUTTER

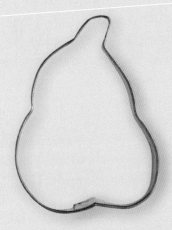

The pear cutter is the smallest one in this book, which makes the cookies great candidates for putting on sticks to make cookie pops. The Pear itself is an ideal cookie for beginners because it uses simple techniques.

Sometimes it's just fun to make cookies that are totally unexpected (see Sardines, page 215; Hair Dryer, page 246; Ship in a Bottle, page 111). Why would you ever make a ham-shaped cookie? It's just silly and it makes people laugh! And you would not likely find a ham cookie cutter anywhere else.

PEAR

● beginner   ○ intermediate   ○ advanced

what you need

TO MAKE THE COOKIES
2½-inch pear cookie cutter

Cookie dough of choice (pages 26–33), prepared, chilled, and rolled out

Cooling racks

TO DECORATE
1 cup Royal Icing (pages 40–42)

Pasteurized egg white or water

Gel food colors: lemon yellow, neon green, whitener, chocolate brown, sunset orange

2 plastic or parchment paper piping bags (page 53)

2 #1 tips

Assorted paintbrushes

Plate or ceramic mixing palette

1. **Make the cookies.** Cut out 24 cookies from the dough. Bake and cool as directed.

2. **Make the lining and flooding icing for the pear and outline.** Mix ¾ cup royal icing in a bowl with lemon yellow, neon green, and whitener gels to make golden yellow. Thin to lining consistency and spoon ¼ cup into a piping bag fitted with a #1 tip. Thin the remaining icing to flooding consistency and cover with plastic wrap. Using the golden yellow lining icing, outline the pear, not including the stem. Let set for 5 minutes.

3. **Make brown lining and flooding icing for the stem; outline and paint in.** Spoon ¼ cup royal icing into a bowl and mix in chocolate brown gel to make brown for the stem. Thin to lining consistency

and spoon 2 tablespoons into a piping bag fitted with a #1 tip. Thin the remaining icing to flooding consistency and cover with plastic wrap. Using the lining icing, outline the stem, touching the base of the stem to the top of the pear. Let set for 5 minutes. Reserve the brown lining icing.

4. **Paint in the pear and stem.** Using a paintbrush and the golden yellow flooding icing, paint in the pear. Using a paintbrush and the brown flooding icing, paint in the stem. Let set for 6 to 8 hours or overnight.

5. **Re-outline the stem. Make watercolors and paint on details.** Using the reserved brown lining icing, re-outline the stem. Squeeze a few dots of

PEAR CONTINUES

sunset orange and chocolate brown gels onto a mixing palette or plate. Using a medium paintbrush, mix a little water into the orange gel to make a watercolor (see page 66). Use it to shade the pear along the left side. Use a paintbrush and water to dilute the brown gel, then paint tiny specks in clusters on the pear. Let set for 15 minutes or until dry.

• MAKES 24 •

HAM

○ beginner ● intermediate ○ advanced

what you need

TO MAKE THE COOKIES
2½-inch pear cookie cutter

Cookie dough of choice (pages 26–33), prepared, chilled, and rolled out

Cooling racks

TO DECORATE
3 cups Royal Icing (pages 40–42)

Pasteurized egg white or water

Gel food colors: whitener, chocolate brown, buckeye brown, bright red, super black

5 plastic or parchment paper piping bags (page 53)

5 #1 tips

Assorted paintbrushes

1. **Make the cookies.** Cut out 24 cookies from the dough. Bake and cool as directed.

2. **Make white lining and flooding icing for the ham bone.** Mix ½ cup royal icing in a bowl with whitener gel to make bright white. Thin to lining consistency and spoon ¼ cup into a piping bag fitted with a #1 tip. Thin the remaining icing to flooding consistency and cover with plastic wrap.

3. **Outline and paint in the ham bone.** Position the cookie so that the stem of the pear is at 10 o'clock. Using the white lining icing, outline the tip of the ham bone. Let set for 5 minutes. Using a paintbrush and the white flooding icing, paint in the ham bone, thinning out the icing where the ham overlaps the bone. Let set for 1 hour. Reserve the white lining and flooding icing.

4. **Make brown lining and flooding icing for the skin; outline and paint in.** While the white icing sets, mix ½ cup royal icing with chocolate brown and buckeye brown gels to make brown for

the skin of the ham. Thin to lining consistency and spoon ¼ cup into a piping bag fitted with a #1 tip. Thin the remaining icing to flooding consistency, add whitener, and cover with plastic wrap. Using the brown lining icing, outline the skin of the ham following the edge of the cookie, making small bumps along both sides and going over the bone. Let set for 5 minutes. Using the brown flooding icing, paint in the ham skin. Let set for 4 to 6 hours.

5. **Make lining and flooding icing for the fat layer; outline and paint in.** Spoon ½ cup royal icing into a bowl, thin to lining consistency, and spoon ¼ cup into a piping bag fitted with a #1 tip. Thin the remaining icing to flooding consistency and cover the bowl with plastic wrap. Using the uncolored lining icing, outline the layer of fat, butting up (page 64) the interior line against the skin line. Make another line ¼ inch inside the outer line. Using a small paintbrush and the flooding icing, paint in the fat ring. Let set for 1 hour.

6. **Make pink flooding icing for the meat; paint in.** Mix ½ cup royal icing in a bowl with bright red, buckeye brown, and whitener gels to make pink for the ham. Thin to flooding consistency. Using a paintbrush, paint in the ham, butting the icing up to the interior line of the fat ring. Let set until hard, 6 to 8 hours or overnight.

7. **Outline and paint in the bone in the ham.** Using the reserved bright white lining icing, outline a small circle in the center of the pink icing.

Let set for 5 minutes. Using a paintbrush and the reserved white flooding icing, paint in the circle. Let set for 1 hour.

8. **Make dark brown and black lining icings; re-outline the ham and make details.** While the icing sets, beat the royal icing at medium low for 30 seconds. Mix ½ cup icing with chocolate brown and buckeye brown gels to make dark brown for re-outlining the ham and making the details on the skin. Thin to lining consistency and spoon it all into a piping bag fitted with a #1 tip. Mix 2 tablespoons icing with super black gel to make black for the inner circle. Thin to lining consistency and spoon it all into a piping bag fitted with a #1 tip. Using the darker brown lining icing, re-outline the skin of the ham, including the line that butts up against the fat ring. Make a grid pattern on the skin, drawing the horizontal lines first, followed by the vertical lines. Using the black lining icing, outline a black circle in the center of the bone in the ham, and fill in with the icing. Let set for 15 minutes or until dry.

FLOWER

○ beginner ● intermediate ○ advanced

what you need

TO MAKE THE COOKIES
2½-inch pear cookie cutter

Cookie dough of choice (pages 26–33), prepared, chilled, and rolled out

Cooling racks

TO DECORATE
2 cups Royal Icing (pages 40–42)

Pasteurized egg white or water

Gel food colors: neon orange, sunset orange, leaf green, neon green, whitener, lemon yellow

6 plastic or parchment paper piping bags (page 53)

6 #1 tips

Assorted paintbrushes

1. **Make the cookies.** Cut out 24 cookies from the dough. Bake and cool as directed.

2. **Make orange lining and flooding icing for the petals.** Mix ½ cup royal icing in a bowl with neon orange and sunset orange gels to make bright orange for the petals. Thin to lining consistency and spoon ¼ cup into a piping bag fitted with a #1 tip. Thin the remaining icing to flooding consistency, add whitener, and cover with plastic wrap.

3. **Outline and paint in the petals.** Position the cookie so that the pear stem is the bottom. Using the orange lining icing, outline the silhouette of the petals of the flower, noting that three are clustered together in the middle. Let set for 5 minutes.

Using a paintbrush and the orange flooding icing, paint in the petals. Let set for 2 to 4 hours.

4. **Make green lining and flooding icing for the leaves; outline and paint in.** While the orange icing sets, mix ½ cup royal icing in a bowl with leaf green and neon green to make green for the stem and leaves. Thin to lining consistency and spoon ¼ cup into a piping bag fitted with a #1 tip. Thin the remaining icing to flooding consistency, add whitener, and cover with plastic wrap. Using the lining icing, outline the stem and leaves, butting (see page 64) the top of the stem to the bottom of the petals and giving the leaves jagged edges by holding the piping tip close to the cookie. Let

set for 5 minutes. Using a paintbrush and the green flooding icing, paint in the stem and leaves. Let set for 2 to 3 hours.

5. **Make dark orange and dark green lining icings to re-outline the petals and stem. Make lemon yellow lining and flooding icing for the center of the flower.** When the orange and green flooding icings are set, spoon ¼ cup royal icing into each of three bowls. Cover two with plastic wrap. To the remaining bowl, add neon orange and sunset orange gels to make dark orange for re-outlining the petals. Thin to lining consistency and spoon it all into a piping bag fitted with a #1 tip. To the second bowl, add leaf green and neon green gels to make dark green for re-outlining the stem and petals. Thin to lining consistency and spoon it all into a piping bag fitted with a #1 tip. To the third bowl, add lemon yellow gel to make lemon yellow for the center of the flower. Thin to lining consistency and spoon ¼ cup into a piping bag fitted with a #1 tip. Thin the remaining icing to flooding consistency, add whitener gel, and cover with plastic wrap.

6. **Outline and paint in the center of the flower. Re-outline the petals, stem, and leaves. Make details.** Using the yellow lining icing, outline an oval for the center of the flower, piping it over the orange icing. Let set for 5 minutes. Using a paintbrush and the yellow flooding icing, paint in the oval. Let set for 1 hour. Meanwhile, use the dark orange lining icing to re-outline the flower petals. Use the dark green lining icing to re-outline the stem and leaves. Pipe a line down the center of each leaf.

7. **Make dark yellow lining icing and re-outline the center.** Mix ¼ cup royal icing in a bowl with lemon yellow gel to make dark yellow. Thin to lining consistency and spoon it all into a piping bag fitted with a #1 tip. Re-outline the yellow center. Holding the bag at a 45-degree angle and touching the tip to the cookie, make tiny dots in the center of the flower. Let set for 1 hour.

HIPPO

○ beginner   ○ intermediate   ● advanced

what you need

TO MAKE THE COOKIES

2½-inch pear cookie cutter

Cookie dough of choice (pages 26–33), prepared, chilled, and rolled out

Cooling racks

TO DECORATE

2 cups Royal Icing (pages 40–42)

Pasteurized egg white or water

Gel food colors: super black, regal purple, whitener, bright red

6 plastic or parchment paper piping bags (page 53)

6 #1 tips

Assorted paintbrushes

1. **Make the cookies.** Cut out 24 cookies from the dough. Bake and cool as directed.

2. **Make black lining and flooding icing for the inside of the mouth.** Mix ¼ cup royal icing in a small bowl with super black gel to make black. Thin to lining consistency and spoon 2 tablespoons into a piping bag fitted with a #1 tip. Thin the remaining icing to thin flooding consistency and cover with plastic wrap.

3. **Outline and paint in the mouth.** Position the cookie so that the pear stem is the hippo's ear. Using the black lining icing, outline the black part of the mouth only on the edge of the cookie between the top and bottom lips. Using a paintbrush and the flooding icing, thinly paint in the black

area of the mouth, thinning out the icing where the tongue and mouth overlap. Let set for 1 hour. Reserve the black lining icing.

4. **Make purple-gray lining and flooding icing for the hippo's head; outline and paint in.** Meanwhile, mix ¾ cup royal icing in a bowl with a toothpick each of super black, regal purple, and whitener gels to make purple-gray for the head. Thin to lining consistency and spoon ¼ cup into a piping bag fitted with a #1 tip. Thin the remaining purple-gray to flooding consistency and cover the bowl with plastic wrap. Using the lining icing, outline the hippo's head, including the open mouth and making a small bump for the nostril and a teardrop shape for the ear. Let set for

5 minutes. Using a paintbrush and the purple-gray flooding icing, paint in the head. Let set until hard, 6 to 8 hours or overnight.

5. **Outline the eye. Make red lining and flooding icing for the tongue; make dark purple lining icing to re-outline the hippo.** Refresh the royal icing on medium low for 30 seconds. Using the reserved black lining icing, outline the eye in a small half-moon shape. Reserve the black lining icing. Spoon ½ cup royal icing into each of two small bowls. Cover one with plastic wrap. To the remaining, add bright red gel to make red for the tongue. Thin to lining consistency and spoon 2 tablespoons into a piping bag fitted with a #1 tip. Thin the remaining red icing to flooding consistency and cover with plastic wrap. To the second bowl, add super black and regal purple gels to make dark purple-gray for re-outlining the hippo. Spoon it all into a piping bag fitted with a #1 tip.

6. **Outline and paint in the tongue. Re-outline the head and make details.** Using the red lining icing, outline the tongue (including under the teeth), butting up (see page 64) the line against the purple-gray rim of the mouth. Let set for 5 minutes. Using a paintbrush and the red flooding icing, paint in the tongue. Let set for 4 to 6 hours. Using the dark purple lining icing, re-outline the head. Outline the interior nostril and the curve of the ear.

7. **Make dark red lining icing and re-outline the tongue. Make white lining and flooding icing for the teeth; outline, paint in, and re-outline. Fill in eye and details.** Spoon ¼ cup royal icing into each of two bowls. Cover one with plastic wrap. To the other, add bright red gel to make dark red. Spoon it all into a piping bag fitted with a #1 tip. To the second bowl, add whitener gel to make white for the teeth. Thin to lining consistency and spoon 2 tablespoons icing into a piping bag fitted with a #1 tip. Thin the remaining icing to flooding consistency and cover with plastic wrap. Using the white lining icing, outline the upper and lower teeth, butting the white lines to the edge of the mouth. Fill in the eye with the tip of the white lining icing. Let set for 5 minutes. Reserve the white lining icing. Using a paintbrush and the white flooding icing, paint in the teeth. Let set for 1 hour. When the white flooding icing is set, use the reserved white lining icing to re-outline the teeth. Using the dark red lining icing, re-outline the tongue. Using the reserved black lining icing, make a dot for the pupil on top of the eye. Let set for 1 hour.

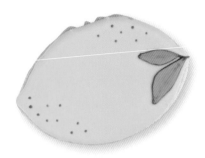

FOOTBALL CUTTER

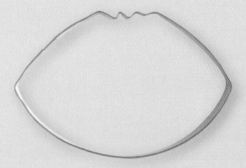

The only challenge I found with the football was deciding which of the many images I came up with to keep in this book. A horse's head, an eyeball, a classic Thanksgiving turkey, a holiday ornament—these are the shapes that got away. Every cookie in this group is perfect for first-time decorators (or experienced ones with little time to spare). Take liberties with the Leaf. Ice it in orange and yellow for autumn. And try the lips in various shades. They're perfect for Valentine's Day.

FOOTBALL

● beginner ○ intermediate ○ advanced

what you need

TO MAKE THE COOKIES
3½-inch football cookie cutter

Cookie dough of choice (pages 26–33), prepared, chilled, and rolled out

Cooling racks

TO DECORATE
2¼ cups Royal Icing (pages 40–42)

Pasteurized egg white or water

Gel food colors: chocolate brown, super black, whitener

3 plastic or parchment paper piping bags (page 53)

3 #1 tips

Assorted paintbrushes

1. **Make the cookies.** Cut out 24 cookies from the dough. Bake and cool as directed.

2. **Make dark brown lining and flooding icing for the football; outline and paint in.** Mix 1½ cups royal icing in a small bowl with chocolate brown and super black gels to make dark brown for the football. Do not make it too dark or the color may dry splotchy. Thin to lining consistency and spoon ¼ cup into a piping bag fitted with a #1 tip. Thin the remaining icing to flooding consistency, add a little whitener, and cover the bowl with plastic wrap. Using the lining icing, outline the silhouette of the football, following the shape of the cookie but leaving the ridged section

bare. Let set for 5 minutes. Using a paintbrush and the flooding icing, paint in the football. Let set until hard, 6 to 8 hours or overnight.

3. **Make white lining and flooding icing for the stripes and lacing; outline and paint in.** Refresh the royal icing on medium low for 30 seconds. Mix ½ cup icing with the whitener gel to make white for the stripes and lacing. Thin to lining consistency and spoon ¼ cup into a piping bag fitted with a #1 tip. Thin the remaining icing to flooding consistency and cover with plastic wrap. Using the lining icing, outline the laces on the top of the football and the stripes at either

FOOTBALL CONTINUES

end. Let set for 5 minutes. Using a paintbrush and the flooding icing, paint in the laces and stripes. Let set until hard, 6 to 8 hours or overnight.

4. **Make darker brown lining icing for the seam and outline.** Mix 2 tablespoons royal icing in a bowl with chocolate brown and super black gels to make a slightly darker brown for the seam. Thin to lining consistency and spoon all of it into a piping bag fitted with a #1 tip. Make the horizontal seam on the football, dipping the line slightly in the middle. Let set for 1 hour.

· MAKES 24 ·

LEAF

● beginner   ○ intermediate   ○ advanced

what you need

TO MAKE THE COOKIES
3½-inch football cookie cutter

Cookie dough of choice (pages 26–33), prepared, chilled, and rolled out

Cooling racks

TO DECORATE
2 cups Royal Icing (pages 40–42)

Pasteurized egg white or water

Gel food colors: leaf green, whitener, chocolate brown, bright red, lemon yellow, super black (or black fine-tipped edible marker)

4 plastic or parchment paper piping bags (page 53)

3 #1 tips

1 #1.5 tip

Assorted paintbrushes

1. **Make the cookies.** Cut out 24 cookies from the dough. Bake and cool as directed.

2. **Make green lining and flooding icing for the leaf; outline and paint in.** Mix 1½ cups royal icing in a bowl with leaf green gel and, if desired, a toothpick of chocolate brown to make a slightly dull green, for the leaf. Thin to lining consistency and spoon ¼ cup into a piping bag fitted with a #1 tip. Thin the remaining icing to flooding consistency, add a little whitener, and cover with plastic wrap. Using the lining icing, outline the leaf, making the edges somewhat jagged. Let set

for 5 minutes. Using a paintbrush and the green flooding icing, paint in the leaf. Let set overnight.

3. **Make dark green lining icing to re-outline the leaf and make the veins.** Refresh the remaining royal icing on medium low for 30 seconds. Mix ¼ cup royal icing with leaf green and chocolate brown gels to make dark green to outline the leaf and make the veins. Thin to lining consistency and spoon all of it into a piping bag fitted with a #1 tip. Re-outline the leaf, then make a line down the center from tip to tip. Make the veins on the cookie from the center line to the edges.

4. **Make red and yellow lining icings for the ladybug and caterpillar.** Mix 2 tablespoons royal icing in a bowl with bright red gel paste to make red for the ladybug. Thin to slightly looser than lining consistency (you want the ladybugs to spread out a bit) and spoon all of it into a piping bag fitted with a #1 tip. Mix 2 tablespoons icing with lemon yellow gel to make bright yellow for the caterpillar. Thin to slightly looser than lining consistency and spoon all of it into a piping bag fitted with a #1.5 tip.

5. **Make the ladybugs and caterpillar; make black dots and lines.** Using the red lining icing, make the ladybugs by setting the piping tip at a 45-degree angle on the cookie and squeezing the piping bag to make a small dot; make the dots slightly different sizes. Using the yellow lining icing, make the caterpillar using the same method and squeezing five or so narrow ovals onto the leaf in an arc, leaving a space after each one. Let set for 10 minutes. To finish the caterpillar, squeeze three additional yellow ovals in between the existing yellow ovals. Squeeze a slightly larger dot at one end for the caterpillar's head. Let set for 30 minutes. Using either a small paintbrush and super black gel to make black watercolor (see page 66) or a black fine-tipped edible marker, paint or draw the dots on the ladybug as well as the stripes and antennae on the caterpillar.

LIPS

● beginner   ○ intermediate   ○ advanced

what you need

TO MAKE THE COOKIES
3½-inch football cookie cutter

Cookie dough of choice (pages 26–33), prepared, chilled, and rolled out

Cooling racks

TO DECORATE
2 cups Royal Icing (pages 40–42)

Pasteurized egg white or water

Gel food colors: bright red, whitener

2 plastic or parchment paper piping bags (page 53)

2 #1 tips

Paintbrush

1. **Make the cookies.** Cut out 24 cookies from the dough. Bake and cool as directed.

2. **Make lining and flooding icing for the lips.** Mix 1½ cups royal icing in a bowl with bright red gel to make red. Thin to lining consistency and spoon ¼ cup into a piping bag fitted with a #1 tip. Thin the remaining icing to flooding consistency, add a little whitener, and cover with plastic wrap.

3. **Outline and paint in the lips.** Using the red lining icing, outline the silhouette of the lips, making sure to shape the upper lip as in the photo. Let set for 5 minutes. Using the paintbrush and the flooding icing, paint in the lips. Let set until hard, 6 to 8 hours or overnight.

4. **Make lining icing to re-outline lips and make detail.** Refresh the royal icing on medium low for 30 seconds. Mix ¼ cup icing with bright red gel paste to make a slightly darker red for re-outlining. Thin to lining consistency and spoon into a piping bag fitted with a #1 tip. Re-outline the lips, then make a horizontal line with a slight dip in the center from tip to tip. Let set for 1 hour.

LEMON

● beginner ○ intermediate ○ advanced

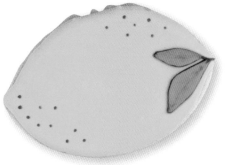

what you need

TO MAKE THE COOKIES
3½-inch football cookie cutter

Cookie dough of choice (pages 26–33), prepared, chilled, and rolled out

Cooling racks

TO DECORATE
2 cups Royal Icing (pages 40–42)

Pasteurized egg white or water

Gel food colors: lemon yellow, whitener, neon green, leaf green, chocolate brown

3 plastic or parchment paper piping bags (page 53)

3 #1 tips

Assorted paintbrushes

1. **Make the cookies.** Cut out 24 cookies from the dough. Bake and cool as directed.

2. **Make yellow lining and flooding icing for the lemon; outline and paint in.** Mix 1½ cups royal icing in a bowl with lemon yellow gel to make yellow. Stir in a drop of whitener. Thin to lining consistency and spoon ¼ cup into a piping bag fitted with a #1 tip. Thin the remaining icing to flooding consistency and cover with plastic wrap. Using the lining icing, outline the lemon, disguising the ridges on the side of the cookie. Using a paintbrush and the flooding icing, paint in the lemon. Let set until hard, 6 to 8 hours or overnight.

3. **Make green lining and flooding icing for the leaves; paint in.** Mix ¼ cup royal icing in a bowl with neon green and leaf green gels to make green for the leaves. Thin to lining consistency and spoon 2 tablespoons into a piping bag fitted with a #1 tip. Thin the remaining icing to flooding consistency, add a little whitener, and cover with plastic wrap. Using the lining icing, outline two leaves on one end of the lemon, then draw a stem from the leaves to the point. Using a paintbrush and the flooding icing, paint in the leaves.

4. **Make brown lining icing for the dots on the lemon; make the dots.** Mix ¼ cup royal icing with chocolate brown gel to make brown. Thin to lining consistency and spoon it all into a piping bag fitted with a #1 tip. Make a few small dots on opposite sides of the lemon, as shown. Let set until hard, about 3 hours.

GIFT TAG CUTTER

When I came up with the idea for this book, I knew I wanted certain cookies included. One was a toaster. So I was thrilled when I noticed that the end of the gift tag resembles not only the chin of Frankenstein's monster and a pile of popcorn, but a slice of bread, too. I worked it out from there by positioning the toaster onto the cookie at a three-quarters view, leaving space for the cord, a detail that really brings it to life.

GIFT TAG

○ beginner ● intermediate ○ advanced

what you need

TO MAKE THE COOKIES
3-inch gift tag cookie cutter

Cookie dough of choice (pages 26–33), prepared, chilled, and rolled out

Cooling racks

TO DECORATE
2 cups Royal Icing (pages 40–42)

Pasteurized egg white or water

Gel food colors: whitener, super black, bright red, gold, chocolate brown

4 plastic or parchment paper piping bags (page 53)

4 #1 tips

Paintbrush

Edible marker (optional)

---

1. **Make the cookies.** Cut out 24 cookies from the dough. Using a straw, punch out a hole where the grommet is on the tag. Bake and cool as directed.

2. **Make white lining and flooding icing for the tag; outline and paint in.** Mix 1¼ cups royal icing in a bowl with whitener gel to make white for the tag. Thin to lining consistency and spoon ¼ cup into a piping bag fitted with a #1 tip. Thin the remaining icing to flooding consistency and cover with plastic wrap. Using the lining icing, outline the gift tag, taking care to make the top and bottom lines parallel. Let set for 5 minutes. Using a large paintbrush and the white flooding icing, paint in the tag. Let set until hard, 6 to 8 hours or overnight.

3. **Make lining icings: gray to re-outline the tag, red for the writing, and brown for the hole.** Refresh the royal icing on medium low for 30 seconds. Spoon ¼ cup icing into each of three bowls. Cover two with plastic wrap. To the remaining bowl, add super black gel to make light gray for outlining the gift tag. Spoon all of it into a piping bag fitted with a #1 tip. To the second bowl, add bright red gel to make red for the writing and lines. Spoon all of it into a piping bag fitted with a #1 tip. To the third bowl, add gold and chocolate brown gels to make golden brown to outline the tag hole. Spoon all of it into a piping bag fitted with a #1 tip.

GIFT TAG CONTINUES

4. **Re-outline the tag; outline the hole; write on the tag.** Using the gray lining icing, re-outline the gift tag. Pipe a second line inside the outer one, leaving a space for the hole. Using the golden brown lining icing, outline the gift tag hole. Using the red lining icing, write "TO" and "FROM," one underneath the other, then pipe a horizontal line next to each word. Let set for 15 minutes or until hard. If desired, add names with edible marker.

• MAKES 24 •

FRANKENSTEIN'S MONSTER

○ beginner ● intermediate ○ advanced

what you need

TO MAKE THE COOKIES
3-inch gift tag cookie cutter

Cookie dough of choice (pages 26–33), prepared, chilled, and rolled out

Cooling racks

TO DECORATE
3 cups Royal Icing (pages 40–42)

Pasteurized egg white or water

Gel food colors: leaf green, neon green, super black, whitener, lemon yellow

3 plastic or parchment paper piping bags (page 53)

3 #1 tips

Assorted paintbrushes

1. **Make the cookies.** Cut out 24 cookies from the dough. Bake and cool as directed.

2. **Make green lining and flooding icing for the face; outline and paint in.** Mix 1 cup royal icing in a bowl with leaf green and neon green gels to make green for the monster's face. Thin to lining consistency and spoon ¼ cup into a piping bag fitted with a #1 tip. Thin the remaining icing to flooding consistency and cover with plastic wrap. Position the cookie so that the short flat side is the top. Using the green lining icing, outline the bottom half of the face, stopping where the

top of the ear meets the face. Using a medium paintbrush and the green flooding icing, paint in the face, thinning out the icing where the hair overlaps the forehead. Let set until hard, 6 to 8 hours or overnight.

3. **Make black lining and flooding icing for the hair; make dark green lining icing for re-outlining the face.** Refresh the royal icing on medium low for 30 seconds. Mix 1 cup icing in a bowl with super black gel to make black for the hair. Thin to lining consistency and spoon ¼ cup into a piping bag fitted with a #1 tip. Thin the remaining black icing to flooding consistency and cover with plastic wrap. Mix ¼ cup royal icing in a bowl with the leaf green and neon green gels to make darker green icing for re-outlining the face. Spoon all of it into a piping bag fitted with a #1 tip.

4. **Outline and paint in the hair and stripes; outline the eyes; make the nose and mouth. Re-outline the ears and chin; make details.** Using the black lining icing, outline the the silhouette of the hair. Outline the two stripes in the hair with wavy vertical lines. Outline the eyes and draw in the nose and mouth. Let set for 5 minutes. Using the darker green lining icing, re-outline the ears and chin. Draw the scar on the forehead and the half-moons in the inner ears. Using a small paintbrush and the black flooding icing, paint in the hair, excluding the gray stripes. Let set until hard, 6 to 8 hours or overnight.

5. **Make gray flooding icing for the stripes and yellow flooding icing for the eyes and paint in.** Spoon ¼ cup royal icing into a small bowl. Add super black and whitener gels to make light gray for the stripes in the hair. Thin to flooding consistency and cover with plastic wrap. To another bowl, add 2 tablespoons of royal icing. Add lemon yellow and whitener gels to make yellow for the eyes. Thin to flooding consistency and cover with plastic wrap. Using a small paintbrush and the light gray flooding icing, paint in the stripes in the hair, butting up (see page 64) the gray icing to the black lining icing. Using another small paintbrush and the yellow flooding icing, paint in the eyes. Let set for 4 to 6 hours. Reserve the black lining icing.

6. **Re-outline the hair, make pupils.** When the flooding icing is set, use the reserved black lining icing to re-outline the hair, then pipe dots on the eyes for pupils.

TOASTER

○ beginner ● intermediate ○ advanced

what you need

TO MAKE THE COOKIES
3-inch gift tag cookie cutter

Cookie dough of choice (pages 26–33), prepared, chilled, and rolled out

Cooling racks

TO DECORATE
2½ cups Royal Icing (pages 40–42)

Pasteurized egg white or water

Gel food colors: super black, whitener, chocolate brown, gold, ivory

5 plastic or parchment paper piping bags (page 53)

5 #1 tips

Assorted paintbrushes

1. **Make the cookies.** Cut out 24 cookies from the dough. Bake and cool as directed.

2. **Make gray lining and flooding icing for the toaster.** Mix 1¼ cups royal icing in a bowl with super black and whitener gels to make gray. Thin to lining consistency and spoon ¼ cup into a piping bag fitted with a #1 tip. Thin the remaining icing to flooding consistency and cover with plastic wrap.

3. **Outline and paint in the toaster.** Position the cookie so that the short flat side is the bottom. Using the gray lining icing, outline the silhouette of the toaster, skipping the part where the bread overlaps. Let set for 5 minutes. Using a medium paintbrush and the gray flooding icing, paint in the toaster, thinning out the icing where the bread overlaps the toaster. Let set until hard, 6 to 8 hours.

4. **Make lining icings: black for the openings and golden brown for the crust.** Refresh the royal icing on medium low for 30 seconds. Spoon ¼ cup icing into each of two bowls. Cover one with plastic wrap. To the other, mix in super black gel to make black for the openings. Thin to lining consistency and spoon all of it into a piping bag fitted with a #1 tip. To the second bowl, add chocolate brown and gold gels to make golden brown for the bread crust. Thin to lining consistency and spoon all of it into a piping bag fitted with a #1 tip.

5. **Outline the openings and fill in. Outline the bread crust.** Using the black lining icing, outline the openings at the top and side of the toaster. Holding the tip close to the cookie, fill in the openings. Let set for 5 minutes. Using the golden

brown lining icing, outline the bread. Let set for 5 minutes.

6. **Make flooding icing for the bread and paint in.** Mix ¼ cup royal icing in a bowl with ivory and whitener gels to make soft white for the bread. Thin to flooding consistency. Using a small paintbrush, carefully paint in the bread. Let set for 4 to 6 hours.

7. **Make lining icings: light gray to re-outline the toaster, white for the cord and details.** Spoon ¼ cup royal icing into each of two bowls. Cover one with plastic wrap. In the remaining bowl, mix super black and whitener gels to make light gray. Thin to lining consistency and spoon it all into a piping bag fitted with a #1 tip. To the second bowl, add whitener gel to make bright white for the toaster cord and shine mark. Thin to lining consistency and spoon into a piping bag fitted with a #1 tip. Using the light gray lining icing, re-outline the toaster, and make the interior line to give the toaster a ¾ perspective. Outline a small rectangle over the black opening on the side for the lever, holding the tip close to the cookie to fill it in. Reserve the gray lining icing. Using the bright white lining icing, make the electrical cord. Make the shine mark on the toaster. Using the reserved gray icing, outline a plug and hold the piping tip close to the cookie to fill it in. Draw in the prongs. Let set for 1 hour.

MAKES 24

MOVIE POPCORN

O beginner ● intermediate O advanced

what you need

TO MAKE THE COOKIES
3-inch gift tag cookie cutter

Cookie dough of choice (pages 26–33), prepared, chilled, and rolled out

Cooling racks

TO DECORATE
3 cups Royal Icing (pages 40–42)

Pasteurized egg white or water

Gel food colors: whitener, bright red, lemon yellow, gold

4 plastic or parchment paper piping bags (page 53)

3 #1 tips

1 #1.5 tip

Assorted paintbrushes

Plate or ceramic mixing palette

MOVIE POPCORN CONTINUES

1. **Make the cookies.** Cut out 24 cookies from the dough. Bake and cool as directed.

2. **Make white lining and flooding icing for the box; outline and paint in.** Mix 1¼ cups royal icing in a bowl with whitener gel to make white. Thin to lining consistency and spoon ¼ cup into a piping bag fitted with a #1 tip. Thin the remaining icing to flooding consistency and cover with plastic wrap. Using the lining icing, outline the silhouette of the popcorn and the box. Let set for 5 minutes. Using a large paintbrush and the white flooding icing, paint in the entire area and let set until hard, 6 to 8 hours or overnight.

3. **Make red lining and flooding icing for the stripes; outline and paint in.** Refresh the royal icing on medium low for 30 seconds. Mix ¾ cup icing in a small bowl with bright red gel to make the red stripes for the box. Thin to lining consistency and spoon ¼ cup into a piping bag fitted with a #1 tip. Thin the remaining icing to flooding consistency and cover with plastic wrap. Using the red lining icing, outline the popcorn box only, making a scalloped edge along the top of the box with five peaks. From the low point of each scallop, make a vertical line slightly on the diagonal to the bottom of the box. Let set for 5 minutes. Using a small paintbrush and the red flooding icing, thinly paint in every other stripe, beginning on the far left. Let set for 4 to 6 hours.

4. **Make white lining icing. Make the popcorn; outline the white stripes.** Spoon ¼ cup royal icing into a bowl. Add whitener to make white icing and thin to lining consistency. Spoon all of it into a pastry bag fitted with a #1 tip. Pipe random white dots in different sizes and clusters above the popcorn box. Leave space for the yellow popcorn. Let set for 10 minutes. Using the white lining icing, outline the white stripes on the box by butting them up to the red outlines. Reserve the remaining lining icing. Let set for 10 minutes.

5. **Make yellow lining icing for bigger popcorn kernels and apply.** Mix ¼ cup royal icing in a bowl with lemon yellow and whitener gels to make pale yellow popcorn. Thin to lining consistency and spoon it all into a piping bag fitted with a #1.5 tip. Make big dots of the icing on top of the white dots, covering the empty spaces. Let set for 5 minutes.

6. **Outline the white stripes. Add more popcorn.** When the white and red stripes have set, use the reserved bag of white lining icing to outline the white stripes on the box. Add more popcorn to the box by piping more white dots on top of the pale yellow dots. Let set for 5 minutes.

7. **Make watercolors for the kernels; paint on.** Squeeze a small dot of gold gel onto a plate or ceramic mixing palette. Using a small paintbrush, mix in a little water to make a watercolor (see page 66). Paint a few dots (sparingly) on the popcorn for kernels. Let set for 10 minutes.

TOMBSTONE CUTTER

From a tombstone cutter comes a rather disparate group of items, each one appealing to me in its own way. I love the quiet simplicity of the Building and the nostalgia that surfaces when looking at the sardine can that is opened with a key (note that it is entirely outlined in black, which makes it look like an illustration). The Tombstone benefits greatly from the cracks around the edges. Making them smooth wouldn't be nearly as haunting.

TOMBSTONE

○ beginner ● intermediate ○ advanced

what you need

TO MAKE THE COOKIES
3-inch tombstone cookie cutter

Cookie dough of choice (pages 26–33), prepared, chilled, and rolled out

Cooling racks

TO DECORATE
2½ cups Royal Icing (pages 40–42)

Pasteurized egg white or water

Gel food colors: leaf green, chocolate brown, whitener, super black, bright red

4 plastic or parchment paper piping bags (page 53)

4 #1 tips

Assorted paintbrushes

1. **Make the cookies.** Cut out 24 cookies from the dough. Bake and cool as directed.

2. **Make green flooding icing for the grass and paint on.** Mix ½ cup royal icing in a bowl with leaf green, chocolate brown, and whitener gels to make green for the grass. Thin to flooding consistency. Using a paintbrush, paint the grass along the bottom of the cookie close to the edge, thinning out the icing where the tombstone overlaps it. Let set until hard, 2 to 4 hours.

3. **Make gray lining and flooding icing for the tombstone.** Refresh the royal icing on medium low for 30 seconds. Mix 1¼ cups icing in a bowl with a toothpick each of super black and whitener gels to make gray for the tombstone. Thin to lining consistency and spoon ¼ cup into a piping bag

fitted with a #1 tip. Thin the remaining icing to flooding consistency and cover with plastic wrap.

4. **Outline the tombstone and paint in.** Using the gray lining icing, outline the tombstone, making indentations here and there to make it look chipped. Let set for 5 minutes. Using a paintbrush and the flooding icing, paint in the tombstone. Let set until hard, 6 to 8 hours or overnight.

5. **Make lining icings: dark gray to re-outline the tombstone and make details, red for the flowers, and dark green for the leaves.** Refresh the royal icing on medium low for 30 seconds. Spoon ¼ cup icing into each of three bowls. Cover two with plastic wrap. In the remaining bowl, add super black and whitener gels to make dark gray to re-outline the tombstone. Spoon all of

it into a piping bag fitted with a #1 tip. To the second bowl, add bright red gel to make red for the flowers. Thin to lining icing and spoon it all into a piping bag fitted with a #1 tip. To the third bowl, add leaf green and a toothpick of super black gel to make dark green for the leaves of the flowers. Spoon it all into a piping bag fitted with a #1 tip.

6. **Re-outline the tombstone and make details; make the leaves; make the flowers.** Using the dark gray lining icing, re-outline the tombstone.

Write in the letters "RIP" and draw in the cracks, touching the tip to the cookie and squeezing gently to make the lines thinner than the outline. Using the dark green lining icing, draw leaves on the grass by holding the piping tip at a 45-degree angle, touching the cookie, and squeezing the piping bag. Let set for 5 minutes. Using the red lining icing, draw the flowers, swirling the tip around on the surface to give the impression of a flower. Let set for 1 hour or until dry.

· · · · · · · · · · · · · · · MAKES 24 · · · · · · · · · · · · · · ·

ONESIE

○ beginner ● intermediate ○ advanced

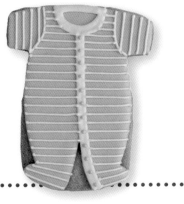

what you need

TO MAKE THE COOKIES
3-inch tombstone cookie cutter

Cookie dough of choice (pages 26–33), prepared, chilled, and rolled out

Cooling racks

TO DECORATE
2¼ cups Royal Icing (pages 40–42)

Pasteurized egg white or water

Gel food colors: neon green, bright blue, whitener, lemon yellow, super black

3 plastic or parchment paper piping bags (page 53)

3 #1 tips

Assorted paintbrushes

1. **Make the cookies.** Cut out 24 cookies from the dough. Bake and cool as directed.
2. **Make green lining and flooding icing for the onesie; outline and paint in.** Mix 1½ cups royal icing in a bowl with neon green, bright blue,

ONESIE CONTINUES

and whitener gels to make pastel green. Thin to lining consistency and spoon ¼ cup into a piping bag fitted with a #1 tip. Thin the remaining icing to flooding consistency and cover with plastic wrap. Position the tombstone cookie upside down so that the grass area is the top. Using the lining icing, outline the silhouette of the onesie. Let set for 5 minutes. Using a paintbrush and the flooding icing, paint in the onesie. Let set until hard, 6 to 8 hours or overnight.

3. **Make yellow lining and flooding icing for the stripes, collar, and placket; outline, paint in, and make stripes.** Refresh the royal icing on medium low for 30 seconds. Mix ½ cup icing in a bowl with a toothpick of lemon yellow gel to make light yellow for the stripes, collar, and placket. Thin to lining consistency and spoon ¼ cup into a piping bag fitted with a #1 tip. Thin the remaining

icing to flooding consistency and cover with plastic wrap. Using the lining icing, outline the collar and placket. Draw the seams where the arms meet the body. Let set for 5 minutes. Make evenly spaced horizontal stripes across the body of the onesie, stopping on the left side of the placket and starting again on the right side of the placket. Make vertical stripes on the sleeves. Using a paintbrush and the flooding icing, paint in the collar and placket. Let set until hard, 2 to 3 hours.

4. **Make gray lining icing for the snaps.** Mix ¼ cup royal icing in a bowl with a toothpick each of super black and whitener gels to make light gray for the snaps. Thin to lining consistency and spoon all of it into a piping bag fitted with a #1 tip. Hold the piping bag at a 45-degree angle to make small dots down the placket, spacing them evenly. Let set for 1 hour.

SARDINES

○ beginner   ○ intermediate   ● advanced

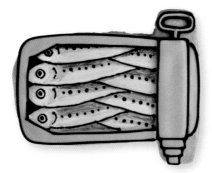

what you need

TO MAKE THE COOKIES
3-inch tombstone cookie cutter

Cookie dough of choice (pages 26–33), prepared, chilled, and rolled out

Cooling racks

TO DECORATE
3 cups Royal Icing (pages 40–42)

Pasteurized egg white or water

Gel food colors: super black, whitener, dark navy, electric pink, lemon yellow, super black, egg yellow, gold

5 plastic or parchment piping bags (page 53)

5 #1 tips

Assorted paintbrushes

Plate or ceramic mixing palette

1. **Make the cookies.** Cut out 24 cookies from the dough. Bake and cool as directed.

2. **Make gray lining and flooding icing for the can; outline and paint in.** Mix 1½ cups royal icing in a bowl with a toothpick each of super black and whitener gels to make light gray. Thin to lining consistency and spoon ¼ cup into a piping bag fitted with a #1 tip. Thin the remaining icing to flooding consistency and cover with plastic wrap. Using the lining icing, outline the silhouette of the sardine tin, including the ends of the rolled-back top but excluding the key. Let set for 5 minutes. Using a paintbrush and the flooding icing, paint in the sardine tin. Let set until hard, 6 to 8 hours or overnight.

3. **Make watercolors for the sardines and paint in.** Squeeze dots of dark navy and electric pink gels onto a plate or ceramic mixing palette. Using a watercolor brush, mix a little water into the navy to make a watercolor (see page 66). Outline the sardines so that they overlap. Paint in the negative space between the sardines. Using a clean paintbrush, mix a little water into the electric pink to make a watercolor. Paint on the bellies and around the gills. Using a clean paintbrush, mix a little water into the navy and shade the upper part of the sardines. Let set to dry 15 minutes.

4. **Make yellow lining icing for the eyes; make dark gray lining and flooding icing for the**

SARDINES CONTINUES

tin. Refresh the royal icing on medium low for 30 seconds. Spoon 2 tablespoons icing into a bowl. Add lemon yellow and whitener gels to make light yellow for the sardines' eyes. Thin to lining consistency and spoon it all into a piping bag with a #1 tip. Into another bowl, spoon ½ cup icing. Add super black gel to make dark gray for outlining the sardine tin. Thin to tight lining consistency and spoon ¼ cup of it into a piping bag fitted with a #1 tip. Thin the remaining icing to flooding consistency and cover with plastic wrap.

5. **Make the eyes. Re-outline the tin; outline the inside rim and key; paint in the rim.** Using the light yellow lining icing, make dots for the sardines' eyes. Using the dark gray lining icing, re-outline the tin, following the edge of the cookie and including the bottom of the rolled-up top. Make a second outline just inside this one, making an angle at the corners and squaring off the corners where the rolled top meets the sardines. Outline the key. Using a paintbrush and the dark gray flooding icing, paint in the rim of the tin. Let set until hard, 6 to 8 hours or overnight.

6. **Make black lining icing for details; make yellow flooding icing for lid.** Refresh the royal icing on medium low for 30 seconds. Spoon ¼ cup icing into a small bowl. Add super black gel to make black for the details on the sardines.

Thin to lining consistency and spoon all of it into a piping bag fitted with a #1 tip. Into the second bowl, spoon ½ cup royal icing. Add egg yellow and gold gels to make yellow-orange for the underside of the rolled top. Thin to lining consistency and spoon ¼ cup into a piping bag fitted with a #1 tip. Thin the remaining icing to flooding consistency, add a little whitener, and cover with plastic wrap.

7. **Outline and paint in the lid. Re-outline the tin and key and make coil details. Re-outline sardines; make eyes and details.** Using the yellow-orange lining icing, outline the silhouette of the rolled top. Let set 5 minutes. Using a paintbrush and the yellow-orange flooding icing, paint in the top. Let set for 2 to 3 hours. Using the black lining icing, re-outline the sardine tin, its inner lip, the key handle, and the rolled top, and make the coil details. Re-outline the sardines by drawing a black outline around each sardine with the tip touching the cookie, then outline each eye and draw in curved lines for the gills. Make dots down the length of each sardine as well as a dot in the eye of each sardine for the pupil. Let set for 1 hour.

BUILDING

○ beginner ● intermediate ○ advanced

what you need

TO MAKE THE COOKIES
3-inch tombstone
cookie cutter

Cookie dough of
choice (pages 26–33),
prepared, chilled, and
rolled out

Cooling racks

TO DECORATE
2¾ cups Royal Icing
(pages 40–42)

Pasteurized egg white
or water

Gel food colors: leaf
green, whitener, bright
red, sunset orange,
chocolate brown, super
black, lemon yellow

6 plastic or parchment
piping bags (page 53)

6 #1 tips

Assorted paintbrushes

1. **Make the cookies.** Cut out 24 cookies from the dough. Bake and cool as directed.

2. **Make lining and flooding icing for the grass; outline and paint in.** Mix ½ cup royal icing in a bowl with leaf green and whitener gels to make green for the grass. Thin to lining consistency and spoon ¼ cup into a piping bag fitted with a #1 tip. Thin the remaining icing to flooding consistency and cover with plastic wrap. Using the lining icing, outline the grass on the bottom of the cookie, including where the curb covers it. Using the green flooding icing, paint in the grass, thining it out where the building overlaps the grass. Let set for 4 to 6 hours.

3. **Make lining and flooding icings: red for the**

building and gray for the sidewalk. Refresh the royal icing on medium low for 30 seconds. Mix 1 cup icing with bright red, sunset orange, and chocolate brown gels to make brick red. Thin to lining consistency and spoon ¼ cup into a piping bag fitted with a #1 tip. Thin the remaining icing to flooding consistency, add whitener, and cover with plastic wrap. Mix ½ cup royal icing in a bowl with a toothpick each of super black and whitener gels to make light gray. Thin to lining consistency and spoon ¼ cup into a piping bag fitted with a #1 tip. Thin the remaining icing to flooding consistency and cover with plastic wrap.

4. **Outline and paint in the building, sidewalk, and entrance path.** Using the brick lining icing,

BUILDING CONTINUES

outline the silhouette of the building, going over the grass. Let set for 5 minutes. Reserve the brick lining icing. Using the light gray lining icing, outline the sidewalk including the path to the entrance. Let set for 5 minutes. Using a paintbrush and the brick flooding icing, paint in the building. Using a paintbrush and the gray flooding icing, paint in the sidewalk and path. Let set until hard, 6 to 8 hours or overnight.

5. **Outline the windows and doors and paint in.** Using the reserved brick lining icing, outline the windows and doors on the building. Make them smaller than they appear—it is very easy to make them too big. Let set for 5 minutes. Refresh the remaining icing on medium low for 30 seconds. Spoon 2 tablespoons of royal icing into each of two bowls. Cover one with plastic wrap. To the other, add lemon yellow and whitener gels to make yellow for the windows. Thin to flooding consistency and cover with plastic wrap. To the second bowl, add chocolate brown to make brown for the door. Thin to flooding consistency and cover with plastic wrap. Using a paintbrush and the yellow flooding icing, paint in the windows. Using another paintbrush and the brown flooding icing, paint in the door. Let set for 30 minutes.

6. **Make lining icings: brick to re-outline the building, black for the door, and gray for the sidewalk.** Spoon ¼ cup royal icing into a bowl. Add chocolate brown, sunset orange, and bright red gels to make dark brick for re-outlining the building. Thin to lining consistency and spoon it all into a piping bag fitted with a #1 tip. Spoon 2 tablespoons of royal icing into each of two bowls. Cover one with plastic wrap. To the first bowl, add super black gel to make black for re-outlining the front door. Thin to lining consistency and spoon it all into a piping bag fitted with a #1 tip. To the other bowl, add super black and whitener gels to make darker gray to re-outline the sidewalk. Thin to lining consistency and spoon it all into a piping bag fitted with a #1 tip.

7. **Re-outline the building, door, and sidewalk.** Using the brick lining icing, re-outline the building, then make the interior line to put it in ¾ perspective. Draw a short line under each window. Using the black lining icing, re-outline the door. Using the dark gray lining icing, re-outline the sidewalk. Let set for 15 minutes or until dry.

HEART CUTTER

Even if you're new to cookie decorating, I'd be surprised if you don't own a heart cutter, which means that you can make at least three other designs from it. And if your cutter is one in a graduated set, you can do even more—make a school of fish, a pumpkin patch, or a field of strawberries.

Simple shapes can be tough to disguise, especially if you don't fiddle with their orientation. These cookies are a little less about disguising the cutter shape than they are about filling it in an unexpected way.

HEART

○ beginner   ● intermediate   ○ advanced

what you need

TO MAKE THE COOKIES
3-inch heart cookie cutter

Cookie dough of choice (pages 26–33), prepared, chilled, and rolled out

Cooling racks

TO DECORATE
3 cups Royal Icing (pages 40–42)

Pasteurized egg white or water

Gel food colors: bright red, electric pink, whitener

2 plastic or parchment piping bags (page 53)

1 #1 tip

1 #1.5 tip

Assorted paintbrushes

1. **Make the cookies.** Cut out 20 cookies from the dough. Bake and cool as directed.

2. **Make red lining and flooding icing; make pink flooding icing.** Mix ¾ cup royal icing in a bowl with bright red gel to make red for the trim. Thin to lining consistency and spoon ¼ cup into a piping bag fitted with a #1 tip. Thin the remaining icing to flooding consistency and cover with plastic wrap. Mix 1½ cups royal icing in a bowl with electric pink and whitener gels to make pink. Thin to flooding consistency and cover with plastic wrap.

3. **Outline the red trim and paint in. Paint in the pink heart.** Using the red lining icing, outline the heart about ¼ inch from the edge. In that ¼-inch space, draw a scalloped edge all the way around the heart, making the bumps big

enough to reach the edge of the cookie. Let set for 5 minutes. Reserve the red lining icing. Using a paintbrush and the red flooding icing, paint in the scallops. Using a paintbrush and the pink flooding icing, paint in the heart. Let set until hard, 6 to 8 hours or overnight.

4. **Make white lining and flooding icing for the center heart.** Refresh the royal icing on medium low for 30 seconds. Mix ¾ cup royal icing in a bowl with whitener gel to make white for the center heart. Thin to lining consistency and spoon ¼ cup into a piping bag fitted with a #1.5 tip. Thin the remaining icing to flooding consistency and cover with plastic wrap.

5. **Outline the central heart. Re-outline the pink heart and trim; make details.** Using the

reserved red lining icing, outline the central heart on top of the pink icing, following the shape of the larger heart. Still using the red lining icing, re-outline the pink heart and the scalloped edge. Let set for 5 minutes. Reserve the red lining icing. With the white lining icing, pipe a dot in the middle of each scallop.

6. **Paint in the white heart; make details.** Using a paintbrush and the white flooding icing, paint in the smaller central heart, using enough icing to make it slightly puffy. Let icing set for 2 hours. Using the reserved red lining icing, holding the piping tip at a 45-degree angle and touching the cookie, make a border of tiny dots around the center heart, butting them up (see page 64) to the outline and spacing them slightly apart so that they do not blend together. Let set for 6 to 8 hours or overnight.

······ MAKES 20 ······

PUMPKIN

● beginner ○ intermediate ○ advanced

what you need

TO MAKE THE COOKIES
3-inch heart cookie cutter

Cookie dough of choice (pages 26–33), prepared, chilled, and rolled out

Cooling racks

TO DECORATE
3½ cups Royal Icing (pages 40–42)

Pasteurized egg white or water

Gel food colors: sunset orange, lemon yellow, whitener, neon green, buckeye brown, leaf green

6 plastic or parchment piping bags (page 53)

6 #1 tips

Assorted paintbrushes

1. **Make the cookies.** Cut out 20 cookies from the dough. Bake and cool as directed.

2. **Make brown lining and flooding icing for the stem; outline and paint in.** Mix ½ cup royal icing in a bowl with buckeye brown gel to make brown for the stem of the pumpkin. Thin to lining consistency and spoon ¼ cup into a piping

PUMPKIN CONTINUES

bag fitted with a #1 tip. Thin the remaining icing to flooding consistency and cover with plastic wrap. Position the cookie so that the heart is upside down. Using the brown lining icing, outline the stem, leaving the bottom unlined where the leaves and pumpkin overlap it. Let set for 5 minutes. Using a paintbrush and the brown flooding icing, paint in the stem, thinning it out where the leaves and pumpkin overlap the stem. Let set for 1 hour.

3. **Make orange lining and flooding icing for the pumpkin; outline and paint in.** Mix 1½ cups royal icing with sunset orange and lemon yellow gels to make orange for the pumpkin. Thin to lining icing and spoon ¼ cup into a piping bag fitted with a #1 tip. Thin the remaining icing to flooding consistency and cover with plastic wrap. Using the orange lining icing, outline the pumpkin, going over the bottom of the stem. Let set for 5 minutes. Using a paintbrush and the orange flooding icing, paint in the pumpkin. Let set until hard, 6 to 8 hours or overnight.

4. **Make green lining and flooding icing for the leaves;. outline and paint in.** Refresh the royal icing on medium low for 30 seconds. Mix ½ cup icing with neon green and leaf green gels to make bright green. Thin to lining consistency and spoon ¼ cup into a piping bag fitted with a #1 tip. Thin the remaining icing to flooding consistency and cover with plastic wrap. Using the green lining icing, outline the leaves, starting each leaf from the top of the pumpkin, piping over the stem and out to the edge of the cookie. Hold the piping tip close to the cookie to make the edges of the leaves slightly ruffled. Let set for 5 minutes. Using a paintbrush and the green flooding icing, paint in the leaves. Let set for 2 hours.

5. **Make lining icings: orange to re-outline the pumpkin, dark green for the leaves, and dark brown for the stem.** Refresh the royal icing on medium low for 30 seconds. Spoon ¼ cup icing into each of three bowls. Cover two with plastic wrap. To the remaining bowl, add sunset orange gel to make dark orange. Thin to lining consistency and spoon it all into a piping bag fitted with a #1 tip. To the second bowl, add leaf green gel to make darker green. Thin to lining consistency and spoon all of it into a piping bag fitted with a #1 tip. To the third bowl, add buckeye brown gel to make darker brown. Thin to lining consistency and spoon it all into a piping bag fitted with a #1 tip.

6. **Re-outline the pumpkin and make the ridges. Re-outline the leaves and make the veins. Re-outline the stem and make details.** Using the darker orange lining icing, re-outline the pumpkin and add the vertical ridges. Let set for 5 minutes. Using the darker green lining icing, re-outline the leaves and add the veins. Make tendrils down the front of the pumpkin, going over the ridges. Using the darker brown lining icing, re-outline the stem, drawing in the details. Let set for 1 hour.

STRAWBERRY

● beginner ○ intermediate ○ advanced

what you need

TO MAKE THE COOKIES
3-inch heart cookie cutter

Cookie dough of choice (pages 26–33), prepared, chilled, and rolled out

Cooling racks

TO DECORATE
2½ cups Royal Icing (pages 40–42)

Pasteurized egg white or water

Gel food colors: bright red, leaf green, neon green, lemon yellow, whitener

4 plastic or parchment paper piping bags (page 53)

4 #1 tips

Assorted paintbrushes

1. **Make the cookies.** Cut out 20 cookies from the dough. Bake and cool as directed.

2. **Make red lining and flooding icing for the strawberry; outline and paint in.** Mix 1½ cups royal icing in a bowl with the bright red gel to make red. Thin to lining consistency and spoon ¼ cup into a piping bag fitted with a #1 tip. Thin the remaining icing to flooding consistency and cover with plastic wrap. Using the lining icing, outline the strawberry, following the shape of the cookie and rounding the tip at the bottom. Let set for 5 minutes. Reserve the red lining icing. Using a paintbrush and the flooding icing, paint in the strawberry. Let set until hard, 6 to 8 hours or overnight.

3. **Make green lining and flooding icing for the leaves; outline and paint in.** Refresh the royal icing on medium low for 30 seconds. Mix ½ cup icing with leaf green and neon green gels to make green. Thin to lining consistency and spoon ¼ cup into a piping bag fitted with a #1 tip. Thin the remaining icing to flooding consistency and cover with plastic wrap. Using the green lining icing, outline the three leaves at the top of the strawberry. Let set for 5 minutes. Using a paintbrush and the green flooding icing, paint in the leaves. Let set for 2 to 3 hours.

4. **Make yellow lining icing and make the seeds.** Mix ¼ cup royal icing with lemon yellow and whitener gels to make yellow for the seeds.

STRAWBERRY CONTINUES

Thin to lining consistency and spoon into a piping bag fitted with a #1 tip. Draw seeds on the strawberry, spacing them evenly apart, and drag the tip toward you to make them tear-shaped.

5. **Make green lining icing to re-outline the leaves; re-outline the strawberry and leaves and make the details.** Mix ¼ cup royal icing with leaf green gel to make darker green. Thin to lining consistency and spoon all of it into a piping bag fitted with a #1 tip. Using the reserved red lining icing, re-outline the strawberry. Using the dark green lining icing, re-outline the leaves and add the veins. Let set for 1 hour.

· · · · · · · · · · · · · · · · MAKES 20 · · · · · · · · · · · · · · · ·

FISH

○ beginner ● intermediate ○ advanced

what you need

TO MAKE THE COOKIES
3-inch heart cookie cutter

Cookie dough of choice (pages 26–33), prepared, chilled, and rolled out

Cooling racks

TO DECORATE
4 cups Royal Icing (pages 40–42)

Pasteurized egg white or water

Gel food colors: leaf green, neon green, whitener, electric pink, lemon yellow, super black (or black edible marker)

6 plastic or parchment paper piping bags (page 53)

6 #1 tips

Assorted paintbrushes

1. **Make the cookies.** Cut out 20 cookies from the dough. Bake and cool as directed.

2. **Make lining and flooding icings: light green for the fish and pink for the fins.** Spoon 1¼ cups royal icing in each of two bowls. Cover one with plastic wrap. To the other, add leaf green, neon green, and whitener gels to make light green. Thin to lining consistency and spoon ¼ cup into a piping bag fitted with a #1 tip. Thin the remaining icing to flooding consistency and cover with plastic wrap. To the second bowl, add electric pink and whitener gels to make medium pink. Thin to lining consistency and spoon ¼ cup into a piping bag fitted with a #1 tip. Thin

the remaining icing to flooding consistency and cover with plastic wrap.

3. **Outline and paint in the fish and fins.** Position the cookie so that the point of the heart is on the left. Leaving space on the top, bottom, and right edge of the cookie for the fins, outline the fish's body using the light green lining icing. Allow the icing to set for 10 minutes. Using the pink lining icing, outline the top, bottom, and tail fins, stopping at the outline of the fish. Let set for 5 minutes. Reserve the pink lining icing. Using a paintbrush and the green flooding icing, paint in the fish's body. Using a paintbrush and the pink flooding icing, paint in the fins. Let set until hard, 6 to 8 hours or overnight. Reserve the pink flooding icing.

4. **Make yellow lining and flooding icing for the stripes, eye, and mouth; outline and paint in.** Refresh the royal icing on medium low for 30 seconds. Mix ½ cup royal icing in a bowl with lemon yellow and whitener gels to make yellow for the stripes, mouth, and eye. Thin to lining consistency and spoon ¼ cup into a piping bag fitted with a #1 tip. Thin the remaining to flooding consistency and cover with plastic wrap. Using the yellow lining icing, outline two stripes, making them slightly curvy and one shorter than the other. Make the outline for the nose and the eye. Let set for 5 minutes. Using a paintbrush and the yellow flooding icing, paint in the stripes and the nose. Add a little whitener to the icing, then paint in the eye. Let set for 2 to 3 hours.

5. **Make dark green lining icing; re-outline the fish and make the mouth and gill.** While the yellow flooding icing sets, mix ¼ cup royal icing with leaf green and neon green gels to make darker green. Thin to lining consistency and spoon it all into a piping bag fitted with a #1 tip. Re-outline the fish's body, excluding the fins and tail but including the nose. Draw a short horizontal line onto the yellow icing for the mouth. Add the green gill under the eye. Let set for 5 minutes.

6. **Outline and paint in the side fin.** Using the reserved pink lining icing, outline the side fin, beginning at the gill and going over one yellow stripe. Let set for 5 minutes. Using a paintbrush and the reserved pink flooding icing, paint in the side fin, stopping at the green gill line. Let set for 4 to 6 hours.

7. **Make dark pink lining icing; re-outline the fins and tail. Make the eye.** Mix ¼ cup royal icing in a bowl with electric pink gel to make darker pink. Thin to lining consistency and spoon it all into a piping bag fitted with a #1 tip. Mix 2 tablespoons royal icing in a bowl with super black gel to make black for the eye, or use a black edible marker. Thin to lining consistency and spoon into a piping bag fitted with a #1 tip. Using the darker pink lining icing, re-outline the fins and tail, then add lines inside the fins and tail. Using the black lining icing, draw a circle inside the yellow circle for the pupil, using the piping tip to fill in the circle with black icing. Let set for 1 hour.

ICE CREAM CONE CUTTER

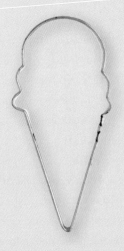

Coming up with designs for this cutter was easy when I positioned it right side up and upside down, but looking at it on its side was another story—until I thought about perspective. The Train might look daunting, but the shape of the cone gets you halfway there. It's like a cheat sheet for learning how to paint in perspective.

The ice cream cone is a fabulous summer cookie. Try adding sprinkles to it while the icing is still wet.

ICE CREAM CONE

○ beginner ● intermediate ○ advanced

what you need

TO MAKE THE COOKIES
4-inch ice cream cone cookie cutter

Cookie dough of choice (pages 26–33), prepared, chilled, and rolled out

Cooling racks

TO DECORATE
2½ cups Royal Icing (pages 40–42)

Pasteurized egg white or water

Gel food colors: gold, chocolate brown, whitener, electric pink, neon green, bright blue

4 plastic or parchment piping bags (page 53)

4 #1 tips

Assorted paintbrushes

---

1. **Make the cookies.** Cut out 24 cookies from the dough. Bake and cool as directed.

2. **Make golden brown lining and flooding icing for the cone; outline and paint in.** Mix ¾ cup royal icing in a bowl with gold, chocolate brown, and whitener gels to make golden brown for the cone. Thin to lining consistency and spoon ¼ cup into a piping bag fitted with a #1 tip. Thin the remaining to flooding consistency, add a little more whitener, and cover with plastic wrap. Using the golden brown lining icing, outline the cone, rounding the tip and leaving bare the top of the cone where the pink ice cream overlaps. Let set for 5 minutes. Reserve the golden brown lining icing. Using a paintbrush and the golden brown flooding icing, paint in the cone, thinning out the icing where the pink overlaps it. Let set for 2 to 3 hours.

3. **Make pink lining and flooding icing for the strawberry scoop; outline and paint in.** Mix ¾ cup royal icing in a bowl with electric pink and whitener gels to make pink. Thin to lining consistency and spoon ¼ cup into a piping bag fitted with a #1 tip. Thin the remaining icing to flooding consistency and cover with plastic wrap. Using the lining icing, outline the strawberry scoop, making a wavy line where it overlaps the cone and leaving the top of the pink scoop unlined. Let set for 5 minutes. Reserve the pink lining icing. Using a paintbrush and the pink flooding icing,

ICE CREAM CONE CONTINUES

paint in the strawberry scoop, thinning out the icing where the mint chocolate chip scoop overlaps. Let set for 2 hours.

4. **Make green lining and flooding icing for the mint scoop; outline and paint in.** Mix ¾ cup royal icing with the neon green, bright blue, and whitener gels to make mint green. Thin to lining consistency and spoon ¼ cup into a piping bag fitted with a #1 tip. Thin the remaining icing to flooding consistency and cover with plastic wrap. Using the green lining icing, outline the mint chocolate chip scoop, making a wavy line on the bottom of the scoop where it overlaps the strawberry scoop. Let set for 5 minutes. Reserve the green lining icing. Using a paintbrush and the mint green flooding icing, paint in the scoop. Let set for 1 hour.

5. **Re-outline the scoops and cone. Make the waffle pattern.** Using the reserved pink lining icing, re-outline the strawberry scoop. Using the reserved green lining icing, re-outline the mint chocolate chip scoop. Using the reserved golden brown lining icing, re-outline the cone, then make the waffle pattern on it by making diagonal lines spaced evenly apart going in one direction, then repeating going in the opposite direction. Let set for 5 minutes.

6. **Make brown lining icing for the chips and draw on.** Refresh the royal icing on medium low for 30 seconds. Mix ¼ cup royal icing with chocolate brown gel to make dark brown for the chocolate chips. Thin to lining consistency and spoon it all into a piping bag fitted with a #1 tip. Draw the chips onto the mint green ice cream, touching the cookie with your tip and squeezing the bag, moving it around slightly to make irregular shapes.

• • • • • • • • • • • • • • • MAKES 24 • • • • • • • • • • • • • • • • •

TRAIN

○ beginner   ○ intermediate   ● advanced

what you need

TO MAKE THE COOKIES
4¼-inch ice cream cone cookie cutter

Cookie dough of choice (pages 26–33), prepared, chilled, and rolled out

Cooling racks

TO DECORATE
4½ cups Royal Icing (pages 40–42)

Pasteurized egg white or water

Gel food colors: super black, whitener, royal blue, leaf green, egg yellow, bright red, lemon yellow

12 plastic or parchment paper piping bags (page 53)

12 #1 tips

Assorted paintbrushes

1. **Make the cookies.** Cut out 24 cookies from the dough. Bake and cool as directed.

2. **Make lining and flooding icings for the train cars.** Spoon ½ cup royal icing into each of four bowls. Cover three with plastic wrap. To the remaining bowl, add a toothpick each of super black and whitener gels to make gray for the front of the train. Thin to lining consistency and spoon ¼ cup into a piping bag fitted with a #1 tip. Thin the remaining icing to flooding consistency and cover with plastic wrap. To the second bowl, add royal blue gel to make blue for two of the train cars. Thin to lining consistency and spoon ¼ cup into a piping bag fitted with a #1 tip. Thin the remaining icing to flooding consistency and cover with plastic wrap. To the third bowl, add leaf green gel to make green for two of the cars. Thin to lining consistency and spoon ¼ cup into a piping bag fitted with a #1 tip. Thin the remaining icing to flooding consistency and cover with plastic wrap. To the fourth bowl, add egg yellow gel to make orange-yellow for one of the cars. Thin to lining consistency and spoon ¼ cup into a piping bag fitted with a #1 tip. Thin the remaining icing to flooding consistency and cover with plastic wrap.

3. **Outline the cars and paint in.** Position the cookie so that the point of the cone is on the right. Using the gray lining icing, outline the silhouette of the front of the train, including the light. Using the blue, green, and orange-yellow lining icings, outline the remaining train cars as pictured, butting up (see page 64) the lines that sit next to each other and making each car progressively smaller as you work from left to right. Be sure to leave enough space at the bottom of the cookie for the wheels. Using the orange-yellow lining icing, outline the two smokestacks on the top of the train. Let set for 5 minutes. Paint in all the cars in their respective colors with the flooding icings. Paint in the smokestacks with orange-yellow flooding icing. Let set until hard, 6 to 8 hours or overnight.

4. **Make lining and flooding icings: pale blue for the windows and red for the wheels.** Refresh the royal icing on medium low for 30 seconds. Spoon ½ cup royal icing into each of two bowls. Cover one with plastic wrap. To the other, add a tiny toothpick of royal blue gel to make pale blue for the windows. Thin to lining consistency and spoon ¼ cup into a piping bag fitted with a #1 tip. Thin the remaining icing to flooding consistency and cover with plastic wrap. To the second bowl, add bright red gel to make red for the wheels. Spoon ¼ cup icing into a piping bag fitted with a #1 tip. Thin the remaining icing to flooding consistency and cover with plastic wrap.

5. **Outline the windows and wheels.** Using the pale blue lining icing, draw the windows on the train cars, making them progressively thinner as

TRAIN CONTINUES

you work from left to right. Let set for 5 minutes. Using the red lining icing, outline the wheels, drawing the tops over the painted cars, making them big enough to touch the bottom edge of the cookie, and making them progressively smaller as you work from left to right. Outline the front wheel of the other side of the train. Let set for 5 minutes.

6. **Paint in the windows and wheels.** Using a paintbrush and the pale blue flooding icing, thinly paint in the windows so that they appear like glass. Using a paintbrush and the red flooding icing, paint in the wheels. Let set for 4 to 6 hours.

7. **Make lining icings to re-outline the cars.** Spoon ¼ cup royal icing into each of four bowls. Cover three bowls with plastic wrap. To the remaining, add super black and whitener gels to make darker gray for re-outlining the front of the train. Thin to lining consistency and spoon it all into a piping bag fitted with a #1 tip. To the second bowl, add royal blue gel to make darker blue to re-outline the blue cars. Thin to lining consistency and spoon it all into a piping bag fitted with a #1 tip. To the third bowl, add leaf green gel to make darker green to re-outline the green cars. Thin to lining consistency and spoon it all into a piping bag fitted with a #1 tip. To the fourth bowl, add egg yellow gel to make darker orange-yellow for re-outlining the orange car. Thin to lining consistency and spoon it all into a piping bag fitted with a #1 tip.

8. **Re-outline the cars and make details.** Using the darker gray lining icing, re-outline the front of the train, adding ovals to indicate the front face and the light. Draw the grate at the bottom so that it is attached to the train and touching the edge of the cookie. Using the remaining re-outlining icings, re-outline the train cars and windows in their respective colors. Re-outline the smokestacks with the darker orange-yellow lining icing.

9. **Make red lining icing to re-outline the wheels; make yellow lining icing for the wheel details.** Spoon ¼ cup royal icing into each of two bowls. Cover one with plastic wrap. To the other, add bright red gel to make red for re-outlining the wheels. Thin to lining consistency and spoon it all into a piping bag fitted with a #1 tip. To the second bowl, add lemon yellow and whitener gels to make yellow for the center of each wheel and the light. Thin to lining consistency and spoon all of it into a piping bag fitted with a #1 tip. Using the red lining icing, re-outline the wheels. Pipe a yellow dot in the middle of each wheel. Using the tip of the yellow icing, fill in the front light. Let set for 1 hour or until dry.

GNOME

○ beginner   ○ intermediate   ● advanced

what you need

TO MAKE THE COOKIES
4¼-inch ice cream cone cookie cutter

Cookie dough of choice (pages 26–33), prepared, chilled, and rolled out

Cooling racks

TO DECORATE
4 cups Royal Icing (pages 40–42)

Pasteurized egg white or water

Gel food colors: bright red, super black, whitener, copper (flesh), royal blue (or blue edible marker)

8 plastic or parchment piping bags (page 53)

8 #1 tips

Assorted paintbrushes

1. **Make the cookies.** Cut out 24 cookies from the dough. Bake and cool as directed.

2. **Make lining and flooding icing for the face; outline and paint in.** Mix ¾ cup royal icing in a bowl with copper (flesh) and whitener gels to make skin tone for the gnome's face. Thin to lining consistency and spoon ¼ cup into a piping bag fitted with a #1 tip. Thin the remaining icing to flooding consistency and cover with plastic wrap. Using the lining icing, outline the ears. Using a paintbrush and the flooding icing, paint in the ears as well as the area of the cookie where the gnome's face will be, thinning out the icing in the areas where the hat, beard, and mustache overlap the face. Let set for 4 to 6 hours.

3. **Make lining and flooding icings: gray for the beard and red for the hat.** Spoon ¾ cup royal icing into each of two bowls. Cover one with plastic wrap. To the other, add super black and whitener gels to make light gray. Thin to lining consistency and spoon ¼ cup into a piping bag fitted with a #1 tip. Thin the remaining icing to flooding consistency and cover with plastic wrap. To the second bowl, add bright red gel to make red. Thin to lining consistency and spoon ¼ cup into a piping bag fitted with a #1 tip. Thin the remaining icing to flooding consistency and cover with plastic wrap.

4. **Outline and paint in the beard, mustache, and hat.** Using the light gray lining icing, outline

GNOME CONTINUES

the silhouette of the beard and mustache, stopping the line at the top of the ears where the hat overlaps. Leave a little area of skin showing under the mustache and above the beard for the lip. Let set for 5 minutes. Using a paintbrush and the light gray flooding icing, paint in the beard and mustache, thinning out the icing where the hat overlaps. Let set for 1 hour. Using the red lining icing, outline the hat, going over the top of the beard and the face. Let set for 5 minutes. Using a paintbrush and the red flooding icing, paint in the hat. Let set until hard, 6 to 8 hours or overnight.

5. **Make lining icings: red for re-outlining the hat, dark gray for the beard, skin tone for the face, and white for the eyes.** Refresh the royal icing on medium low for 30 seconds. Spoon ¼ cup royal icing into each of three bowls. Cover two with plastic wrap. To the remaining one, add super black and whitener gels to make darker gray for re-outlining the beard. Spoon it all into a piping bag fitted with a #1 tip. To another bowl, add copper (flesh) gel to make darker skin tone. Thin to lining consistency and spoon it all into a piping bag fitted with a #1 tip. To the third bowl, add bright red gel for re-outlining the hat. Thin to lining consistency and spoon into a piping bag fitted with a #1 tip. Spoon 2 tablespoons of royal icing into a small bowl. Add whitener to make white for the eyes. Thin to lining consistency and spoon it all into a piping bag fitted with a #1 tip.

6. **Re-outline the ears, lip, beard, and mustache; make details. Make flooding icing for the nose.** Using the skin tone lining icing, re-outline the ears and lip. Draw the inner ear and outline the nose, going over the mustache and leaving the top of the nose unlined. Let set for 5 minutes. Reserve the skin tone lining icing. Mix 2 tablespoons royal icing in a bowl with copper (flesh) gel to make slightly darker skin for the nose. Thin to flooding consistency; with a paintbrush, paint in the nose. Using the darker gray lining icing, re-outline the beard and mustache and draw lines on the beard and mustache to indicate hair. Make the eyebrows, holding the tip at a 45-degree angle and touching the cookie. Using the white lining icing, make dots for the eyes. Let set for 1 hour. Reserve the white lining icing.

7. **Re-outline the nose. Make lining icing for the pupils.** Using the reserved darker skin tone lining icing, re-outline the nose. Mix 2 tablespoons royal icing in a bowl with royal blue gel to make blue for the pupils. Thin to lining consistency and spoon it all into a piping bag fitted with a #1 tip. For the pupil, squeeze a blue dot into each eye or use blue edible marker. Using the reserved white lining icing, make a white dot on the edge of each blue dot. Let set for 15 minutes or until dry.

POSY

○ beginner ● intermediate ○ advanced

what you need

TO MAKE THE COOKIES
4¼-inch ice cream cone cookie cutter

Cookie dough of choice (pages 26–33), prepared, chilled, and rolled out

Cooling racks

TO DECORATE
3¼ cups Royal Icing (pages 40–42)

Pasteurized egg white or water

Gel food colors: bright blue, whitener, leaf green, lemon yellow

6 plastic or parchment piping bags (page 53)

6 #1 tips

Assorted paintbrushes

1. **Make the cookies.** Cut out 24 cookies from the dough. Bake and cool as directed.

2. **Make light blue lining and flooding icing for the paper cone; outline and paint in.** Mix ¾ cup royal icing in a bowl with bright blue and whitener gels to make light blue. Thin to lining consistency and spoon ¼ cup into a piping bag fitted with a #1 tip. Thin the remaining icing to flooding consistency and cover with plastic wrap. Using the lining icing, outline the paper cone, stopping where the leaves overlap. Let set for 5 minutes. Using a paintbrush and the flooding icing, paint in the cone, thinning out the icing where the leaves overlap. Let set for 4 to 6 hours.

3. **Make green lining and flooding icing for the leaves; outline and paint in.** Mix ¾ cup royal icing in a bowl with leaf green gel to make green. Thin to lining consistency and spoon ¼ cup into a piping bag fitted with a #1 tip. Thin the remaining icing to flooding consistency, add a little whitener, and cover with plastic wrap. Using the lining icing, outline the silhouette of the leaves all over the bare part of the cookie, going over the blue paper cone. Let set for 5 minutes. Using a paintbrush and the flooding icing, paint in the leaf area. Let set until hard, 4 to 6 hours or overnight.

4. **Make white lining and flooding icing for the flowers; make dark green lining icing to re-outline the leaves. Outline the flowers and paint in.** Refresh the royal icing on medium low

POSY CONTINUES

for 30 seconds. Spoon ½ cup icing into a bowl. Cover one with plastic wrap. Add whitener gel to make white. Thin to lining consistency and spoon ¼ cup into a piping bag fitted with a #1 tip. Thin the remaining icing to flooding consistency and cover with plastic wrap. Spoon ¼ cup icing into a small bowl. Add leaf green gel to make the darker green and thin to lining consistency. Spoon it all into a piping bag fitted with a #1 tip. Using the white lining icing, outline the flowers on top of the green icing, keeping the tip close to the surface. Let set for 5 minutes. Using a paintbrush and the white flooding icing, paint in the flowers. Let set for 3 hours. Reserve the white lining icing.

5. **Re-outline the leaves and draw in more; re-outline the flowers.** While the white flooding icing sets, use the darker green lining icing to re-outline the leaves and draw in more leaves around the flowers, filling up any bare green spaces in between. Using the reserved white lining icing, re-outline the flowers, outlining the individual petals. Let set for 5 minutes.

6. **Make lining icings: darker blue to re-outline the cone; lemon for the center of the flowers. Re-outline the cone and make interior lines; make the center of the flowers.** Spoon ¼ cup royal icing into each of two bowls. Cover one with plastic wrap. To the other, add bright blue gel to make darker blue. Thin to lining consistency and spoon it all into a piping bag fitted with a #1 tip. To the remaining bowl, add lemon yellow gel and whitener to make bright yellow. Thin to lining consistency and spoon it all into a piping bag fitted with a #1 tip. Using the darker blue lining icing, re-outline the blue paper cone, then make a slightly curved line along the length of the right side of the cone. Using the yellow lining icing, make dots for the centers of some of the flowers, squeezing the piping bag gently and moving the tip around in the dot for texture. Let set for 1 hour or until dry.

SQUARE CUTTER

I could go on forever with a square. But I must have been hungry when I chose these, because they all relate to food. The success of the Egg on Toast is the result of a happy accident: I painted the bread with white flooding icing, which didn't ring true for toast, so I scraped it off with an offset spatula—and the result was exactly the texture I had been looking for!

I had fun with the other cookies, making the peanut butter icing the consistency of real peanut butter and using confectioners' sugar to make a pile of chalk dust on the Chalkboard. The key to the slice of Swiss Cheese? Getting the color just right.

CHALKBOARD

● beginner   ○ intermediate   ○ advanced

what you need

TO MAKE THE COOKIES
3-inch square cookie cutter

Cookie dough of choice (pages 26–33), prepared, chilled, and rolled out

Cooling racks

TO DECORATE
2¼ cups Royal Icing (pages 40–42)

Pasturized egg white or water

Gel food colors: super black, whitener, gold, chocolate brown, egg yellow

2 plastic or parchment paper piping bags (page 53)

2 #1 tips

Assorted paintbrushes

Confectioners' sugar, sifted

1. **Make the cookies.** Cut out 18 cookies from the dough. Bake and cool as directed.

2. **Make black flooding icing for the chalkboard and paint in.** Mix 1¼ cups royal icing in a bowl with super black to make black for the chalkboard. Thin to loose flooding consistency and, using a paintbrush, thinly paint the surface of the cookie with the icing, thinning it out to within a ¼ inch of the edge. Let set for 2 hours or until dry.

3. **Make brown lining and flooding icing for the frame; outline and paint in.** Mix ¾ cup royal icing with gold, chocolate brown, egg yellow, and whitener gels to make light brown for the frame. Thin to lining consistency and spoon ¼ cup into a piping bag fitted with a #1 tip. Thin

the remaining icing to flooding consistency and cover with plastic wrap. Using the brown lining icing, outline the outer and inner edges of the chalkboard frame, leaving a ⅛-inch edge around the cookie. Let set for 5 minutes. Using a paintbrush and the flooding icing, carefully paint in the frame. Let set for 2 hours.

4. **Make white lining icing for the chalk; write on the board and make the chalk.** Mix ¼ cup royal icing with whitener gel to make chalk white. Thin to tight lining consistency and spoon it all into a piping bag fitted with a #1 tip. To "write" words on the chalkboard, use the piping bag like a pencil, dragging its tip on the surface of the chalkboard. Let set for 5 minutes. Pipe two short, fat lines on the base

of the frame to mimic chalk. Using your fingers, gently dab a little confectioners' sugar along the bottom edge of the chalkboard, then brush a small pile to one side to mimic chalk dust. Using your finger, dab a little more around the words. Let set for 30 minutes or until dry.

OPEN-FACED PEANUT BUTTER SANDWICH

● beginner   ○ intermediate   ○ advanced

what you need

TO MAKE THE COOKIES
3-inch square cookie cutter

Cookie dough of choice (pages 26–33), prepared, chilled, and rolled out

Cooling racks

TO DECORATE
3½ cups Royal Icing (pages 40–42)

Pasteurized egg white or water

Gel food colors: sunset orange, chocolate brown, egg yellow, whitener, lemon yellow, gold

1 plastic or parchment paper piping bag (page 53)

1 #1.5 tip

Offset spatula or butter knife

Paintbrush

1. **Make the cookies.** Cut out 18 cookies from the dough. Bake and cool as directed.
2. **Make brown lining icing for the crust; make off-white flooding icing for the bread.** Mix ¼ cup royal icing in a bowl with sunset orange, chocolate brown, egg yellow, and whitener gels to make brown for the crust. Thin to slightly looser than lining consistency and spoon it all into a piping bag fitted with a #1.5 tip. Mix 1¾ cups royal icing in a bowl with lemon yellow and whitener gels to make off-white for the bread.

OPEN-FACED PEANUT BUTTER SANDWICH CONTINUES

Thin to flooding consistency and cover with plastic wrap.

3. **Outline the crust and paint in the bread.** Using the brown lining icing, outline the slice of bread using the full surface of the cookie, making indentations, and rounding the corners to mimic a slice of bread. Let set for 5 minutes. Using a paintbrush and the off-white flooding icing, paint in the bread, butting up (see page 64) the icing to the crust. Let set until hard, 6 to 8 hours or overnight.

4. **Make the "peanut butter" and spread it on the bread.** Refresh the royal icing on medium low for 30 seconds. Mix 1½ cups icing in a bowl with chocolate brown, gold, and whitener gels to make brown for the peanut butter. Thin the icing just to spreadable peanut butter consistency. Using an offset spatula or butter knife, spread the peanut butter onto the bread, leaving a rim of the white bread showing. Don't worry about being neat; the icing looks more realistic if it's a little messy! Let set for 4 to 6 hours or until dry.

· · · · · · · · · · · · · · MAKES 18 · · · · · · · · · · · · · ·

EGG ON TOAST

● beginner ○ intermediate ○ advanced

what you need

TO MAKE THE COOKIES
3-inch square cookie cutter

Cookie dough of choice (pages 26–33), prepared, chilled, and rolled out

Cooling racks

TO DECORATE
3½ cups Royal Icing (pages 40–42)

Pasteurized egg white or water

Gel food colors: sunset orange, chocolate brown, egg yellow, whitener, lemon yellow

3 plastic or parchment paper piping bags (page 53)

2 #1 tips

1 #1.5 tip

Offset spatula or butter knife

Assorted paintbrushes

1. **Make the cookies.** Cut out 18 cookies from the dough. Bake and cool as directed.

2. **Make brown lining icing for the crust and** outline it. Mix ¼ cup royal icing with sunset orange, chocolate brown, egg yellow, and whitener gels to make brown for the bread crust.

Thin to lining consistency and spoon it all into a piping bag fitted with a #1.5 tip. Outline the bread slice, using the full surface of the cookie, making indentations on the left and right sides, and rounding the corners to resemble a slice of bread. Let set for 30 minutes.

3. **Make off-white flooding icing for the bread and paint on.** Mix ¾ cups royal icing with a toothpick of lemon yellow to make off-white for the bread. Using a paintbrush, paint a *very* thin layer of the flooding icing inside the crust; you want the texture of the cookie to show through to mimic the air holes of a slice of toast. Use the side of a butter knife or offset spatula to wipe away excess icing, scraping right down to the cookie to exaggerate the texture. Let set for 30 seconds.

4. **Make white lining and flooding icing for the egg white; outline and paint in.** Mix 1½ cups royal icing with whitener gel to make egg white. Thin to lining consistency and spoon ¼ cup into a piping bag fitted with a #1 tip. Thin the remaining icing to flooding consistency and cover the bowl with plastic wrap. Using the white lining icing, outline the egg white on the bread slice. Let set for 5 minutes. Using a paintbrush and the white flooding icing, paint in the egg white. Let set until hard, 4 to 6 hours or overnight.

5. **Make yellow lining and flooding icing for the yolk; outline and paint in.** Refresh the royal icing on medium low for 30 seconds. Mix ¾ cup icing in a bowl with egg yellow gel to make egg yolk yellow. Thin to lining consistency and spoon ¼ cup into a piping bag fitted with a #1 tip. Thin the remaining icing to thick flooding consistency and cover with plastic wrap. Using the lining icing, outline a circle on the egg white. Let set for 5 minutes. Using a paintbrush and the flooding icing, paint in the yolk, making it slightly puffy to mimic a real egg yolk. Let set until hard, 6 to 8 hours or overnight.

SWISS CHEESE

● beginner ○ intermediate ○ advanced

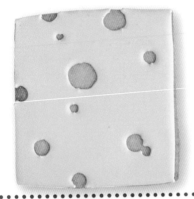

what you need

TO MAKE THE COOKIES
3-inch square cookie cutter

Cookie dough of choice (pages 26–33), prepared, chilled, and rolled out

Cooling racks

TO DECORATE
2 cups Royal Icing (pages 40–42)

Pasteurized egg white or water

Gel food colors: lemon yellow, egg yellow, whitener

1 plastic or parchment paper piping bag (page 53)

1 #1 tip

Paintbrush

1. **Make the cookies.** Cut out 18 cookies from the dough. Bake and cool as directed.

2. **Make lining and flooding icing for the cheese.** Mix 2 cups royal icing in a bowl with tiny toothpicks of lemon yellow, egg yellow, and whitener gels to make light yellow for the cheese. Thin the icing to lining consistency and spoon ¼ cup into a piping bag fitted with a #1 tip. Thin the remaining icing to flooding consistency and cover with plastic wrap.

3. **Outline the cheese and paint in.** Using the lining icing, pipe the edges of the cheese slice, making irregularly shaped holes in the edges. Outline holes of various sizes in random places on the interior of the cookie. Let set for 5 minutes. Using a paintbrush and the flooding icing, paint in the interior of the slice, around the holes. Let set until hard, 6 to 8 hours or overnight.

BASEBALL CAP CUTTER

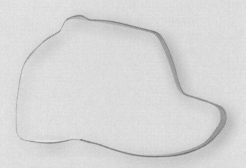

A cap, a sneaker, a hair dryer; the challenge here was to find a way to use this cookie vertically. Then I "saw" the chair, and though it seemed simple, it turned out to be a rather challenging cookie because of its three-quarters perspective. It helps to outline the cutter on a piece of paper first and practice drawing the interior lines—the arms, seat cushion, and top of the skirt—with your piping bag to get a feel for where they go. If you're not comfortable painting in such slender stripes for the fabric, use an edible pen to make them.

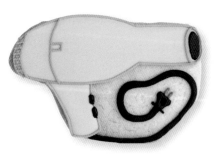

BASEBALL CAP

● beginner ○ intermediate ○ advanced

what you need

TO MAKE THE COOKIES
3-inch baseball cap cookie cutter

Cookie dough of choice (pages 26–33), prepared, chilled, and rolled out

Cooling racks

TO DECORATE
1½ cups Royal Icing (pages 40–42)

Pasteurized egg white or water

Gel food colors: lemon yellow, egg yellow, whitener, navy blue

3 plastic or parchment paper piping bags (page 53)

3 #1 tips

Assorted paintbrushes

1. **Make the cookies.** Cut out 24 cookies from the dough. Bake and cool as directed.

2. **Make the yellow lining and flooding icing for the baseball cap; outline and paint in.** Mix ¾ cup royal icing in a small bowl with lemon yellow and egg yellow gels to make bright yellow for the baseball cap. Thin to lining consistency and spoon ¼ cup into a piping bag fitted with a #1 tip. Thin the remaining icing to flooding consistency and cover with plastic wrap. Using the lining icing, outline the silhouette of the yellow part of the cap only, leaving room for the button on the top. Let set for 5 minutes. Using a medium paintbrush and the flooding icing, paint in the yellow part of the cap. Let set until hard, 6 to 8 hours or overnight.

3. **Make blue lining and flooding icing for the brim and button; outline and paint in.** Mix ½ cup royal icing in a bowl with navy blue gel to make navy blue for the brim of the cap. Thin to lining consistency and spoon ¼ cup into a piping bag fitted with a #1 tip. Thin the remaining icing to flooding consistency, add a little whitener, and cover with plastic wrap. Using the lining icing, outline the edge of the brim, leaving bare the area where the brim meets the cap. Outline the button on the top of the cap. Let set for 5 minutes. Reserve the navy blue lining icing. Using a small paintbrush and the flooding icing, paint in the brim and the button. Let set until hard, about 4 hours.

4. **Make darker yellow lining icing and**

re-outline the cap. Re-outline the brim and button; make details. Refresh the royal icing on medium low for 30 seconds. Mix ¼ cup icing with lemon yellow and egg yellow gels to make the orange-yellow for re-outlining the hat. Thin to lining consistency and spoon it all into a piping bag fitted with a #1 tip. Re-outline the cap only, then make two curved lines for the seams. Using the reserved navy blue lining icing, re-outline the brim and button. Draw a tiny circle in each of the two panels on the cap for air vents. Let set for 5 minutes.

MAKES 24

HIGH-TOP SNEAKER

○ beginner ● intermediate ○ advanced

what you need

TO MAKE THE COOKIES
3-inch baseball cap cookie cutter

Cookie dough of choice (pages 26–33), prepared, chilled, and rolled out

Cooling racks

TO DECORATE
2 cups Royal Icing (pages 40–42)

Pasteurized egg white or water

Gel food colors: bright blue, super black, whitener

4 plastic or parchment paper piping bags (page 53)

4 #1 tips

Assorted paintbrushes

Blue edible marker (optional)

1. **Make the cookies.** Cut out 24 cookies from the dough. Bake and cool as directed.

2. **Make blue lining and flooding icing for the sneaker; outline and paint in the tongue.** Mix 1 cup royal icing in a bowl with bright blue to make sky blue for the sneaker. Thin to lining consistency and spoon ¼ cup into a piping bag fitted with a #1 tip. Thin the remaining icing to flooding consistency and cover with plastic wrap. Using the lining icing, outline the top and right side of the sneaker's tongue, stopping at the white toe cap. Let set for 5 minutes. Reserve the sky blue lining icing. Using a small paintbrush and the flooding icing, paint in the tongue, thinning out the icing where the toe cap and side of the shoe

HIGH-TOP SNEAKER CONTINUES

overlap it. Let set for 2 hours. Cover the remaining blue flooding icing with plastic wrap and reserve.

3. **Outline the sneaker and paint in.** Using the reserved sky blue lining icing, outline the body of the sneaker, overlapping the tongue and stopping where it meets the white sole. Using a medium paintbrush and the reserved flooding icing, paint in the sneaker, thinning out the icing where the white sole overlaps. Let set for 6 to 8 hours or overnight.

4. **Make gray lining icing for the eyelets; draw in.** Refresh the royal icing on medium low for 30 seconds. Mix 2 tablespoons icing with a toothpick each of super black and whitener gels to make metal gray for the eyelets. Thin to lining consistency and spoon it all into a piping bag fitted with a #1 tip. Draw six tiny circles along the curve of the sneaker where the laces go, spacing them an equal distance apart. Let set for 5 minutes.

5. **Make white lining and flooding icing for the sole, toe cap, and logo; outline and paint in. Draw in the stitching and the laces.** Mix ¾ cup royal icing in a bowl with whitener gel to make white for the sole, shoelaces, and logo. Thin to lining consistency and spoon ¼ cup into a piping bag fitted with a #1 tip. Thin the remaining icing to flooding consistency and cover with plastic wrap. Using the white lining icing, outline the sole and toe cap. Draw a circle on the side of the shoe for the logo. Draw short, evenly spaced dashes along the top and right side of the body of the sneaker to make the stitching. Make the bottom five laces, beginning at the eyelets and touching down at the edge of the tongue, squeezing hard and moving slowly to make fatter lines. Make the top lace by starting inside the eyelet and curving slightly down the side of the sneaker, squeezing hard to make fatter lines. Touch down, then squeeze a bit more gently to make the plastic end of the lace (or you won't be able to lace your sneaker!). Outline the rest of the laces going across the tongue as above. Using a paintbrush and the white flooding icing, paint in the sole, toe cap, and circle. Let set until hard, 6 to 8 hours or overnight.

6. **Make lining icing for the star.** Refresh the royal icing on medium low for 30 seconds. Mix 2 tablespoons icing with bright blue gel to make light blue for the star. Thin to lining consistency and spoon into a piping bag fitted with a #1 tip. Outline a star on the white circle by drawing or dragging the tip on the surface. Let set for 10 minutes. Alternatively, use a blue edible marker.

CHAIR

○ beginner   ○ intermediate   ● advanced

what you need

TO MAKE THE COOKIES
3-inch baseball cap cookie cutter

Cookie dough of choice (pages 26–33), prepared, chilled, and rolled out

Cooling racks

TO DECORATE
1½ cups Royal Icing (pages 40–42)

Pasteurized egg white or water

Gel food colors: whitener, super black, bright red

2 plastic or parchment paper piping bags (page 53)

2 #1 tips

Assorted paintbrushes

Plate or ceramic mixing palette

Red edible marker (optional)

1. **Make the cookies.** Cut out 24 cookies from the dough. Bake and cool as directed.

2. **Make white lining and flooding icing for the chair; outline and paint in.** Mix 1 cup royal icing in a bowl with whitener gel to make bright white. Thin to lining consistency and spoon ¼ cup into a piping bag fitted with a #1 tip. Thin the remaining icing to flooding consistency and cover with plastic wrap. Position the cookie so that the brim of the cap is the top. Using the lining icing, outline the silhouette of the chair, making the bottom wavy by holding the piping tip a bit closer to the cookie. Let set for 5 minutes. Using a medium paintbrush and the white flooding icing, paint in the chair. Let set until hard, 6 to 8 hours or overnight.

3. **Make black lining icing and re-outline the chair and details.** Refresh the icing on medium low for 30 seconds. Mix ¼ cup icing in a bowl with super black gel to make black for outlining the chair. Thin to tight lining consistency and spoon all of it into a piping bag fitted with a #1 tip. Re-outline the silhouette of the chair, then make the lines for the arms, seat cushion, and skirt with the tip hovering slightly above the cookie. Let set for 10 minutes.

4. **Make red watercolor for the stripes and paint on.** Squeeze a dot of bright red gel onto a plate or ceramic mixing palette. Using a small paintbrush, mix in a little water to make a watercolor (see page 66). Using a watercolor brush, paint the stripes

CHAIR CONTINUES

on the chair, making them equidistant from one another. Keep your brush as dry as possible to avoid getting the black lines wet (this can cause the color to bleed). Let set for 30 minutes. Alternatively, use red edible marker to draw in the stripes.

•••••••••••••••••••••••••• MAKES 24 ••••••••••••••••••••••••••

HAIR DRYER

○ beginner   ● intermediate   ○ advanced

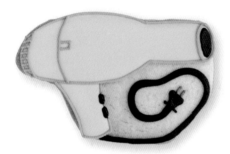

what you need

TO MAKE THE COOKIES
3-inch baseball cap cookie cutter

Cookie dough of choice (pages 26–33), prepared, chilled, and rolled out

Cooling racks

TO DECORATE
1½ cups Royal Icing (pages 40–42)

Pasteurized egg white or water

Gel food colors: neon green, whitener, super black

4 plastic or parchment paper piping bags (page 53)

4 #1 tips

Assorted paintbrushes

Green edible marker (optional)

1. **Make the cookies.** Cut out 24 cookies from the dough. Bake and cool as directed.

2. **Make green lining and flooding icing for the hair dryer; outline and paint in.** Mix ¾ cup royal icing in a bowl with neon green gel to make lime green for the hair dryer. Thin to lining consistency and spoon ¼ cup into a piping bag fitted with a #1 tip. Thin the remaining icing to flooding consistency, add a little whitener, and cover with plastic wrap. Turn the cookie upside down, so that the top of the hat is the bottom. Using the green lining icing, outline the silhouette of the hair dryer. Let set for 5 minutes. If you like, you can draw the silhouette on with edible marker first. Using a medium paintbrush and the flooding icing, paint in the hair dryer. Let set until hard, 6 to 8 hours or overnight.

3. **Make black lining and flooding icing for the cord and plug; outline, paint in, and make details.** Refresh the royal icing on medium low for

30 seconds. Mix ¼ cup icing in a bowl with super black gel to make black for the cord, buttons, and nose of the dryer. Thin to lining consistency and spoon it all into a piping bag fitted with a #1 tip. Using the lining icing, make the power cord by first making one curvy line then butting a second line up against it (see page 64). Next, draw in the plug. Make the oval at the nose of the dryer and fill it in. Make the two buttons on the handle. Let set for 5 minutes.

4. **Make dark green lining icing and re-outline the hair dryer.** Meanwhile, mix ¼ cup royal icing in a bowl with neon green gel to make a dark neon green for outlining the dryer. Thin to lining consistency and spoon it all into a piping bag fitted with a #1 tip. Re-outline the hair dryer. Make the interior details. Let set for 5 minutes.

5. **Make gray lining icing for the plug's prongs and draw them in.** Mix 2 tablespoons royal icing with super black and whitener gels to make gray for the plug's prongs. Thin to lining consistency and spoon it all into a piping bag fitted with a #1 tip. Draw the prongs at the end of the plug. Let set for 20 minutes.

FROG CUTTER

This grouping features metallic gold and watercolors for effect. It's rare for me to embellish my cookies with anything sparkly—I apply shiny dust only when I think it's required, as it is for the angel's halo. If you like more shine, add some pearl dust to her wings.

Using watercolors for the fishbowl gives the illusion that there's real water in it. This is especially true in contrast to the opaque icing on the other parts of the cookie.

I particularly love that this group features three animals, or four if you count the fish!

FROG

○ beginner ● intermediate ○ advanced

what you need

TO MAKE THE COOKIES
3-inch frog cookie cutter

Cookie dough of choice (pages 26–33), prepared, chilled, and rolled out

Cooling racks

TO DECORATE
2 cups Royal Icing (pages 40–42)

Pasteurized egg white or water

Gel food colors: neon green, sunset orange, gold, whitener, lemon yellow, chocolate brown, super black, electric pink

5 plastic or parchment paper piping bags (page 53)

5 #1 tips

Assorted paintbrushes

1. **Make the cookies.** Cut out 24 cookies from the dough. Bake and cool as directed.

2. **Make green lining and flooding icing for the frog; outline and paint in.** Spoon ¾ cup royal icing into a bowl and mix with neon green, sunset orange, and gold gels to make green. Thin to lining consistency and spoon ¼ cup into a piping bag fitted with a #1 tip. Thin the remaining icing to flooding consistency, add a little whitener, and cover with plastic wrap. Using the lining icing, outline the silhouette of the frog along the edges of the cookie. Along the bottom, outline four individual toes for each webbed foot and three fingers of each hand. Make a curved horizontal line across the face for the mouth. Make the lines on the inside of the frog's arms to separate them from the yellow belly. Let set for 5 minutes. Using a small paintbrush and the green flooding icing, paint in the top of the head above the mouth line and the arms and legs.

3. **Make light yellow flooding icing for the belly and paint in.** Mix ½ cup royal icing in a bowl with a toothpick each of lemon yellow and whitener gels to make light yellow for the frog's belly and thin to flooding consistency. Using a small paintbrush, paint in the belly area, butting the icing up (see page 64) to the green outline. Let set until hard, 6 to 8 hours or overnight.

4. **Make yellow lining and flooding icing for the frog's eyes; outline and paint in.** Refresh the royal icing on medium low for 30 seconds.

FROG CONTINUES

Mix ¼ cup icing in a bowl with lemon yellow gel to make darker yellow for the eyes. Thin to lining consistency and spoon 2 tablespoons into a piping bag fitted with a #1 tip. Thin the remaining icing to flooding consistency and cover with plastic wrap. Using the lining icing, outline the frog's eyes. Let set for 5 minutes. Using a small paintbrush and the yellow flooding icing, paint in the eyes. Let set for 1 hour.

5. **Make dark green lining icing, re-outline the frog, and make details.** Meanwhile, mix ¼ cup royal icing with neon green and chocolate brown gels to make dark green to re-outline the frog. Thin to lining consistency and spoon it all into a piping bag fitted with a #1 tip. Re-outline the frog, going above the eyes, and re-outline the mouth.

Re-outline the arms and three fingers. Do not re-outline where the arms meet the neck.

6. **Make lining icings for the black eyes and pink tongue and draw in.** Spoon 2 tablespoons royal icing into each of two bowls. Cover one with plastic wrap. To the other, add super black gel to make the black for the eyes. Thin to lining consistency and spoon it all into a piping bag fitted with a #1 tip. To the second bowl, add electric pink gel to make pink for the tongue. Thin to lining consistency and spoon it all into a piping bag fitted with a #1 tip. Using the black lining icing, make black circles on the eyes for pupils. Using the pink lining icing, make the frog's tongue sticking out of the corner of his mouth. Let set for 10 minutes or until dry.

········· **MAKES 24** ·········

CAT AND FISH

○ beginner ● intermediate ○ advanced

what you need

TO MAKE THE COOKIES
3-inch frog cookie cutter

Cookie dough of choice (pages 26–33), prepared, chilled, and rolled out

Cooling racks

TO DECORATE
2½ cups Royal Icing (pages 40–42)

Pasteurized egg white or water

Gel food colors: sunset orange, whitener, bright blue, royal blue, gold, chocolate brown, neon green, super black

6 plastic or parchment paper piping bags (page 53)

6 #1 tips

Assorted paintbrushes

Plate or ceramic mixing palette

1. **Make the cookies.** Cut out 24 cookies from the dough. Bake and cool as directed.

2. **Make light orange lining and flooding icing for the cat; outline and paint in.** Spoon ½ cup royal icing into a bowl and mix with sunset orange gel to make light orange. Thin to lining consistency and spoon ¼ cup into a piping bag fitted with a #1 tip. Thin the remaining to flooding consistency, add a little whitener, and cover with plastic wrap. Using the lining icing, outline the silhouette of the cat's head and body, stopping where the body meets the top edge of the fishbowl. Using a medium paintbrush and the light orange flooding icing, paint in the cat, thinning the icing where the bowl overlaps. Let set until hard, 6 to 8 hours or overnight.

3. **Make lining and flooding icings: pale blue for the water and royal blue for the shelf.** Refresh the royal icing on medium low for 30 seconds. Spoon ½ cup icing into each of two bowls. Cover one with plastic wrap. To the other, add a tiny toothpick of bright blue gel to make palest blue for the water. Thin to lining consistency and spoon ¼ cup into a piping bag fitted with a #1 tip. Thin the remaining icing to flooding consistency and cover with plastic wrap. To the second bowl, add royal blue to make royal blue to outline the shelf. Thin to lining consistency and spoon ¼ cup into a piping bag fitted with a #1 tip. Thin the remaining icing to flooding consistency, add a little whitener, and cover with plastic wrap.

4. **Outline the fishbowl and shelf and paint in.** Using the pale blue lining icing, outline the fishbowl. Let set for 5 minutes. Using the royal blue lining icing, outline the shelf, butting up (see page 64) the top line to the bottom line of the fishbowl. Let set for 5 minutes. Using a medium paintbrush and the pale blue flooding icing, paint in the fishbowl. Using a medium paintbrush and the royal blue flooding icing, paint in the shelf. Let set until hard, 6 to 8 hours or overnight.

5. **Make watercolors for the cat and fishbowl details. Paint on.** Squeeze dots of sunset orange, chocolate brown, bright blue, gold, neon green, and super black gels onto a plate or ceramic mixing palette. Using a watercolor brush, mix a little water into each color to make watercolors (see page 66). Use the sunset orange to paint on the cat's stripes, and use the chocolate brown for the ears. Use the bright blue for the water in the fishbowl, the chocolate brown mixed with gold for the sand, the neon green for the seaweed, and the sunset orange for the goldfish.

6. **Make lining icings: chocolate brown to re-outline the cat and blue for the shelf. Make white lining and flooding icing for the fishbowl and eyes.** Spoon ¼ cup icing into each of two bowls. Cover one with plastic wrap. To the remaining, add chocolate brown and sunset orange gels to make chocolate brown for re-outlining the cat. Thin to lining consistency

CAT AND FISH CONTINUES

and spoon it all into a piping bag fitted with a #1 tip. To the other bowl, add royal blue gel to make dark blue to re-outline the shelf. Thin to lining consistency and spoon it all into a piping bag fitted with a #1 tip. To a third bowl, spoon ½ cup icing and add whitener to make white to re-outline the fishbowl. Thin to lining consistency and spoon all but 2 tablespoons into a piping bag fitted with a #1 tip. Thin the remaining white icing to flooding consistency and cover with plastic wrap.

7. **Re-outline the cat, fishbowl, and shelf. Paint in the eyes. Draw details.** Using the brown lining icing, re-outline the cat's head and body. Draw in the eyes and nose. Let set for 5 minutes. Using the white lining icing, re-outline the fish-bowl. Using the dark blue lining icing, re-outline the shelf and draw the interior lines. Using a small paintbrush or a toothpick and the white flooding icing, fill in the eyes. Let set until hard, 1 hour.

8. **Make watercolor for the cat's eyes. Paint on.** Using a watercolor brush, mix a little water into gold gel on a plate or ceramic mixing palette to make watercolor for the cat's eyes. Paint in the eyes. Let set for 10 minutes or until dry. Mix a little super black gel with water as above to make black watercolor for the cat's pupils. Paint tiny dots for the pupils. Let set for 10 minutes or until dry.

· **MAKES 24** ·

COW'S HEAD

○ beginner   ● intermediate   ○ advanced

what you need

TO MAKE THE COOKIES
3-inch frog cookie cutter

Cookie dough of choice (pages 26–33), prepared, chilled, and rolled out

Cooling racks

TO DECORATE
2¼ cups Royal Icing (pages 40–42)

Pasteurized egg white or water

Gel food colors: buck-eye brown, whitener, copper (flesh), super black

5 plastic or parchment paper piping bags (page 53)

5 #1 tips

Assorted paintbrushes

1. **Make the cookies.** Cut out 24 cookies from the dough. Bake and cool as directed.

2. **Make lining and flooding icings: brown for the cow's head and light pink for the nose.** Spoon ½ cup royal icing into each of two bowls. Cover one with plastic wrap. To the remaining, add buckeye brown gel to make brown for the cow's head. Thin to lining consistency and spoon ¼ cup into a piping bag fitted with a #1 tip. Thin the remaining icing to flooding consistency, add a little whitener, and cover with plastic wrap. To the second bowl, add copper (flesh) to make light pink for the cow's nose. Thin to lining consistency and spoon ¼ cup into a piping bag fitted with a #1 tip. Thin the remaining to flooding consistency, add a little whitener, and cover with plastic wrap.

3. **Outline the muzzle, nose, and head. Make interior lines.** Using the light pink lining icing, outline the cow's nose, rounding the two bumps at the bottom for the chin. Let set for 5 minutes. Using the brown lining icing, outline the silhouette of the cow's head just to where it meets the nose. Round out the cheekbones instead of following the edge of the cookie. Make two wavy lines down the middle of the head where the white marking will go. Let set for 5 minutes.

4. **Paint in the dark sides of the head and the nose.** Using a medium paintbrush and the brown flooding icing, paint in the left and right sides of the head. Let set for 10 minutes or until dry. Using another medium paintbrush and the light pink flooding icing, paint in the cow's nose. Let set until hard, 6 to 8 hours or overnight.

5. **Make white lining and flooding icing and paint in the white marking.** Refresh the royal icing on medium low for 30 seconds. Mix ½ cup icing with whitener to make white for the marking. Thin to lining consistency and spoon ¼ cup into a piping bag fitted with a #1 tip. Reserve the white lining icing. Thin the remaining icing to flooding consistency. Using a small paintbrush and the white flooding icing, paint in the white marking on the cow's head, butting the white icing up to the brown (see page 64). Let set until hard, 3 to 4 hours or overnight.

6. **Make lining icings: darker pink to re-outline the nose and dark brown for the head; make black flooding icing for the eyes.** Spoon ¼ cup royal icing into each of two bowls. Cover one with plastic wrap. To the other bowl, add copper (flesh) to make darker pink to re-outline the cow's nose. Thin to lining consistency and spoon it all into a piping bag fitted with a #1 tip. To the second bowl, add buckeye brown and super black gel to make dark brown to re-outline the cow's head. Thin to lining consistency and spoon 3 tablespoons into a piping bag fitted with a #1 tip. Add additional super black gel to the remaining dark brown icing to make black for the cow's eyes. Thin to flooding consistency and cover with plastic wrap.

COW'S HEAD CONTINUES

7. **Re-outline the head and nose; draw in details. Paint in eyes and nostrils.** Using the dark brown lining icing, re-outline the cow's head, leaving the nose unlined. Draw in the ears, eyes, and nostrils. Let set for 5 minutes. Using the darker pink lining icing, re-outline the nose, making two arches around the nostrils and a curved line to separate the nose from the chin. Using a small paintbrush and the black flooding icing, thinly paint in the eyes and the nostrils. Let set for 1 hour or until hard. Using the reserved white lining icing, make dots on the eyes for the pupils. Let set for 10 minutes or until dry.

· MAKES 24 ·

ANGEL

○ beginner   ○ intermediate   ● advanced

what you need

TO MAKE THE COOKIES
3-inch frog cookie cutter

Cookie dough of choice (pages 26–33), prepared, chilled, and rolled out

Cooling racks

TO DECORATE
2¾ cups Royal Icing (pages 40–42)

Pasteurized egg white or water

Gel food colors: whitener, buckeye brown, gold, ivory, super black

Edible gold luster dust

Vodka or lemon extract

6 plastic or parchment paper piping bags (page 53)

6 #1 tips

Assorted paintbrushes

1. **Make the cookies.** Cut out 24 cookies from the dough. Bake and cool as directed.

2. **Make white lining and flooding icing for the wings.** Mix ¾ cup royal icing in a bowl with whitener to make white for the wings. Thin to lining consistency and spoon ¼ cup into a piping bag fitted with a #1 tip. Thin the remaining icing to thin flooding consistency and cover with plastic wrap.

3. **Outline and paint in the wings.** Turn the

cookie upside down so the frog's head is on the bottom. Using the white lining icing, outline the silhouette of the wings, leaving bare the areas where the head and robe overlap. Let set for 5 minutes. Using a medium paintbrush and the white flooding icing, paint in the wings, thinning out the icing where the head and robe overlap them. Let set until hard, 6 to 8 hours or overnight.

4. **Make lining and flooding icings: brown for the face and beige for the robe.** Refresh the royal icing on medium low for 30 seconds. Spoon ½ cup icing into a bowl; add buckeye brown and gold gels to make brown for the angel's skin. Thin to lining consistency and spoon ¼ cup into a piping bag fitted with a #1 tip. Thin the remaining icing to flooding consistency, add whitener, and cover with plastic wrap. Into the other bowl, spoon ¾ cup icing. Add a toothpick of ivory gel to make beige for the angel's robe. Thin to lining consistency and spoon ¼ cup into a piping bag fitted with a #1 tip. Thin the remaining icing to flooding consistency and cover with plastic wrap.

5. **Outline the head, robe, and feet.** Using the brown lining icing, outline the head, leaving the top of the cookie bare for the hair and the halo. Let set for 5 minutes. Reserve the brown lining icing. Using the beige lining icing, outline the robe, letting the lines touch the neck. Let set for 5 minutes. Using the reserved brown lining icing, outline the feet poking out from under the robe, letting the lines touch the bottom of the robe.

Let set for 1 hour or until dry. Reserve the brown lining icing.

6. **Paint in the face, feet, and robe.** Using a small paintbrush and the brown flooding icing, paint in the face and feet. Using a medium paintbrush and the beige flooding icing, paint in the robe. Let set until hard, 6 to 8 hours or overnight.

7. **Make black lining and flooding icing for the hair, facial features, and hands; make dark beige lining icing to re-outline the robe.** Refresh the royal icing on medium low for 30 seconds. Spoon ¼ cup royal icing into each of two bowls. Cover one with plastic wrap. To the other, add super black gel to make black for the hair, facial features, and hands. Thin to tight lining consistency and spoon 2 tablespoons into a piping bag fitted with a #1 tip. Thin the remaining icing to flooding consistency and cover with plastic wrap. To the second bowl, add ivory gel to make darker beige to re-outline the robe. Thin to lining consistency and spoon it all into a piping bag fitted with a #1 tip.

8. **Outline and paint in the hair and make details. Re-outline the robe. Make the hands and re-outline the feet.** Using the black lining icing, outline the hair around the face and draw in the eyes and mouth. Let set for 5 minutes. Using the darker beige lining icing, re-outline the robe and make the sleeves. Let set for 5 minutes. Using the reserved brown lining icing, make the hands by squeezing hard and piping slowly to make two

ANGEL CONTINUES

fat lines. Re-outline the feet. Using a small paint-brush and the black flooding icing, paint in the hair. Let set for 3 to 4 hours or until hard.

9. **Make white lining icing and re-outline the wings and make details. Outline and dust the halo.** Refresh the royal icing on medium low for 30 seconds. Spoon ¼ cup icing into a bowl and mix with whitener to make white to re-outline the wings and make the details. Thin to lining consistency and spoon all of it into a piping bag fitted with a #1 tip. Re-outline the wings and make the details of the feathers. Outline the oval halo on the angel's head. Let set for 15 minutes. Combine a little gold luster dust with vodka or lemon extract in a small bowl. Stir with a small paintbrush and paint the halo with the gold luster dust. Let set for 5 minutes.

TEACUP CUTTER

Two cookie designs in this group—the Teacup and the Stork—feature wet-on-wet dots, a technique used when you want dots to appear as part of the material and not rise above it.

You can use this technique on other cookies in the book such as the Heart (page 220), Wedding Cake (page 165), and Easter Bunny (page 87).

TEACUP

● beginner ○ intermediate ○ advanced

what you need

TO MAKE THE COOKIES
2¾-inch teacup cookie cutter

Cookie dough of choice (pages 26–33), prepared, chilled, and rolled out

Cooling racks

TO DECORATE
3 cups Royal Icing (pages 40–42)

Pasteurized egg white or water

Gel food colors: whitener, sunset orange, chocolate brown, gold

5 plastic or parchment paper piping bags (page 53)

4 #1 tips

1 #1.5 tip

Assorted paintbrushes

1. **Make the cookies.** Cut out 24 cookies from the dough. Bake and cool as directed.

2. **Make white lining and flooding icing for the saucer; outline and paint in.** Mix 1 cup royal icing in a bowl with whitener gel to make white. Thin to lining consistency and spoon ¼ cup into a piping bag fitted with a #1 tip. Thin the remaining icing to flooding consistency and cover with plastic wrap. Using the white lining icing, outline the saucer, leaving the area bare where the teacup overlaps the saucer. Let set for 5 minutes. Using a medium paintbrush and the flooding icing, paint in the saucer, thinning the icing where the teacup overlaps. Let set until hard, 6 to 8 hours or overnight.

3. **Make orange lining and flooding icing for the teacup; make white icing for the polka dots.** Refresh the royal icing on medium low for 30 seconds. Mix 1 cup royal icing with sunset orange gel to make orange for the teacup. Thin to lining consistency and spoon ¼ cup into a piping bag fitted with a #1 tip. Thin the remaining to flooding consistency, add whitener, and cover with plastic wrap. Mix ¼ cup royal icing with whitener gel to make white for the polka dots. Thin to a consistency that's slightly looser than lining icing but not as loose as flooding icing. Spoon into a piping bag fitted with a #1.5 tip and set aside.

4. **Outline and paint in the teacup. Make the dots.** Using the orange lining icing, outline the silhouette of the teacup without the handle, going over the top of the saucer and including the foot of the cup. Next, outline the handle. Let set for

5 minutes. Using a medium paintbrush and the orange flooding icing, paint in the teacup including the handle. While the icing is still wet, use the loose white lining icing to drop dots into the orange icing of the teacup, spacing them to create a polka-dot pattern—you can make them where the tea will go because they will be covered. Let set for 4 to 6 hours.

5. **Make lining and flooding icing for the tea. Make orange lining icing and re-outline the cup; make details.** Refresh the royal icing on medium low for 30 seconds. Mix ½ cup icing with chocolate brown and gold gels to make light brown for the tea. Thin to lining consistency and spoon ¼ cup into a piping bag fitted with a #1 tip. Thin the remaining icing to thin flooding consistency, add whitener, and cover with plastic wrap. Mix ¼ cup royal icing in a bowl with sunset

orange gel to make darker orange to re-outline the teacup. Thin to lining consistency and spoon it all into a piping bag fitted with a #1 tip. Using the darker orange lining icing, re-outline the teacup, including the foot and handle, and pipe an oval for the mouth of the teacup. Re-outline the saucer and pipe another oval inside the saucer around the foot of the teacup.

6. **Outline the tea and paint in.** Using the light brown lining icing, outline the top edge of the tea, just below the back lip of the teacup. Let set for 5 minutes. Using a medium paintbrush and the light brown flooding icing, paint in the tea, butting the icing up (see page 64) to the outline of the front lip of the teacup. Let set until hard, 2 to 3 hours.

ROTARY PHONE

○ beginner ● intermediate ○ advanced

what you need

TO MAKE THE COOKIES
2¾-inch teacup cookie cutter

Cookie dough of choice (pages 26–33), prepared, chilled, and rolled out

Cooling racks

TO DECORATE
2½ cups Royal Icing (pages 40–42)

Pasteurized egg white or water

Gel food colors: royal blue, whitener

3 plastic or parchment paper piping bags (page 53)

3 #1 tips

Assorted paintbrushes

1. **Make the cookies.** Cut out 24 cookies from the dough. Bake and cool as directed.

2. **Make lining and flooding icing for the phone; outline and paint in.** Mix 1¼ cups royal icing in a bowl with royal blue and whitener gels to make light blue for the telephone. Thin to lining consistency and spoon ¼ cup into a piping bag fitted with a #1 tip. Thin the remaining icing to flooding consistency and cover with plastic wrap. Turn the cookie upside down so the teacup's saucer is at the top. Using the lining icing, outline the silhouette of the phone, including the receiver, taking care to leave space under it. Let set for 5 minutes. Using a medium paintbrush and the light blue flooding icing, paint in the phone. Let set until hard, 6 to 8 hours or overnight.

3. **Make lining icing to re-outline the phone and make details; make flooding icing for the dial pad. Re-outline and paint in.** Refresh the royal icing on medium low for 30 seconds. Mix ½ cup royal icing in a bowl with royal blue and whitener gels to make a darker blue to re-outline the phone. Spoon ¼ cup into a piping bag fitted with a #1 tip. Thin the remaining icing to flooding consistency and cover with plastic wrap. Mix ¼ cup royal icing with royal blue and whitener gels to make lighter blue for the background of the dial. Thin to flooding consistency and cover with plastic wrap. Using the darker blue lining icing, re-outline the phone, then make the details on the receiver, the rectangles that hold it up, the curved line at the bottom of the phone, and the cord.

Draw a big circle in the middle of the phone. Let set for 5 minutes. Reserve the darker blue lining and flooding icing. Using a small paintbrush and the lighter blue flooding icing, paint in the circle. Let set until hard, 3 to 4 hours.

4. **Make white lining and flooding icing for the dial; outline and paint in.** Refresh the royal icing on medium low for 30 seconds. Mix ½ cup icing with whitener gel to make white for the dial. Thin to lining consistency and spoon ¼ cup into a piping bag fitted with a #1 tip. Thin the remaining to flooding consistency and cover with plastic wrap. Using the white lining icing, draw a smaller circle inside the lighter blue circle. Let set for 5 minutes. Using a small paintbrush and the white flooding icing, thinly paint in the circle. Let set until hard, 2 hours.

5. **Draw details; paint in.** When the white flooding icing is set, use the reserved darker blue lining icing to draw a small circle in the middle of the white circle. Use the tip to draw the finger holes on the white icing. Using another small paintbrush and the reserved darker blue flooding icing, paint in the small circle.

· MAKES 24 ·

GRADUATION CAP

● beginner ○ intermediate ○ advanced

what you need

TO MAKE THE COOKIES
2¾-inch teacup cookie cutter

Cookie dough of choice (pages 26–33), prepared, chilled, and rolled out

Cooling racks

TO DECORATE
2 cups Royal Icing (pages 40–42)

Pasteurized egg white or water

Gel food colors: regal purple, whitener, egg yellow

Black fine-tipped edible marker (optional)

3 plastic or parchment paper piping bags (page 53)

3 #1 tips

Assorted paintbrushes

GRADUATION CAP CONTINUES

1. **Make the cookies.** Cut out 24 cookies from the dough. Bake and cool as directed.

2. **Make lining and flooding icing for the cap; outline and paint in.** Mix 1¼ cups royal icing in a bowl with regal purple gel to make deep purple for the cap. Thin to lining consistency and spoon ¼ cup into a piping bag fitted with a #1 tip. Thin the remaining to flooding consistency, add whitener, and cover with plastic wrap. Turn the cookie upside down so the teacup's saucer is at the top. Using the purple lining icing, outline the silhouette of the cap, leaving space on the left side of the cookie for the tassel. Let set for 5 minutes. Reserve the purple lining icing. Using a large paintbrush and the purple flooding icing, paint in the cap. Let set until hard, 6 to 8 hours or overnight.

3. **Make white lining icing to re-outline the cap and make details; make yellow lining and flooding icing for the tassel. Re-outline, outline, and paint in.** Refresh the royal icing on medium low for 30 seconds. Mix ¼ cup icing with whitener gel to make white for re-outlining the cap. Thin to lining consistency and spoon all of it into a piping bag fitted with a #1 tip. Mix ½ cup royal icing in a bowl with egg yellow gel to make orange-yellow for the tassel. Thin to lining consistency and spoon ¼ cup into a piping bag fitted with a #1 tip. Thin the remaining icing to flooding consistency, add whitener, and cover with plastic wrap. Using the white lining icing, re-outline the cap and include the detail to square off the top. Make an oval in the center of the top of the cap for the button. Let set for 5 minutes. Using the orange-yellow lining icing, outline the silhouette of the tassel, then connect it to the cap with a line to the button. Let set for 5 minutes. Reserve the orange-yellow lining icing. Using a small paintbrush and the orange-yellow flooding icing, paint in the tassel. Let set for 1 hour.

4. **Re-outline the tassel and draw in details.** Using the reserved orange-yellow lining icing, re-outline the tassel and draw in the lines for texture. Let set for 15 minutes. Using the reserved dark purple lining icing, make a line across the tassel for the tie. Alternatively, use a black fine-tipped edible marker to draw the line.

STORK

○ beginner   ● intermediate   ○ advanced

what you need

TO MAKE THE COOKIES
2¾-inch teacup cookie cutter

Cookie dough of choice (pages 26–33), prepared, chilled, and rolled out

Cooling racks

TO DECORATE
2¾ cups Royal Icing (pages 40–42)

Pasteurized egg white or water

Gel food colors: whitener, royal blue, sunset orange, super black

7 plastic or parchment paper piping bags (page 53)

6 #1 tips

1 #1.5 tip

Black fine-tipped edible marker (optional)

1. **Make the cookies.** Cut out 24 cookies from the dough. Bake and cool as directed.

2. **Make lining and flooding icings: white for the stork and light blue for the bag; outline and paint in the stork.** Mix 1 cup royal icing in a bowl with whitener gel to make white. Thin to lining consistency and spoon ¼ cup into a piping bag fitted with a #1 tip. Thin the remaining icing to flooding consistency and cover with plastic wrap. Mix ½ cup royal icing in a bowl with royal blue and whitener gels to make light blue for the stork's sack. Thin to lining consistency and spoon ¼ cup into a piping bag fitted with a #1 tip. Thin the remaining icing to flooding consistency and cover with plastic wrap. Position the cookie so that the teacup's handle is at the top. Using the white lining icing, outline the silhouette of the stork, not including the beak. Follow the curve of the top and right edge of the cookie for the head, neck, and wing. Draw bumps along the bottom right edge of the cookie for feathers. Leave enough space on the left side of the cookie for the sack. Let set for 5 minutes. Using a medium paintbrush and the white flooding icing, paint in the stork. Let set for 4 to 6 hours.

3. **Outline the sack and paint in. Make loose white lining icing for the dots; make dots.** While the white flooding icing sets, use the light blue lining icing to outline the sack so that it reaches the bottom left edge of the cookie. Let set for 5 minutes. Mix ¼ cup royal icing in a bowl

STORK CONTINUES

with whitener to make white for the polka dots. Thin to a consistency that's slightly looser than lining icing but not as thin as flooding icing. Spoon all of it into a piping bag fitted with a #1.5 tip. Using a medium paintbrush and light blue flooding icing, paint in the sack. While the icing is still wet, use the bag of looser white lining icing to drop small white dots of icing into the light blue flooding icing. Space the white dots apart so they make a polka-dot pattern on the sack. Let set until hard, 6 to 8 hours or overnight.

4. **Make orange lining and flooding icing for the beak; make gray lining icing to re-outline the stork. Outline, paint in, and re-outline.** Refresh the royal icing on medium low for 30 seconds. Mix ¼ cup royal icing in a bowl with sunset orange gel to make bright orange for the beak. Thin to lining consistency and spoon 2 tablespoons into a piping bag fitted with a #1 tip. Thin the remaining icing to flooding consistency and cover with plastic wrap. Mix ¼ cup royal icing with a toothpick each of super black and whitener gels to make light gray for re-outlining the stork. Spoon it all into a piping bag fitted with a #1 tip. Using the orange lining icing, outline the silhouette of the beak, going over the sack for the top of the beak and stopping

at the sack for the bottom of the beak. Let set for 5 minutes. Using a small paintbrush and the orange flooding icing, paint in the beak. Let set for 1 hour. Meanwhile, using the light gray lining icing, re-outline the stork, then make the feather details and the lines indicating the wing and the head.

5. **Make lining icings: darker orange to re-outline the beak and darker blue for the sack. Re-outline and make details.** Spoon 3 tablespoons royal icing into each of two bowls. Cover one with plastic wrap. To the remaining, add sunset orange gel to make a darker orange to re-outline the beak. Thin to lining consistency and spoon it all into a piping bag fitted with a #1 tip. To the second bowl, add royal blue and whitener gels to make darker blue to outline the sack. Thin to lining consistency and spoon it all into a piping bag fitted with a #1 tip. Using the darker orange lining icing, re-outline the beak and make a line to separate the top and bottom and a dot for the nostril. Using the darker blue lining icing, re-outline the sack, moving around the beak. Using the darker blue or lighter gray lining icing, make a dot for the stork's eye. Alternatively, use a black fine-tipped edible marker to draw in the eye. Let set for 10 minutes or until dry.

MOON CUTTER

Oddly, the moon, though one of the simplest cookies in this book, was particularly difficult to get right. I went through at least 12 different color combinations before I was satisfied. The golden moon needed the navy outline to give it that feel of midnight sky.

All four cookies in this group remind me of summer. When you make the Banana Split, personalize it with your favorite ice cream flavors!

MOON

● beginner   ○ intermediate   ○ advanced

what you need

TO MAKE THE COOKIES
3-inch moon cookie cutter

Cookie dough of choice (pages 26–33), prepared, chilled, and rolled out

Cooling racks

TO DECORATE
1½ cups Royal Icing (pages 40–42)

Pasteurized egg white or water

Gel food colors: lemon yellow, whitener, royal blue

2 plastic or parchment paper piping bags (page 53)

2 #1 tips

Large paintbrush

1. **Make the cookies.** Cut out 24 cookies from the dough. Bake and cool as directed.

2. **Make yellow lining and flooding icing; outline the moon and paint in.** Mix 1 cup royal icing in a small bowl with lemon yellow gel to make yellow for the moon. Thin to lining consistency and spoon ¼ cup into a piping bag fitted with a #1 tip. Thin the remaining icing to flooding consistency, add a little whitener, and cover with plastic wrap. Using the lining icing, outline the moon along the edge of the cookie, making an indent for the lips and chin. Let set for 5 minutes.

Using a large paintbrush and the flooding icing, paint in the moon. Let set until hard, 6 to 8 hours or overnight.

3. **Make blue lining icing and re-outline the moon; draw in the eye.** Refresh the royal icing on medium low for 30 seconds. Mix ¼ cup icing in a bowl with royal blue gel to make blue to re-outline the moon. Thin to lining consistency and spoon all of it into a piping bag fitted with a #1 tip. Re-outline the moon and draw a half circle for the eye. Draw a few short lines perpendicular to the eye for the eyelashes. Let set for 1 hour.

BAT

● beginner ○ intermediate ○ advanced

what you need

TO MAKE THE COOKIES
3-inch moon cookie cutter

Cookie dough of choice (pages 26–33), prepared, chilled, and rolled out

Cooling racks

TO DECORATE
1½ cups Royal Icing (pages 40–42)

Pasteurized egg white or water

Gel food colors: super black, bright red

2 plastic or parchment paper piping bags (page 53)

2 #1 tips

Medium paintbrush

1. **Make the cookies.** Cut out 24 cookies from the dough. Bake and cool as directed.

2. **Make black lining and flooding icing for the bat.** Mix 1 cup royal icing in a bowl with super black gel to make black. Thin to lining consistency and spoon ¼ cup into a piping bag fitted with a #1 tip. Thin the remaining black icing to flooding consistency and cover with plastic wrap.

3. **Outline the bat and paint in.** Position the cookie so that the arc of the moon is the top. Using the black lining icing, outline the bat, excluding the claws, following the edge of the cookie along the wings, and making three scallops along the bottom of each. Reserve the black lining icing. Using a medium paintbrush and the black flooding icing,

paint in the bat. Let set until hard, 6 to 8 hours or overnight.

4. **Re-outline the bat and make details.** Using the reserved lining icing, re-outline the bat. Draw the ribs on the bat's wings by piping lines from the tips of the shoulders to the scallop points at the bottom of each wing. Make claws by drawing three short lines on either side of the body.

5. **Make red lining icing and make the eyes.** Refresh the royal icing on medium low speed for 30 seconds. Spoon 2 tablespoons icing into a bowl and mix in bright red gel to make red for the eyes. Thin to lining consistency and spoon it all into a piping bag fitted with a #1 tip. Make two red dots for the eyes. Let set for 30 minutes.

WATERMELON SLICE

● beginner ○ intermediate ○ advanced

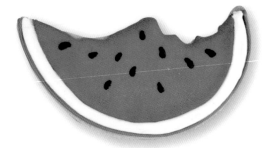

what you need

TO MAKE THE COOKIES
3-inch moon cookie cutter

Cookie dough of choice (pages 26–33), prepared, chilled, and rolled out

Cooling racks

TO DECORATE
1½ cups Royal Icing (pages 40–42)

Pasteurized egg white or water

Gel food colors: bright red, whitener, teal green, leaf green, super black

4 plastic or parchment paper piping bags (page 53)

4 #1.5 tips

Assorted paintbrushes

1. **Make the cookies.** Cut out 24 cookies from the dough. Bake and cool as directed.

2. **Make lining and flooding icings: pink for the watermelon and white for the rind; make green lining icing for the skin.** Spoon ½ cup royal icing into each of two bowls. Cover one with plastic wrap. To the other bowl, add bright red gel to make watermelon pink. Thin to lining consistency and spoon ¼ cup into a piping bag fitted with a #1.5 tip. Thin the remaining icing to flooding consistency, add whitener, and cover with plastic wrap. To the second bowl, add whitener gel to make bright white for the rind. Thin to lining consistency and spoon ¼ cup into a piping bag fitted with a #1.5 tip. Thin the remaining

icing to flooding consistency and cover with plastic wrap. Mix ¼ cup royal icing in a bowl with teal green, leaf green, and whitener to make green for the skin. Thin to lining consistency and spoon all of it into a piping bag fitted with a #1.5 tip.

3. **Outline the watermelon and rind and paint in. Outline the skin.** Position the cookie so that the moon's arc is the bottom and the face is the top. Using the pink lining icing, outline the pink part of the melon, making a jagged line along the top of the cookie. Let set for 5 minutes. Using the white lining icing, outline the rind, butting the line (see page 64) adjacent to the pink up against it and leaving ⅛ inch along the bottom edge for the green skin. Using a medium paintbrush and

the pink flooding icing, paint in the watermelon. Using a small paintbrush and the white flooding icing, paint in the rind, taking care to keep the white icing from spilling over into the pink and using enough icing so that the colors are level. Using the green lining icing, outline the green skin, butting the green line up to the white line as closely as possible. Let set until hard, 6 to 8 hours or overnight.

4. **Make black lining icing for the seeds; draw in.** Refresh the royal icing on medium low for 30 seconds. Mix ¼ cup icing with super black gel to make black. Thin to lining consistency and spoon into a piping bag fitted with a #1.5 tip. Turn the cookie so that the jagged side is the bottom and, holding the tip against the cookie at a 45-degree angle, draw seeds by squeezing the bag then pulling away quickly to make the shape of teardrops. Let set for 1 hour.

· · · · · · · · · · · · · · · · · · · MAKES 24 · · · · · · · · · · · · · · · · ·

BANANA SPLIT

○ beginner   ○ intermediate   ● advanced

what you need

TO MAKE THE COOKIES
3-inch moon cookie cutter

Cookie dough of choice (pages 26–33), prepared, chilled, and rolled out

Cooling racks

TO DECORATE
3 cups Royal Icing (pages 40–42)

Pasteurized egg white or water

Gel food colors: chocolate brown, electric pink, neon green, bright blue, lemon yellow, whitener, super black, bright red

11 plastic or parchment paper piping bags (page 53)

11 #1 tips

Assorted paintbrushes

1. **Make the cookies.** Cut out 24 cookies from the dough. Bake and cool as directed.

2. **Make the lining and flooding icings for the chocolate and mint ice cream scoops.** Spoon

BANANA SPLIT CONTINUES

¼ cup royal icing into each of two bowls. Cover one with plastic wrap. To the other bowl, mix in chocolate brown gel to make brown for the chocolate ice cream. Thin to lining consistency and spoon 2 tablespoons into a piping bag fitted with a #1 tip. Thin the remaining icing to flooding consistency and cover with plastic wrap. To the second bowl, mix in neon green and bright blue gels to make mint green for the mint chocolate chip ice cream. Thin to lining consistency and spoon 2 tablespoons into a piping bag fitted with a #1 tip. Thin the remaining icing to flooding consistency and cover with plastic wrap.

3. **Outline the chocolate and mint scoops and paint them in.** Position the cookie so that the moon's arc is the bottom and the face is the top. Using the brown lining icing, outline the top of the chocolate scoop, stopping where it meets the banana and the strawberry scoop. Do the same with the mint green. Let set for 5 minutes. Using the flooding icings, paint in the chocolate and mint scoops, thinning out the icing where it goes behind the bananas, bowl, and strawberry scoop. Let set for 2 to 3 hours.

4. **Make light yellow and pale pink lining and flooding icings for the bananas and the strawberry scoop; outline and paint in.** Spoon ¼ cup royal icing into each of two bowls. Cover one with plastic wrap. To the other bowl, add a tiny toothpick each of lemon yellow and whitener gels to make pale yellow for the bananas. Thin to lining consistency and spoon 2 tablespoons into a piping bag fitted with a #1 tip. Thin the remaining icing to flooding consistency and cover with plastic wrap. To the remaining bowl, add a toothpick of electric pink gel to make pink for the strawberry ice cream. Thin to lining consistency and spoon 2 tablespoons into a piping bag fitted with a #1 tip. Thin the remaining icing to flooding consistency and cover with plastic wrap. Using the pale yellow lining icing, outline the bananas on either end of the cookie. Using the pink lining icing, outline the strawberry scoop to the tip of the cookie. Let set for 5 minutes. Reserve the lining icings. Using a paintbrush and the yellow flooding icing, paint in the bananas, thinning the icing at the bottom where the bowl overlaps. Using the pink flooding icing, paint in the strawberry scoop in the same way. Let set for 3 to 4 hours.

5. **Make gray lining and flooding icing for the bowl; outline and paint in.** Mix ½ cup royal icing in a bowl with a toothpick of super black and a drop of whitener gel to make gray for the bowl. Thin to lining consistency and spoon ¼ cup into a piping bag fitted with a #1 tip. Thin the remaining icing to flooding consistency and cover with plastic wrap. Using the gray lining icing, outline the silhouette of the ice cream bowl including the foot of the bowl. Let set for 5 minutes. Using a paintbrush and the gray flooding icing, paint in the bowl. Let set for 2 to 3 hours or until hard.

6. **Re-outline the bananas. Make lining icings:**

pink to re-outline the strawberry scoop and dark brown for the chocolate; make super dark brown lining and flooding icing for the fudge. Using the reserved pale yellow lining icing, re-outline the bananas. Refresh the royal icing on medium low for 30 seconds. Spoon ¼ cup icing into each of three bowls. Cover two with plastic wrap. To the remaining bowl, mix in chocolate brown gel to make darker brown to re-outline the chocolate scoop. Thin to lining consistency and spoon all of it into a piping bag fitted with a #1 tip. To the second bowl, add electric pink gel to make darker pink to re-outline the strawberry scoop. Thin to lining consistency and spoon all of it into a piping bag fitted with a #1 tip. To the third bowl, mix in chocolate brown and super black gels to make super dark brown for the fudge sauce. Thin to lining consistency and spoon 2 tablespoons into a piping bag fitted with a #1 tip. Thin the remaining icing to flooding consistency and cover with plastic wrap.

7. **Re-outline the chocolate scoop and draw details. Outline the fudge and paint in; draw in the chips.** Using the dark brown lining icing, re-outline the scoop of chocolate ice cream. Draw a few squiggles on the scoop to give it texture. Using the super dark brown lining icing, outline the fudge on the strawberry scoop, making an irregular line along the top to make the whipped cream look realistic and a more exaggerated curvy line on the bottom to mimic drips. Draw in the chips

on the mint ice cream. Let set for 5 minutes.

8. **Paint in the fudge. Make bright pink lining icing to re-outline the strawberry scoop and draw details.** Spoon ¼ cup royal icing into a bowl. Add electric pink to make bright pink to re-outline the strawberry scoop. Spoon it all into a piping bag fitted with a #1 tip, re-outline the strawberry scoop, and draw in details. Using a small paintbrush and the super dark brown flooding icing, paint in the fudge. Reserve the bright pink lining icing. Let set for 3 to 4 hours.

9. **Make white lining icing for the whipped cream; make dark gray for re-outlining the bowl.** Spoon ¼ cup royal icing into each of two bowls. Cover one with plastic wrap. To the other bowl, add whitener gel to make white for the whipped cream. Thin to lining consistency and spoon all of it into a piping bag fitted with a #1 tip. To the remaining bowl, add a toothpick of super black and a drop of whitener gels to make darker gray to re-outline the bowl. Thin to lining consistency and spoon all of it into a piping bag fitted with a #1 tip.

10. **Top with the whipped cream and re-outline the bowl. Make the cherry.** Using the white lining icing, squeeze some whipped cream above the hot fudge. Using the darker gray lining icing, re-outline the bowl. Let set for 30 minutes or until dry. Using the reserved bright pink lining icing, make a cherry on top of the whipped cream. Let set for 2 to 3 hours or until dry.

CONNECT THE COOKIE TO ITS CUTTER!

Can you figure out which cookie came from which cutter? The answers are below.

1.

a.

2.

b.

3.

c.

4.

d.

ANSWERS: 1. b; 2. d; 3. a; 4. c

PACKING AND SHIPPING COOKIES

There is nothing worse than finding out that after all the time and effort you put in to making your amazing cookies, they've arrived at their destination broken—I speak from experience here.

It is 100 percent possible to ship even the most fragile cookies if you are careful. I have a client who tells me that the cookies she orders from me are packed as if they are pieces of fancy china. I ship the most fragile cookies—those with slender appendages—across the country with no breakage, so I know it can be done. Just think: *padding, padding, padding.*

what you need

Cellophane bags (sized to fit cookies) or waxed paper

Ribbon, tape, or stickers to close the cello bags

Scissors

Decorative box to pack cookies in (cake or bakery box, large cookie tin)

Bubble wrap

Corrugated cardboard box for shipping (2 inches larger on all sides than the decorative box) to hold the smaller box

Padding material (plain newsprint, tissue paper)

Packing tape

1. **Wrap the cookies.** Insert each cookie into an appropriately sized bag. Gather the cellophane at the top of the bag so that the folds of the bag do not obscure the front of the cookie. Wrap ribbon around the gather and tie into a bow in such a way that it does not cover the front of the cookie.

You can also just make a knot, which is simple and clean. Trim the ribbon ends with scissors. Instead of a ribbon, you can secure the bag shut with tape or a sticker. Alternatively, wrap each cookie in waxed paper.

2. **Package the cookies.** If I'm delivering cookies myself, I pack them in a bakery box with sheets of waxed tissue in between each layer. If I'm going to ship them, I like to pack the cookies in their cellophane bags directly into a corrugated cardboard box. First, cut strips of bubble wrap twice the length of the cookie. Wrap each cookie in bubble wrap. Pad the bottom of the box with several layers of crumpled plain tissue or newsprint to ensure that the cookies never touch the hard walls or the bottom of the box. Tap your fingers lightly against the padding; if you can feel the cardboard, add more padding. Arrange the cookies on their sides, upright, rather than laying flat in the box, allowing one cookie to rest against the next. If you've tied the cellophane bags with a ribbon, alternate the orientation of each (top to bottom, bottom to top) so the ribbons don't pile up together. Make sure you leave 1½ to 2 inches between the cookies and the walls of the box; this prevents the cookies from breaking if the box is damaged en route.

3. **Add more layers of crumpled tissue if necessary to prevent the cookies from moving around in the box.** Hold the box closed and shake it; if you

hear or feel no movement, the cookies are safe to ship. If the cookies move around, add more protective crumpled tissue. Seal the box and ship.

Tip: Be sure the cookies are packed firmly but gently against each other, pressed tightly enough to keep them upright but not so tight that they break.

STORING COOKIES

Generally I make my cookies right before I am going to use them. They taste best when they are at their freshest. But if you do want to store them, here is what I suggest.

Decorated cookies should be *completely* dry before storing. I use the Ball Pin Test to be sure. Poke a pin onto the surface of the cookie—if it doesn't puncture the surface, the cookie is thoroughly dry. Once they are dry, you can store decorated cookies at room temperature between sheets of waxed paper in an airtight container for 2 weeks or in the refrigerator for up to a month.

To freeze cookies, which keeps them freshest, wrap each one in a resealable plastic bag or tied cellophane bag. Place in a freezer-safe container and freeze for up to 3 months. To thaw, leave the container out at room temperature. Because the cookies are in bags, any condensation that takes place will happen on the bag and not the cookie.

SOURCES

SUR LA TABLE
800 243 0852
www.surlatable.com
Almost all the cutters used in the book, baking ingredients including King Arthur gluten free multipurpose flour, bakeware (baking sheets, pastry cloth, rolling pins, rolling pin rings, parchment, sifters, whisks, spatulas, mixing bowls, measuring tools, scales), decorating tools (Wilton food coloring, Wilton silver and gold pearl decorating dust, edible markers, tip brush, Ateco piping tips, disposable pastry bags, parchment triangles), packaging supplies (cellophane bags, boxes), lollipop sticks

KING ARTHUR FLOUR
800 827 6836
www.kingarthurflour.com
Baking ingredients (gluten free multipurpose flour, whole wheat flour, xanthan gum), lollipop sticks, edible markers, box of 8 assorted AmeriColor soft gel paste food colors, cookie cutters, bakeware (baking sheets, parchment paper half sheets, etc.)

WILTON INDUSTRIES
888 373 4588
www.wilton.com
Cookie cutters, bakeware, decorating tools (food coloring, fine-tip edible markers, tip brush, piping tips, disposable piping bags, etc.), packaging supplies (cellophane bags), meringue powder, lollipop sticks

PFEIL & HOLING
718 545 4600
www.cakedeco.com
Bakeware, decorating tools (PME scriber needle tool, Chefmaster and AmeriColor food coloring, luster and pearl dusts), meringue powder, isomalt nibs, lollipop sticks

BERYL'S
800 488 2749
703 256 6951
www.beryls.com
Decorating tools (PME piping tips, edible markers), packaging supplies (cellophane bags, boxes)

N.Y. CAKE AND BAKING SUPPLIES
56 West 22nd Street
New York, NY 10010
212 675 2253
www.nycake.com
Cookie cutters, bakeware (rolling pin rings, parchment paper), decorating supplies (PME, Ateco, and Wilton piping tips, parchment triangles, disposable pastry bags, AmeriColor food coloring, edible markers, luster dusts), packaging supplies, isomalt nibs

CONFECTION CRAFT
3936 N Williams Ave.
Portland, OR 97227
503 505 0481
www.confectioncraft.com
Natural food coloring and sprinkles

INDIA TREE

www.indiatree.com
Carried by various retailers and online sources
Natural food colorings and sprinkles

WHOLE FOODS MARKET

www.wholefoodsmarket.com
Baking ingredients (Bob's Red Mill all-purpose gluten free flour, Deb's dried egg whites, pasteurized egg whites, xanthan gum, nondairy butter, vegan sugar, vegan confectioners' sugar, Ener-G egg replacer, extracts, etc.)

BOB'S RED MILL

13521 SE Pheasant Ct.
Milwaukie, OR 97222
800 349 2173
503 654 3215
www.bobsredmill.com
Gluten free all-purpose flour, whole wheat flour, evaporated cane sugar (vegetarian), egg replacer, xanthan gum

MICHAELS

800 642 4235
www.michaels.com
Art and craft supplies (paintbrushes, X-ACTO knives, Fiskars scissors, pliers, etc.), cookie cutters, decorating supplies (disposable piping bags, piping tips, etc.), packaging supplies (cellophane bags, boxes)

OFF THE BEATEN PATH

866 756 6543
www.cookiecutter.com
Cookie cutters, cookie cutter aluminum strips, bakeware, decorating supplies

THE LITTLE FOX FACTORY

www.thelittlefoxfactory.com
Cookie cutters (excellent assortment)

FANCY FLOURS

406 587 0118
www.fancyflours.com
Cookie cutters, bakeware, decorating tools, packaging supplies

ULINE

800 295 5510
www.uline.com
Packaging and shipping supplies (boxes, cellophane bags, bubble wrap, tape, etc.)

CONFECTIONERY HOUSE

518 279 3179
www.confectioneryhouse.com
Bakeware, decorating supplies, cookie cutters

SUGARCRAFT

513 896 7089
www.sugarcraft.com`
Cookie cutters, bakeware, decorating tools (Chefmaster, AmeriColor, and Wilton food coloring; luster dusts; piping tips), packaging supplies (cellophane bags, boxes, etc.)

DIFFICULTY LEVEL INDEX

The index below ranks decorated cookies by their respective levels of decorating difficulty. Each cookie cutter in the book includes four cookies with varying levels of difficulty.

ADVANCED

ACKNOWLEDGMENTS

I would like to thank my friends at Stonesong Press especially: Judy Linden, my agent, has been excited about my idea for this book from the very beginning. She generously encouraged and guided me every step of the way. Ellen Scordato paid attention to so many details and kept things running smoothly. Thank you also to Sarah Passick for her involvement.

I am indebted to Karen Murgolo, my editor at Grand Central Publishing, for her belief in and enthusiasm for this project. Thanks to Pippa White and Tareth Mitch, also at Grand Central Publishing, and to my copy editor Deri Reed.

Many thanks to Amy Sly for her playful book design, and to Jennifer Causey for her extraordinary photography.

To the photo assistant Chaunte Vaughn and prop stylist Kalen Kaminski: Thank you for all your help during the shoot.

Thank you to my writer, Kathleen Hackett, for her talent, patience, and sense of humor.

To Andrea Vuocolo, who tested and helped develop these recipes, and to recipe testers Debra Lee and Monica Buchwald, thank you.

Thanks and love to my daughter, Dena Paige Fisher, for her design ideas and always-honest feedback.

Thank you to Kim Messano, Alison Greenberg, Katie Haigler, Daphne Brucculeri, Lisa Abitbol, Abby Ballin, Rona Hunter, and Dana James for their various contributions.

To my husband, Ron, thanks for adapting to my crazier than normal work shedule.

A special thanks goes to Jessica Tsai, my incredibly talented assistant who has contributed more than anyone else to this book. From cookie designing to writing recipes, she has worked with me tirelessly every step of the way, and I can't imagine having done this without her.

INDEX

ABOUT THE AUTHOR

Artist-turned-baker Patti Paige, creator and owner of Baked Ideas, a custom bakery in New York City, has appeared nationally on Food Network's *Barefoot Contessa* ("How the Cookie Crumbles") and the Cooking Channel's *FoodCrafters*. Her cookies have filled the pages of *O, The Oprah Magazine*, *Martha Stewart Weddings*, *Sweet Paul*, the *New York Times*, and *Brides* magazine, among others. Patti has conducted cookie decorating workshops at Williams-Sonoma, the Sweet Paul Makerie, and other locations. Her work has been showcased with *Hello, Cupcake!*'s Karen Tack and Alan Richardson, and her diverse group of clients has included Alicia Keys, David Hyde Pierce, Tiffany & Co., Crayola, *Gourmet* magazine, the Metropolitan Museum of Art, and Hillary Clinton. Patti lives in New York City with her husband.